Strategy of the Spirit

'An account of the explosive growth of the most extensive contemporary Protestant missionary endeavor and of the man whose career and outlook gave it form.'

Strategy of the Spirit

J. Philip Hogan
and the growth of the
Assemblies of God worldwide
1960–1990

Everett A. Wilson

regnum

First published in the UK 1997 by Paternoster Press

03   02   01   00   99   98   97   7   6   5   4   3   2   1

Paternoster Press is an imprint of Paternoster Publishing,
P.O. Box 300, Carlisle, Cumbria CA3 0QS

British Library Cataloguing in Publication Data

A catalogue record for this book is available from the British Library.

ISBN 1-870345-23-1

This book is printed using Suffolk New Book paper which is 100% acid free

Typeset by WestKey Ltd, Falmouth, Cornwall
Printed in Great Britain by Clays Ltd, Bungay, Suffolk

In memory of my parents

Ruben Archer Wilson
(1906–1993)
and
Harriet Porter Wilson
(1907–1967)

Ordained Assemblies of God ministers
who believed that
ministry should by synonymous with integrity.

Contents

Foreword

This book is about a missionary general. J. Philip Hogan's visionary and decisive leadership has given shape and facilitated the growth and stability of the farther reaching global revival movement in the twentieth century – now frequently termed by church historians 'the Pentecostal century'. In a recent BBC interview when I was asked about the reasons for the tragic and protracted crisis in former Yugoslavia (which used to be my homeland) and the failure of the international community there and in other places, I pointed to the crisis of leadership in our broken world. Everywhere we see the consequences of the lack of leadership marked by the fundamental trio of qualities: clarity of vision, moral conviction and will to act when most appropriate. Asked by the interviewer to illustrate, and attempted to express the indescribable pain of Bosnia, where I ministered at that time, I appealed to World War II history: 'You 'Britishers' should understand: there are too many Chamberlains around and no Churchill to be found!'

J. Philip Hogan was a Churchill in the arena of the post-World War II history of missions. In his personality and ministry, as this book shows, we have ample evidence of that unique combination of vision, conviction and courage. His commitment to the global extent of the call of God and to the normality of Bibilcal revelation was matched by a rare grasp of history and a first-rate mind, sharp to perceive and quick to discern the issues of the day. A man of strong convictions and courageous action, Hogan was not afraid to face new challenges and to adapt to change. 'The world has changed and so must we – anchored to the rock, but geared to the times,' he would state his missiological philosophy. This attitude has enabled him to engineer several strategic ministries and efficient instruments for the evangelization of the world.

Hogan was a missionary leader who understood quicker than many of his evangelical colleagues that the church's dynamic center is moving from the North Atlantic Nations to the younger and more vital churches of Latin America, Asia and Africa. This recognition that Christianity, especially the Pentecostal branch, has become during his tenure a predominantly non-Western movement, is at the very core of his founding vision of the World Assemblies of God Fellowship, of which he rightfully became the first chairman. He was urging his American friends to celebrate the internationalization of the Gospel as the fulfillment of Jesus' prophecy that 'this Gospel shall be preached in the whole world as a testimony to all nations' (Matt. 24:14), and to recognize and adjust to this shift of the mission 'power base' to the Third World with emergence of a new generation of strong non-Western leaders.

Though recognized widely as a leader with a comprehensive vision and as an efficient administrator, Hogan was at the same time a man of prayer whose life was fully surrendered to the living God and open to the natural and supernatural guidance of his Spirit. His Christian walk and ministry are marked by a simple, trusting, prinicipled faith in the Lord of the Harvest and a full dependance on the Holy Spirit, the true executive of the mission of Jesus in our world. 'Above all human instrumentality, the sovereignty of the Holy Spirit stands in bold relief' is the apt summary of his theology of mission. He captures and expresses it in a more personal statement along with an incredible prophetic boldness in the following statement: 'I am persuaded to believe that after taking advantage of every tool, pursuing every possible human plan, all one needs to do to find plenty of service is simply to follow the leading of the Spirit. When one engages this truth and begins to live by its principles, there will be whole communities, whole cities, whole nations, whole cultures, and whole segments of pagan religions that will suddenly be thrust open to the Gospel witness.'

Dr. Wilson, the author of this book about the "life and times of J. P. Hogan" combines a vivid and panoramic narrative of the ground-breaking events and key personalities in the Assemblies of God denominational and missions history with a nuanced analysis of complex, and at times contradictory, social, economic and political developments. The result is a thouroughly reserached and superbly written contextual biography providing us with a thoughtful and highly readable portrait of 'Brother Hogan' – as most of us consistently and respectfully call him. This pioneering study is essential reading for all who wish to understand the Pentecostal movement at its best – as a modern missionary phenomenon energized by the indispensible Spirit of God for the supreme task of the world evangelization. It can also be profitably read as a 'case study' of a servant-leader whose life and work provide ample evidence of how a God-given vision, combined with focused energy and dogged persistence, can prevail in the battles against all institutional inertia, administrative procrastination, ecclesiastical provincialism and missionary mediocrity. Both the author of this book and his subject powerfully challenged all of us who are followers of the risen Lord at the threshold of the third millenium to be and to do 'our utmost for His highest'.

Peter Kuzmic

Acknowledgments

An assessment of the contribution of Dr J. Philip Hogan to twentieth-century missions would have been difficult without his understanding and support. When I was invited to undertake the following study, I felt that his contribution could hardly be reduced to a personal profile or even a record of his administrative achievement. The remarkable growth of the Assemblies of God overseas churches during his tenure as director of the Division of Foreign Missions (DFM) and the implications this has for an understanding of Pentecostal missiology demanded a broader treatment. I appreciate the tolerance and patience with which he allowed me to set his life and ministry in a global context so that readers may understand the enormity of his contribution and the representativeness of his own spiritual journey. A careful reading of his extensive publications and of the committee minutes that record the difficult decisions he had to make, as well as observing his independence of action and spirit, have only reinforced my respect for him. My thanks to his wife Virginia, their daughter Lynne, and other family members whose recollections, opinions, and tolerance with my probing intrusions have made this work possible.

J. Philip Hogan has had a host of colleagues who have also been his friends and admirers. Their suggestions and recollections have been invaluable. Among these is Joyce Wells Booze. As editor, writer, journalism professor and promoter of missions, she is a person with extraordinary vision whose strategic role in the DFM in recent years probably cannot be overstated. Joyce Booze has rendered an incomparable service through her concern for developing the DFM archives, and her willingness to give me access to these sources has provided, apart from the perspectives of J. Philip Hogan himself, the bulk of the information necessary for this book. Her colleague, Adele Flower Dalton, a former missionary and a Central Bible Institute classmate of J. Philip and Virginia Hogan, as well as being the daughter of J. Roswell Flower, the first missionary director of the Assemblies of God, was generous in helping me reconstruct Hogan's career. Gloria Robinett, the DFM archivist, was extremely helpful, and Ruth Greve Homer was especially candid and insightful in helping me assess Hogan's early years.

Further this project would have been impossible without the support of Loren Triplett, successor to J. Philip Hogan as executive director of the DFM, and a friend of many years. Other executive officers were also generous in their assistance, especially George O. Wood, the DFM field directors Don Corbin, Robert W. Houlihan, Jerry L. Parsley, John Bueno, and the DFM financial officer Jerry Burgess. My thanks to these colleagues who trusted me with their opinions, recollections, and access to archival materials without knowing precisely what use would be made of my research. Of course they are absolved of any responsibility for my errors and misinterpretations, even while I must acknowledge that my efforts would have been far less authoritative and reliable without their cooperation.

My special thanks to Gary B. McGee. His excellent scholarship and profound understanding of the Pentecostal phenomenon is the necessary starting point for any treatment of Assemblies of God missions. His colleague, Wayne Warner, director of the Assemblies of God archives, and the members of his staff were extremely helpful, as were the personnel of several libraries in Springfield, Missouri. Grant Wacker, a friend of many years, and known for his substantial contribution to Pentecostal studies, has made my process of reconstructing these developments even more productive and enjoyable than they otherwise would have been.

My colleagues at Southern California College and the editors of Regnum Books, International – Murray Dempster, Douglas Petersen and Byron Klaus – are to be thanked for their confidence in asking me to undertake a project that probably has turned out to be far more extensive and complicated than the one that they envisioned at the outset. George P. Wood offered valuable insights and critical assistance in preparing the manuscript, and Mary Wilson, the SCC head librarian, was very helpful in directing me to difficult to access sources.

Finally, my most profound thanks go to my family for their collective support and individual suggestions. Dr Lewis F. Wilson, a Pentecostal scholar of merit, his wife Lenore, and my sister Alice Alford and her husband David read the manuscript at various stages. My brother Noel and his wife Ruth Marshall Wilson provided the needed perspective and critical comments about select topics, as did my brother Ruben and his wife Laura Wilson, and my sister Priscilla Taylor. My wife Lois and our children, Alan and Karen Wilson, Tom and Annette Balch, and Kristi and Jason Garcia, all contributed to the project with their logistical and moral support. For us the Pentecostal movement has far less to do with recollections of past glories and current triumphs than with the values and virtues we saw displayed in the lives of our parents and grandparents to whom this work is dedicated. Their examples of consistency of character and transparency of motives helped us evaluate the sometimes bewildering developments within the movement and nurtured our own spiritual development. As slightly older ministerial colleagues of J. Philip and Virginia Hogan, they lived during the events described in Hogan's story and their experiences provided the background essential for interpreting the historical panorama of Assemblies of God missions.

Everett A. Wilson
San José, Costa Rica
February, 1997

Introduction: A Vine of God's Own Planting

The very characteristics of ecstatic religious behavior – ceremonial association, decentralized structure, unconventional ideology, opposition to established structures – which might appear to be marks of a sect of misfits and dropouts, are indeed the features which combine to make Pentecostalism a growing, expanding, evangelistic religious movement of change.

Luther P. Gerlach.[1]

J. Philip Hogan

On an icy February morning in 1995 J. Philip Hogan met me in his modestly furnished second-story office across the street from the US Assemblies of God headquarters in Springfield, Missouri. We were going to talk about the growth of the Assemblies of God and his role in its global expansion. The stereotypical images of high-profile religious figures, whether grave, unctuous, charismatic, or otherworldly, hardly apply to J. Philip Hogan. At over eighty years of age, and having served thirty years as the executive leader of what became the world's most extensive Protestant missionary operation, Hogan's movements are measured, but his regular features, strong hands, set jaw, penetrating hazel eyes, tanned complexion, and gray-streaked dark hair, to say nothing of his pointed boots and the cut of his clothes, convey as much as anything the image of strength and virility.

And there is no mistaking Hogan's magisterial style or the intensity of his convictions. Courteous and kind, with a sincere if restrained warmth in his manner, he is a man with a mission, with a hard-edged concern for high performance that is impossible to conceal. Curious then that most people who have worked with him – or for him – hold him in esteem, even with affection, and as well admire him for what the Division of Foreign Missions (DFM) accomplished during his years of leadership.

As Hogan talks – about his past, his administration, his views on world missions – he intermittently tilts forward, slightly lowering his

---

[1] Luther P. Gerlach, 'Pentecostalism: Revolution or Counter-Revolution' in *Religious Movements*, 685.

head and peering from under arched eyebrows with intimidating directness. He sometimes pauses for emphasis, cocking his head to one side as he targets his listener for the next verbal volley. His resonant voice is forceful, occasionally overbearing. His phrases flow in deliberate, carefully articulated syllables slightly softened by a Midwestern intonation. When, at the end of our initial interview, Phil Hogan stands, his posture is erect, slightly tensed, giving him a military bearing not typical of glad-handing Pentecostal preachers. J. Philip Hogan, the type-A personality whose long ministerial career was linked with the most prominent Pentecostals of his era, is a key figure in the sometimes incredible account of the achievements of the Assemblies of God overseas missionary program.

Although few people better represent the worldwide, twentieth-century Pentecostal movement or have left a more indelible mark on its development, J. Philip Hogan's contribution was that of an in-the-trenches leader rather than of an icon. Hogan is far too direct, too transparent to remain on a pedestal. His congenial, down-to-earth practicality, his intense, principled seriousness, his ability to dream big dreams and take big risks, his keen focus and spiritual sensitivity, his administrator's 'bottom line' mentality, his admiration for powerful writing and forceful arguments, his concern with the 'larger picture' and with philosophical foundations – all are features that mark the man. One is left with the feeling that his experience, stretching over most of the twentieth century, provides a kind of access map to the protean nature of the Pentecostal movement, especially as it has taken root and grown rapidly overseas.

The global expansion of the Division of Foreign Missions (DFM)

Few people, even among those who were acquainted with the work of the Assemblies of God Foreign Missions Department (renamed the Division of Foreign Missions in 1963), could have foreseen the meteoric rise of the program under the leadership of J. Philip Hogan, executive director from 1 January 1960 to 31 December 1989. From an effective but largely unrecognized denominational endeavor the DFM's extension and influence virtually exploded over these thirty years. Before the end of his tenure as director J. Philip Hogan would oversee a US denominational missions agency at work in 124 countries whose budget was exceeded in the United States only by that of the Southern Baptist Convention. Under Hogan's leadership the DFM created the largest-in-volume foreign-language press in the United States and was also instrumental in the formation of one of the world's largest private primary and secondary educational systems. Professional ministerial training programs were set up for almost a quarter of a million Assemblies of God pastors and lay leaders around the world as, during the course of

Hogan's tenure, the DFM solicited and disbursed a billion missionary dollars. More importantly, during these thirty years Hogan would oversee the formation of one of the world's larger Christian associations, the World Assemblies of God Fellowship, now embracing an estimated twenty-five million adherents.

This astonishing impact of the Pentecostals' approach to missionary work has received remarkably little recognition even in missionary circles. As the Pentecostal message took root in a variety of cultures and circumstances, the collective impact after three decades of Hogan's leadership was scarcely noticed. Only by tabulating the country-by-country developments can an observer acquire some appreciation for the mission's extensive influence. Handbooks publishing statistics of the world's missions fields, such as Patrick Johnstone's *Operation World* and the directories of the Missionary Advanced Research Center (MARC), however, indicate that in a large number of countries the largest or second largest group of Christians is not the product of a European state church or one of the historical mainline American denominations or one of the newer evangelical groups benefiting from generous American funding. Rather, the world missions leader appears to be a still young, dynamic movement that is often thought of as simply an overseas expression of the 'old-time religion.' Actually the movement is something new and autonomous, in each country taking on a unique character. An Assemblies of God national church is listed as the largest or the second largest Protestant denomination in almost a quarter of the countries of the world, making it clearly one of the most effective vehicles for extending the historical Christian faith in our time. This tabulation takes no note of those other countries where the Assemblies of God has substantial, dynamic churches, although other denominational groups have larger numbers of congregations, adherents, and institutional assets.[2]

When the DFM was created in the second decade of the twentieth century, there was little reason to suspect that the mission would lead to anything more than what the missionaries and supporting members themselves had anticipated: small, gathered churches – a remnant of

---

[2] A cognate church of the US Assemblies of God is the Protestant group with the largest number of adherents in Argentina, Brazil, Bulgaria, Burkina Faso, Costa Rica, El Salvador, France, Guatemala, Honduras, Iran, Italy, the Marshall Islands, Mauritius, Mozambique, Nicaragua, Panama, Peru, Portugal, Uruguay, and Zimbabwe. The group is the second largest evangelical church in a number of other countries, including American Samoa, Aruba, Benin, Bolivia, the Dominican Republic, Guyana, Liberia, Madagascar, Mexico, the Netherlands Antilles, New Caledonia, Nigeria, Paraguay, Poland, Senegal, Sierra Leone, Singapore, South Africa, South Korea, Sri Lanka, Venezuela and Zaire. The Iglesia de Dios Pentecostal, the largest Protestant denomination in Puerto Rico, was an affiliate of the Assemblies of God from its origins in 1916 to 1953. Presently, the second largest church in membership in Puerto Rico is the Asambleas de Dios. Patrick Johnstone, *Operation World*.

believers – the result of a final proclamation of the gospel prior to the anticipated eschatological end of the age.

Instead, while Assemblies of God constituents continue to hold that the 'end is nearer than when they first believed' (a reference to Romans 13:11), they need not wait to learn about the results of their cumulative labors – they already know the outcome. Rather than hoping against hope that their own faith will be vindicated, and that the 'latter rain' (the end-times revival that they claimed to have perceived and experienced) will produce a church made up of every tribe, language, people, and nation, the Pentecostals have gradually seen the promise of Peter's message at Pentecost unfold before their eyes.

The missiology of the DFM

The place of J. Philip Hogan as a missionary leader stems from the emphasis that all along has given Pentecostalism its essential character. If Pentecostals have often been considered essentially tongues-speaking fundamentalists, the Assemblies of God emphasized, as did other Pente-costals, the indispensability of the individual's crisis experience as the energizing force of the Christian faith and the coordinating principle of the church. The natural consequences for missionary work of such an emphasis was precisely what the church growth specialist Donald McGavran recognized in assessing the movement's expansion around the world. 'The Pentecostals,' McGavran observed, 'teach that God the Holy Spirit acts powerfully through ordinary Christians.'

> He has chosen the weak and often foolish things of this world to put to shame the wise, the strong, and those of long educational pedigrees. Pentecostals have more new congregations [groups made up of recent converts] than most denominations – and *trust them more* [McGavran's emphasis].[3]

The DFM went beyond discharging an obligatory 'white man's burden' to save the lost and beyond systematically fulfilling the Great Commission in a Sherwin Williams-like 'covering the globe' with the gospel. Rather, the Pentecostals undertook something radically different and audacious, the spawning of embryonic national churches, from the outset complete, fully formed units which, however small and apparently

---

[3] Donald McGavran, 'What Makes Pentecostal Churches Grow,' *Church Growth Bulletin* 13, no. 3 (1977): 97–99. A similar missiological position was advocated by the highly regarded missionary historian Stephen Neill in 'Building the Church on Two Continents,' *Christianity Today* (18 July 1980): 18–23. Neill said in an interview that the aim from the very start 'should be to root the church in the [cultural] soil.' From the start the plan should be to make a 'really indigenous church' where the Western personnel would gradually fade out. He added, however: 'It's going to take time. I reckon 20 years before you've really got even the outline of a church, and probably 50 before you've got a church that can stand on its own feet' (20).

vulnerable, were free-standing outposts of the body of Christ, ultimately responsible for their own administration, support, extension, and institutional development.

Pentecostal missionary work, no matter how similar in appearance to the efforts of other missions, thus soon acquired its own distinguishable character. Rather than extending an American ecclesiastical operation overseas, missionaries whetted the spiritual appetites of the peoples among whom they worked by sharing the testimonies and the emphases which had already given rise to virtually spontaneous Pentecostal movements in the United States, Europe, Latin America and elsewhere during the early part of the twentieth century. Pentecostals did not export made-in-the-USA religion; they devoted their efforts to preaching that God's provision was more than adequate for human needs. Subsequently, they encouraged and nurtured the groups that came into being, groups that were not beholden to them and over which they wielded only moral authority. Expressed in biological terms the emerging church, for Pentecostals, ideally is born fully formed without having to undergo further metamorphosis. Like a vertebrate, held erect by its own backbone, it need never – should never – be either acephalous or parasitic. 'The overseas church from the start,' Hogan says with deliberate emphasis, 'should be independent of foreign assistance for its essential structure, leadership and resources.'[4]

This organic concept of the missionary church, one that grows at its own initiative in its own cultural environment with only tentative external assistance, permits the emerging church, no matter how humble, to develop spiritual muscle and experience a trust in God that does not suffer from nominalism or imitation. Each national church may be expected to adapt to local circumstances, address its own concerns, forge its own faith. During its formation such a church recapitulates the growth process to ensure its complete, balanced development without demeaning servility, slavish copying, and limiting dependence.

Comparisons of Pentecostal missions with other Protestant efforts

While Pentecostals must be cautious in assessing their role – their operating assumption is that no sectarian group can claim a monopoly on the operation of the Holy Spirit – there are several empirical indications that Assemblies of God missionary work, energized by its distinctive missiology, has developed appreciably differently from other missions. For one thing, studies undertaken by church growth researchers have found that its missionary-to-adherents ratio is far lower than for most missions. The *Latin American Church Growth* study (1969) compared the proportion of missionaries supported by each group with the proportion of adherents

---

[4] JPH, letter to author, 8 February 1995.

they reported. The figures showed that the missions that had invested the most in missionaries had actually produced the least growth. Pentecostals, with about 10 per cent of the overseas missionary force, produced two-thirds of the adherents.[5] While these statistics require explanation (e.g., many missions are service or social welfare agencies which by their nature would produce few local congregations; also, the statistics given for Latin America include several large Pentecostal movements that received virtually no missionary support), the inference is that Pentecostal missionary undertakings are indeed different from those of other groups. For example, detailed follow-up studies of the ratios of missionaries to national pastors and congregations in Central America in the 1990s indicate that earlier findings have become even more pronounced – whereas the absolute number of missionaries had changed little in thirty years, the church has experienced rapid growth, further reducing the ratio of missionaries to churches and members.[6]

Theoretical expectations of missionary growth

Another perspective on worldwide Pentecostal church growth is provided by examining the theoretical expectations of social movements. Typically, social and political movements do not simply gain new adherents indefinitely. They grow only so long as they satisfy the needs of a specific, finite population, and decline because they reach some kind of logical growth limit, because they become internally inflexible, or because they have achieved their goals.[7] In fact, overseas Pentecostal churches in many

---

[5]   Five Categories of Missions Agencies at work in Latin America (1969)
The Proportion of Missionary Force and Percentage of Adherents

Type of Mission	Percentage of Combined Missionary Force	Percentage of Evangelical Adherents
Historic Denominations	44.8	25.5
Faith Missions	32.4	1.5
New Evangelical Missions	10.3	3.4
Pentecostals	9.8	63.3
Adventists	2.7	6.3

Source: Read, Monterroso, Johnson, *Latin American Church Growth*, 58.

[6]   Douglas Petersen, 'The Formation of Popular, National Autonomous Pentecostal Churches in Central America,' *Pneuma: The Journal of the Society of Pentecostal Studies* 16 (spring 1994): 23–48.

[7]   William Bruce Cameron holds that 'some movements fail for lack of a felt need for their wares, others because of more effective competition from rival agencies, and still others by working themselves out of a job.' William Bruce Cameron, *Modern Social Movements*, 25–33. While Cameron denies that a 'characteristic life cycle of movements'

instances have plateaued, and some fields have showed little yield after years of effort. But the net increases reported for these national movements often have greatly exceeded theoretical expectations.

During Hogan's tenure as director the adherents of overseas Assemblies of God churches registered a remarkably consistent cumulative increase of more than 10 per cent per year. At this rate growth would be – and was – exponential. Membership would double in only eight years, triple in twelve years and quadruple in just fifteen years. Such a development could hardly be considered typical and, as religious, political, and social action movements go, would have to be considered sustainable for only a brief time. But the Assemblies of God increased on the average by 12 per cent per year, sustained over three decades without indication of net decline.[8]

The Pentecostal phenomenon

That fact that the Pentecostal groups have grown worldwide through the aggregation of numerous, often small, national groups under one loosely knit denominational umbrella hardly detracts from their significance. How could often tiny, overlooked, or discounted national religious movements, generally drawn from the marginal social sectors, gain such large followings and exercise such responsible and effective administrative control over their own affairs with relatively little foreign assistance? Herein lies the secret of Pentecostal missionary effectiveness: not in the successful development of a US organization, but in the vitality of its corresponding overseas churches.

The following account of J. Philip Hogan's career reveals much about the Pentecostal phenomenon itself, for his story is intertwined with the story of an emerging global church that unites remarkably disparate peoples in a dynamic Christian faith.

---

can be found, he acknowledges the effort other sociologists have made to identify patterns of growth and decline. While each movement is unique, precluding predictive statements about its rise and fall, something like development and disintegration are regularly observed in an assortment of social movements. The extensive theoretical literature on religious sects and other movements, including the life cycles of social protest movements, is reviewed succinctly in *International Encyclopedia of the Social Sciences*. See especially the articles by Thomas F. O'Dea, 'Sects and Cults,' (14:130–136), and Joseph R. Gusfield, 'Social Movements: The Study,' (14:445–452). In reference to the 'career of social movements,' Gusfield points out that the 'idealism and missionary zeal of spontaneous emotional commitment to a cause tends to be "corrupted" by the tendency of all organizations to become "ends-in-themselves" ' (14:449).

[8] By way of comparison, at a growth-rate of 3 per cent, a given population would double within a generation. Obviously, Assemblies of God overseas growth is itself a phenomenal development and much greater than that of any other contemporary mission anywhere for sustained periods of time or covering so many fields.

[1]

On the Threshold

In 1959 no map of American religion would include anything called Pentecostal except at the margins or in the ecological niches. Pentecostalism then was simply a cluster of lower-class denominations perceived as being a branch of Fundamentalism.

Martin Marty[1]

Looking in

The Twenty-eighth General Council of the Assemblies of God attracted little notice when it convened in San Antonio, Texas, in August 1959. The meeting, at which Thomas F. Zimmerman and J. Philip Hogan were elected to the offices of general superintendent and director of the Division of Foreign Missions respectively, came at the beginning of a major missionary advance that would thereafter stand as a watershed in the denomination's development.

Apart from the energy and qualifications the new officers brought to their positions, they represented the coming to leadership of men and women whose experience in the Pentecostal movement dated back to the 1930s and '40s. J. Philip Hogan's mature world-view, values, and aspirations, like those of his ministerial colleagues, were shaped by times of crisis. Having witnessed among their own small circle of associates the impact of the full gospel emphases, the new leaders had confidence in their message and the promise it held for a society that seemed destined to self-destruct, confidence formed during the tragedies and uncertainties of economic depression, increasing racial tension, the Holocaust, a crusading global war, the beginnings of the Cold War, and demographic dislocation. But despite its growing confidence the Assemblies of God, like other Pentecostal organizations, was largely unknown and over-looked. As the nation's twenty-seventh largest religious body in membership, the denomination commanded few resources, seemed to offer few benefits to other Protestant groups, and posed no particular threat to the religious establishment.[2]

---

[1] Marty, *A Nation of Behavers*, 106

[2] The monumental study of American religion undertaken by Sydney E. Ahlstrom emphasized the Holiness origins of Pentecostalism with little further comment beyond

A problem of denominational identity

The person on the street in the 1950s, as well as informed clerics, sociologists, journalists, and other observers of American religion, attributed little importance to the Pentecostals. They were simply too out of rhythm with the American mainstream to deserve serious consideration. The standard source of information about such groups, Elmer T. Clark's *The Small Sects in America*, then on the shelves of many American public libraries, described the Assemblies of God in a chapter along with the Church of Jesus Christ of the Latter-day Saints and Father Divine's Peace Mission.[3] The Pentecostals came in for even less attention in Will Herberg's classic *Protestant, Catholic, Jew*, where they were cited only in passing as an example of small-town churches that served 'outsider' migrant laborers.[4]

Worse still for the members' fragile sense of denominational identity, journalists were uncertain about the spelling of the Pentecostals' generic name, often writing it as 'Pentacostal' (an error that still occurs with surprising frequency) as though it were somehow akin to 'Pentagon.'[5] Moreover, the name 'Assemblies of God' presented a problem even for the membership, despite the leadership's efforts to standardize usage with commercially produced church signs and an authorized logo – a matter that was taken up at the 1959 San Antonio General Council.[6] Since the name gave no hint of the group's theological commitments, journalists and editors were uncertain whether to list the group in denominational directories and sociological treatments under the 'A's' or along with the 'Pentacostal' religious fringe.

Furthermore, the standard index of popular reading, the *Reader's Guide to Periodical Literature*, over a period of six years from March 1957 to

---

noting the group's amazing capacity for evangelism. He subsumed the Pentecostals with other sectarian movements that tended to follow an ascending-descending life cycle. Sydney E. Ahlstrom, *A Religious History*, 819–822, 1059–1060, 1065–66, 1086n.

[3] Elmer T. Clark, *Small Sects*, 106, 107.

[4] Will Herberg, *Protestant, Catholic, Jew*, 217, 218. Herberg drew on the analysis of Walter R. Goldschmidt, 'Class Denominationalism in Rural California Churches,' *The American Journal of Sociology* 49, no. 4 (1944).

[5] Inconsistent usage also resulted from ambiguity about whether the term should be capitalized, a proper noun referring to a discrete membership, or whether, in lower case, it referred generically to anyone inclined to charismatic (a term then not widely used) utterances.

[6] Officially, it was a collective noun referring to the Assemblies of God denomination, but many members used it to refer to an individual congregation, each of which in this sense was an 'Assembly of God.' In the early years of the denomination, when envelopes were usually hand addressed, abbreviations of the denominational name, such as 'Ass. of God,' were frequent – and undoubtedly provided letter carriers with considerable amusement.

February 1963, out of 100,000 citations listed only six articles on Pentecostals, two of which were about Pentecostals in Latin America and one
about Pentecostals in Indian reservations in Montana. In the latter article
the author complained that the poorly educated Pentecostal missionaries
had a lifestyle 'much the same as the Indians,' enabling them to identify
with their hosts better than could the highly trained missionaries of other
denominations. 'The civilizing influence of the [major denominations]
was once great,' the author observed. 'Why then do the mainline
Protestant churches turn a deaf ear to the missionary challenge today and
leave the field to a quasi-Protestant group?'[7]

The *Reader's Guide* entry by Arthur Gilbert, an American rabbi who
journalistically covered the 1961 meeting of the World Pentecostal
Fellowship in Jerusalem, observed that most Israelis who dealt with the
Pentecostals were impressed by their goodness, simplicity, and fervor.
They appeared to be like the Hasidim among the Jews. Some Israelis
'empathized with the Pentecostals' sense of themselves as a "separate
people," ' reported Gilbert, 'a people rebuffed by intolerant, "respectable"
Christians.' As for the Pentecostal delegates, Gilbert reported, they
reserved their most enthusiastic responses for speakers who identified
themselves as 'having roots in denominational Christianity but who have
now come to realize that the Pentecostal experience alone provides the
church with power to overcome the corruption, the utter nothingness of
contemporary civilization.'[8]

For the reading public, the Pentecostals did not even provide the
fascination of the flag-rejecting Jehovah's Witnesses or the allegedly
polygamist Mormons, about whom there were dozens of articles. The
closest Pentecostals could come to notoriety was in a few exposés of
how serpents were used in meetings of the Kentucky snake handlers.[9]

---

[7] Vern Dusenberry, 'Montana Indians and the Pentecostals,' *Christian Century* (23 July
1958): 851, 852.

[8] Arthur Gilbert, 'Pentecost Among the Pentecostals,' *Christian Century* (28 June 1961): 794–796.

[9] Clark, *Small Sects*, 106, 107. Clark introduced the 'charismatic sects' with a discussion
of 'bizarre practices,' including 'snake cults,' although he acknowledged that these were
by no means representative of the Pentecostal movement (pp. 98, 99). In the authoritative
Dictionary of Pentecostal and Charismatic Movements (hereafter *DPCM*), the several items
included in the bibliography of the article on 'Serpent Handling' indicate that the topic
had continuing fascination for journalists at least into the 1970s. See Harold D. Hunter,
'Serpent Handling,' in *DPCM*, 777, 778. *DPCM*, interestingly, gives approximately as
much space (about 1000 words) to the subject as is devoted to either Charles Parham,
who is usually considered to be the founder of the modern Pentecostal movement, or to
evangelist Jimmy Swaggart. The article notes that endangerment of one's health to
demonstrate special spiritual grace or power occurred on occasion throughout church
history prior to the rise of Pentecostalism and notes that the Pentecostals generally have
repudiated such presumptuous practices.

Pentecostals, for many Americans, were best understood as a caricature of the sentimental, religious nostalgia aroused by recollections of summer tent revivals, grandma's worn Bible, and certain old camp-meeting songs.

Pentecostals, fundamentalists and evangelicals

The Protestant fundamentalists represented by Carl McIntire, Bob Jones, Jr., and John R. Rice, along with many other less well-known figures – some of whom were considered aggressive and contentious – had long since declared their unmitigated objection to Pentecostals, opposing efforts other than their own to unify the conservative wing of American Protestantism.[10] Fundamentalists seemed to reserve their most sarcastic caricatures for the 'tongues-people.' 'When the hound dog took some stray buckshot intended for the jack-rabbit,' said a popular radio preacher with a chuckle, 'it took off howling – just like a Pentecostal!' Sarcasm and diatribes notwithstanding, the Pentecostals usually identified with their fundamentalist antagonists' unflinching biblicism, apparently unbothered by ostracism and satisfied that were the fundamentalists able to see the light, those 'fiery sons of thunder' would probably themselves make good Pentecostals.

The evangelical wing of conservative Protestantism had taken a kinder view of the Pentecostal movement. Evangelist Billy Graham's Presbyterian medical-missionary father-in-law, L. Nelson Bell, as well as the pastor of Boston's upscale Park Street Congregational Church, Harold John Ockenga, *Christianity Today's* Carl Henry, Fuller Theological Seminary's Harold Lindsell, and at least a few other prominent evangelical figures knew that Protestant Christianity rose or fell on the revelational, suprarational gospel message. These evangelical statesmen recognized that Pentecostals affirmed the historical faith, even if they were not always as articulate and reasoning as was desirable, and although the more extreme among them sometimes engaged in questionable practices.

But if Pentecostals felt ignored, their initiatives and persistence showed that more than a little vitality lay behind these modest congregations with their curious practices. In August 1959, when *Life* magazine ran an article referring to the Sunday school as the 'most wasted' hour of the week, Assemblies of God pastors and lay leaders – many of whom attended the San Antonio General Council – felt vindicated for the high priority they had placed on improving Christian education by emphasizing graded

---

[10]   Edith L. Blumhofer, *Assemblies of God*, vol. 2, *Since 1941*, 16–29. Blumhofer indicates, however, that the fundamentalists' antipathy to Pentecostals was most pronounced after Pentecostal leaders rejected overtures to join with them in reforming the right-wing of American Protestantism.

Sunday school literature, teacher training seminars, and national and regional Sunday school conferences.[11]

The Pentecostal movement, whose demise had been frequently predicted in earlier decades, had demonstrated remarkable staying power and, ever since the economic depression of the 1930s, had shown more than merely incidental growth.[12] The problems brought by war in the 1940s became often opportunities for the crisis-oriented movement, as demographic changes brought many more Americans into contact with Pentecostal-type experiential Christianity. After the war, several of J. Philip Hogan's Bible school associates who had served as military chaplains returned to assume pastoral or denominational positions with broadened world-views and a newly found ability to adapt their message to the times.

Having long sat on the sidelines, singing literally and figuratively 'I'm going through – I'll take the way with the Lord's despised few,' the Pentecostals rebounded from World War II with enthusiasm and purpose. Recognition from the newly formed National Association of Evangelicals, the launching of their national radio ministry Revivaltime, relief activities in cooperation with the National Council of Churches' Church World Service, and involvement in the struggle of the Italian Pentecostals to gain their civil rights all tended to reflect the Pentecostals' growing institutional and moral strength, if not necessarily their theological acceptability.[13] It is not too much to say that there was a growing sence of hope, satisfaction, and even confidence within the movement.

The beginnings of recognition

If recognition and respect from the outside had been slow in coming, the Pentecostals often seemed oblivious or simply unconcerned about it. 'Some people say we Pentecostals are uncouth,' roared an executive officer to an attentive audience in the early 1960s. 'Folks,' he continued confidently – if ungrammatically – 'I'll have you know we have lots of couth!' The fact was that the constituents of the Assemblies of God believed wholeheartedly that they had found something worthy of their

---

[11] Ronald C. Doll, 'Should We Close the Sunday School,' *Christianity Today* (31 August 1959): 3–5. See W. Schroder, 'Our Troubled Sunday Schools,' *Life* (11 February 1957).

[12] Robert Mapes Anderson has analyzed the 1930s as a turning point in Pentecostal growth, making use of the US Bureau of the Census, *Religious Bodies, 1936*, 3 vols. (Washington, D.C.: Government Printing Office, 1941), in his *Vision of the Disinherited*. Although Anderson's explanations about the origins of the movement in the social hostility of the marginal and immigrant populations has been repeatedly questioned, his discussion of the early years of the movement remains one of the most thorough and insightful yet to appear.

[13] The emergence of the Assemblies of God in Italy and its relationship to the DFM is treated in Chapter 7.

commitment. They had seen and felt too much of a personally reassuring faith to take social slights seriously. There were, moreover, encouraging indications that in religious circles some sensitive people from other traditions were beginning to understand the reason for the Pentecostals' enthusiasm and tenacity. In the National Association of Evangelicals the Assemblies of God had acquired respect.[14] Already Noel Perkin, Secretary of the DFM, had been elected to serve as president of the National Association's missionary arm, the Evangelical Foreign Missions Association. The days when standard reference sources categorized the Pentecostals as an off-brand cult were not left behind, but the religious world – and members of the movement themselves – had begun to recognize that what they had long believed and witnessed could not be ignored indefinitely. The Pentecostal movement, on the basis of the increasing tempo of its forward progress, appeared to be on the threshold of a major advance.

By 1959 the emergence of the Assemblies of God, as well as other Pentecostal groups, had made a few journalists re-examine their 'Holy Roller' stereotypes of Pentecostals. An evangelist at an Assemblies of God district meeting the previous year, in the middle of his energetic sermon, held aloft a copy of *Coronet* magazine to show his audience an article titled 'The Old Time Religion Comes Back.' 'The fastest-growing Protestant religion today is the Pentecostal movement,' wrote Richard Carter.

> [Its] members used to be nicknamed 'Holy Rollers,' but they have become too important to remain a target of derision. In barely a half century, this dynamic young version of old-time fundamentalism, which has produced spectacularly successful leaders such as Oral Roberts and the late Aimee Semple McPherson, has won the devotion of at least 2,000,000 Americans of every racial and religious origin and, through zealous foreign missionary work, has gained thousands of converts on every continent.[15]

The president of New York's prestigious Union Theological Seminary, Henry P. Van Dusen, in June 1958 in *Life* magazine took up the same theme. He asserted that the kind of religion he called 'the third force' came closer to the traditional faith than the sometimes perfunctory liturgies of the traditional Christian churches. Perhaps the Pentecostals were on the 'fringe,' retorted Van Dusen, 'but on the fringe of what?'

> Perhaps on the fringe of traditional churches, but not necessarily on the fringe of Christendom. Many features of this 'new' Christianity bear striking resemblance to the life of the earliest Christian churches as revealed in the New Testament. Peter and Barnabas and Paul might find themselves more at

---

14 It may be argued that acceptance of the Assemblies of God had more to do with the organization's size and resources than acquiescence to its beliefs and practices. Blumhofer, *The Assemblies of God*, 2:16–29.

15 Richard Carter, 'The Old Time Religion Comes Back,' *Coronet* 43 (February 1958): 125–30.

home in a Holiness service or at a Pentecostal revival than in the formalized and sophisticated worship of other churches, Catholic or Protestant.[16]

Thus one of the nation's leading churchmen not only affirmed the Pentecostals' ecclesiastical legitimacy but also commended their spiritual intensity. Pentecostals were becoming, at least for a few observers, a topic of conversation. They offered a dynamic religious alternative. Their values, practices and associations seemed appropriate to the needs of a good many people. At times they demonstrated vision, daring, and initiative related, apparently, to their stirring encounters with God at a church altar, a rousing worship service, or a cottage prayer meeting. But whatever other religious groups thought of them, Pentecostals found their experiences satisfying and their emphases vindicated. While the years ahead brought greatly increased recognition and opportunity, the future of the movement as it would eventually emerge could scarcely have been imagined when ministers and lay delegates gathered at the organization's biennial business meeting in August 1959.

It was against this backdrop that J. Philip Hogan, successful as an Assemblies of God evangelist and pastor, and with a creditable if brief missionary career aborted by the closing of China, found himself on his return to the United States in office as Promotional Director of the Division of Foreign Missions. This newly created position required him to develop the basic tools and policies needed for placing the agency's appeals before its denominational constituents. While at age forty-three Hogan was sufficiently mature, experienced, and well-known to occupy a national office, there were no guarantees that in the future he would be considered for the directorship of the DFM when the incumbent leader, the venerated Noel Perkin, retired. Less than two years earlier, Emil Balliet, recently the pastor of the flagship Central Assembly in Springfield, Missouri, had been named as the assistant to Perkin, obviously to groom him for the position in a system that tended to leave room for few surprises.

A little-recognized Assemblies of God landmark

Likely few of the men and women *en route* to San Antonio realized the importance of what was happening in their movement. Virtually unobserved and without comment, the Assemblies of God had just recently achieved one of the most important landmarks in its half-century history: the growth of the overseas membership in the aggregate to exceed that of the American counterpart. Sometime after the mid-1950s, before such statistics were routinely published, the combined memberships of Assem-

---

[16]   Henry P. Van Dusen, 'Force's Lessons for Others,' *Life* (9 June 1958). Flattered by this recognition, Pentecostals seemed to overlook the fact that Van Dusen lumped them with Seventh-day Adventists, Jehovah's Witnesses, and some non-Christian groups.

blies of God overseas national organizations surpassed the membership of the denomination in the United States.[17]

This notable overseas growth was the result of a commitment to missionary effort since the church's beginnings in 1914. Missions for most Pentecostals had never been merely the dutiful fulfillment of an obligation. The missionary task for many came close to being their movement's organizational reason-for-being. With members drawn disproportionately from ethnic and immigrant populations, cultural frontiers had never been either the threat or the restrictive barriers for the Assemblies of God that they sometimes had been for other Protestant denominations. Moreover, the charisma of tongues, believed by some adherents in the early days of the movement to be the ability to speak a language that one had never learned, had consecrated cross-cultural communication even when the language had to be learned.[18] It was not only or even primarily at home where the Pentecostal message had to be proclaimed. Both because spiritually hungry people overseas were often more responsive to the message and because the handicaps of cross-cultural ministry and uncertain times forced missionaries to demonstrate extraordinary power, the

[17]

Table 4.
Comparative Growth of the Assemblies of God.
US and Overseas Constituencies, 1951–1960

Year	Churches	Membership	Sunday School	Overseas Adherents
1951	5,950	318,478	N/A	N/A
1952	5,950	318,478	599,872	N/A
1953	6,362	370,118	710,220	N/A
1954	6,396#	N/A	N/A	426,937*
1955	6,400	370,118	N/A	N/A
1956	7,170	400,000	775,100	N/A
1957	7,320	400,047	805,182	N/A
1958	7,916	470,361	878,000	627,598**
1959	8,104	482,352	893,530	919,704**
1960	8,088	505,552	922,663	949,034**

Source: The *Yearbook of American Churches* and *Key* (2nd quarter 1961), 3; **Assemblies of God Biennial Report, 1985, 25. #Division of Home Mission, National Council of the Churches of Christ in the US, 'Churches and Church Membership in the United States,' series B, no. 8 (1956): 2. Since the Sunday school statistics for the US Assemblies of God were probably more comparable to the reported overseas adherents than were published memberships, the year when the aggregate overseas national Assemblies of God organizations overtook the US membership was probably 1959, precisely the year J. Philip Hogan was elected Director of the Division of Foreign Missions.

[18] When xenoglossy (the term used to describe the ability to speak a modern language without having learned it) failed the early twentieth-century missionaries, who found themselves unable to communicate once they had arrived at their foreign stations, Pentecostals still held the conviction that the shortness of time made their reaching the unevangelized imperative. See Russell Spittler, 'Glossolalia,' *DPCM*, 335–341.

Pentecostal emphases were especially appropriate and appreciated overseas.[19] These incentives, along with the need to proclaim the good news
globally prior to the imminent Second Coming, necessarily made the
whole world the Pentecostals' sphere of operations.[20]

The 1959 General Council

The hotels in San Antonio began to fill with Assemblies of God members
the day before the General Council began on Wednesday, 26 August. As
the delegates entered the 6,000-seat Municipal Auditorium for the initial
evening meeting, the hall was decorated with the large blue-and-gold
Assemblies of God logo, over which hung a banner with the council theme,
'Forward with Christ.' Following official greetings from Associate Justice
Clyde Smith of the Texas Supreme Court, General Superintendent Ralph
M. Riggs, himself a former missionary, brought the keynote message based
on the convention theme. 'What we call the Great Commission,' he told
his audience, 'could just as aptly be termed the "Big Appointment." Christ
made an appointment to meet with His disciples in Galilee and "in all the
world" – and He met them. Today He waits just as surely to meet us
wherever we go as witnesses to this glorious gospel.'[21]

The audience was next invited to witness the production of the
denomination's radio program *Revivaltime*, a minor miracle, given the
difficulty fundamentalists had in securing network air time in the face of
establishment opposition. Featuring C. Morse Ward, a bombastic radio
speaker, the program was scheduled for release on the ABC network the
following Sunday evening. It would reach into homes of Assemblies of
God constituents throughout the nation and would be rebroadcast to a
few English-speaking radio audiences abroad. 'Across the nation and
around the world,' announcer Bartlett Peterson proclaimed with enthusiasm after the opening notes of the theme were sung by the choir, 'it's
Revivaltime!' The moment gave the modest assembly a sense of corporate
pride. Even if the claim of being heard around the world was then
exaggerated, it would soon, increasingly, become a reality.

The next morning Superintendent Riggs called order to the first
business session. The moment had arrived to announce the outcomes
of the various elections and the fate of the proposed resolutions
appearing in the published agenda. The possibility of substantial change
was more than a matter of 'cloakroom speculation.' The planned

---

[19]   Some Pentecostal evangelists through the years may have deliberately used overseas
mass campaigns to advance their reputation, given the ease of attracting large crowds, the
greater openness to mystical phenomena, and the spontaneous response to their messages.
[20]   Non-Pentecostal missionary agencies had long alleged that the group frequently
lacked respect for the comity agreements that parceled out overseas territories to given
missions to avoid competition and duplication of effort.
[21]   'General Council Chronicle,' *Pentecostal Evangel* (11 October 1959): 5.

retirement of J. Roswell Flower, the general secretary who had served the General Council since its inception in 1914, and missionary secretary Noel Perkin's previous decision to retire at the end of the biennium required the Council in session to elect replacements. Given some of the progressive policies and measures supported by the incumbent superintendent Ralph M. Riggs, including the founding of an Assemblies of God liberal arts college, emphasis on catechetical literature for children, and plans for a denominational seminary, the mood generally was for moving more slowly, retrenching, and reaffirming more traditional policies and leadership styles. The elections raised the possibility of major changes with uncertain consequences.

To open the session Superintendent Riggs invited Thomas F. Zimmerman to read a telegram from President Dwight D. Eisenhower: 'Gathered from all parts of the nation and united in one faith, you can accomplish much together. I am sure you will be inspired to advance in the service of God and neighbor. Best wishes for a fine meeting.' In response to this 'kind message from the President,' the convention voted to send a suitable reply. The message and its response – both pro forma – reflected what was obvious: that what went on in the biennial meeting of a Pentecostal denomination was hardly of primary importance in the life of the nation.[22]

Having taken care of the formalities, the council addressed the real issues for which they had gathered, namely the reports of the executive officers which indicated, among other findings, that the movement was growing at a slower annual rate than in previous years. Perhaps as a direct result, on Friday morning occurred one of the more unusual developments in General Council annals. In the task of electing a general superintendent for the following four years, the meeting failed to return the incumbent to office. The succeeding electoral ballots confirmed what was immediately conjectured, namely Ralph Riggs would be replaced by the younger, more charismatic Thomas F. Zimmerman. Having elected a new general superintendent, the next drama to unfold was the election of the director of the DFM.

J. Philip Hogan and Global Conquest

On Saturday afternoon three names were placed in nomination for the post of missionary director, namely Emil Balliet, J. Philip Hogan, and Melvin Hodges. Hodges, the Field Director for Latin America and the Caribbean, had emerged as the denomination's leading missionary theoretician. After Noel Perkin expressed his feeling that 'the responsibilities of the office should be placed on younger shoulders,' the first electoral ballot was cast with none of the nominees receiving a two-thirds

---

[22] Ibid., 5, 6.

majority.[23] Emil Balliet received 407 votes, J. Philip Hogan received 405, and Melvin Hodges 285. A second electoral ballot was cast before adjournment, with the results not to be formally announced until the business session of the following Monday.

Late that evening, the Hogan's phone rang at their rented home in south Springfield, Missouri. Virginia, concerned about caring for their daughter Lynne, and not wanting the family budget to bear the expense of attending the meeting, had remained in Springfield. The call was to report that her husband was running strong; that there was a good possibility that he would be elected to succeed Noel Perkin.

Sentiments scarcely covered by a veneer of rationalizations, loyalties, and commitments threatened to erupt within Virginia Hogan. She tried to sort out her feelings: pride in her husband and appreciation for the respect shown him helped keep in check the ominous fears of losing him to endless travel, prolonged meetings, disrupted schedules, and separation – perhaps for weeks at a time. The executive career of Virginia Hogan's father, Gayle Lewis, one of the assistant superintendents, had demonstrated the personal sacrifice and unreasonable demands such a position could make on a person's time, priorities, and privacy. She had observed what her mother had endured and what she, as a daughter, had experienced in having to share her father unduly with his work. 'Why me?' The question had been asked, often in even more difficult situations. But was there never a respite from the demands, the intrusions, the uncertainty, and the loneliness? She knew that she would work out the misgivings and put on a smile when her own feelings had to give place to the greater good. Should she have gone to the council? Then again, she couldn't have – she was needed at home. Maybe Emil Balliet would still be elected. Clearly he had been groomed for the position. Of course her husband would bring excellent qualifications to the office, but she was not prepared to face all the implications of his possible election.[24]

On Sunday afternoon two hundred missionaries in national dress paraded through the hall to the strains of 'Onward Christian Soldiers' toward the seats provided for them on the platform. The main feature of the missionary rally was J. Philip Hogan's presentation of the newly unveiled 'Global Conquest' program, prelude to an offering to be taken in all Assemblies of God churches and reported at the council. Offerings reported by telephone amounted to $56,000, with another $20,000 in cash and pledges during the afternoon service – encouraging support, but hardly sums that guaranteed a greatly accelerated overseas missionary effort. Hogan's inspiring presentation, however, could hardly be overlooked as balloting for the missions director continued the next day.

---

[23]   Ibid., 9.

[24]   Virginia Hogan's feelings were well founded. At the time of her husband's retirement, their friend Paul Lowenburg wrote in her praise that she had waited for her husband through the years 'at the end of a thousand runways.'

On Monday morning the business session resumed at 9:30 a.m. with Thomas F. Zimmerman, the general superintendent-elect, presiding. On the fourth electoral ballot J. Philip Hogan received 835 of the 1195 votes cast, the required two-thirds majority for election. In fact, Hogan's election by this time should not have been a surprise. He had been acquiring an increasingly important place in the DFM's operation since he came aboard as promotional secretary in 1953. In contrast with the aging executives who received, primarily, veneration, Hogan and Zimmerman represented energy, action, and results. Although in the following years Hogan's keen perception of the fundamental issues, his good judgment, decisiveness, initiative, and willingness to take responsibility showed him to be a strong leader who continued to gain increasing respect throughout his tenure, at the time Hogan had no guarantee of either success or recognition. Instead he faced hard work, increasing pressures, concerns, challenges, and difficult problems demanding immediate solutions.

An uncertain future

Given their global vision, the Pentecostals had to face the same overwhelming world problems that kept statesmen, intellectuals, scientists, and generals sleepless. Not only did disruptive world conditions make missionary efforts uncertain and sometimes hazardous; they also presented a challenge even to the maintaining of conventional approaches. The end of colonialism, rising antipathy to the West, continuing strong ideological tensions, and the loss of financial advantage with the rise of industrial powers outside North America and Europe made traditional missionary efforts increasingly less viable. Moreover, established policies and approaches to missionary work were frequently called into question. Hogan's success as a missionary leader would have to be achieved despite a number of handicaps originating both from within and without the Pentecostal movement.

If the Pentecostals proclaimed the Acts of the Apostles to be normative even in the twentieth century, they had to demonstrate that their beliefs could produce the same apostolic impact. In effect, rather average men and women, compelled by uncharacteristic vision, courage, and confidence, had to place themselves in positions where either their faith and initiative were vindicated or their sincere, generally sacrificial efforts went for naught. If the next years proved to be extremely successful for J. Philip Hogan and the DFM, their achievement was accomplished despite discouraging, faith-testing situations, and without reassurance – except for their own inner sense of God's accompanying presence.

[2]

Profile of a Pentecostal

The manners in vogue among the 'Assemblies of God' recall the amenity of the early Christians. Even when unacquainted, Holy Rollers salute each other as 'friend' and 'brother.' They shake hands, sometimes they piously kiss. 'Glory, Hallelujah! Praise the Lord!' Their faces shine.

Jules Bois[1]

The making of a leader

When J. Philip Hogan retired from his administrative office in 1990, the shadow of his influence had been cast over the development of a Pentecostal national church in more than a hundred countries of the world. In his moral support of national leaders, the development of pastoral training schools, the recruitment and placement of missionary personnel, and in his inspiring sermons and financial support for strategic projects, he had played a key role in promoting, nurturing, and advising a movement that, having been counted in hundreds of thousands of adherents in 1960, was numbered in tens of millions in 1990. Throughout his lengthy tenure, however, even more important than his tangible contributions were the strength of character, the spiritual sensitivity, the focused vision that characterized his firm but sensitive leadership.

Leadership, crucial in any organization, has received exaggerated attention among Pentecostals. These believers have often accepted the elevation of a given figure as a divine appointment, 'God's man' or 'God's woman' for a given challenge – as Ralph Riggs gave way to Thomas F. Zimmerman at the San Antonio General Council in 1959. The fact remains that leaders have invariably been men and women who have risen within the ranks, subject to the approval of their peers. Thus, popularly elected Pentecostal leaders tend to be a product of the movement, mirroring its strengths and weaknesses.

There are more than a few ironies in viewing Phil Hogan as a representative Pentecostal. A man of strong feelings and commitments, he rarely displayed the volatility and emotional excesses usually ascribed to adherents of the movement. A man who did as much as any twenti-

---

[1] Jules Bois, 'The New Religions of America,' *The Forum* 73 (February 1925):145–155.

eth-century figure to promote, structure, and represent the Assemblies of God around the world, his family had little association with the group until they enrolled two of their sons in the school of the denomination's headquarters in Springfield, Missouri, in 1933. As an executive leader who had a good grasp of historical development and an insatiable hunger for learning, Hogan's early years were spent in a culturally disadvantaged environment.

Since J. Philip Hogan grew up in rural America, in a way of life that even then was disappearing, his development appears to be as much influenced by the traditional values and demands of farm life as by features that have been considered distinctively Pentecostal. During the years of his DFM leadership his associates were constantly reminded of his origins, the influences that in later years were detectable in his language, thinking, and down-to-earth practicality.[2] Hogan's years as an evangelist, pastor, missionary, and missions staff member provide a profile of his professional performance, but his administrative approaches and the many crisis decisions he made as director of the DFM were based on something more fundamental – the experiences and influences that shaped his early years.

While Hogan was on hand to observe the emergence of the twenti-eth-century Pentecostal movement, a time filled with colorful personali-ties and the tug-and-pull of heated religious controversies, his own spiritual development seems to have been little affected by the maelstrom around him, evidence of a frame of mind encouraged by the Pentecostal emphases on subjective experience. While spectators saw the emotional-ism of participants, and the religiously sophisticated the alleged tenuous-ness in the movement's theology, Pentecostals like Hogan found assurance in their personally vindicated faith, a confidence that persisted and spread as it found new contexts in a spiritual renewal of global proportions.

---

[2] At J. Philip Hogan's retirement, his colleagues presented him with a small red book reminiscent of the philosophical bible of Maoist Communism, *Quotations from Chairman Mao Tsetung*. The gleanings of Hogan's remarks, the 'Quaint Sayings of Chairman Ho,' were represented as those remarks that have 'challenged and instructed us . . . in sermons, presentations, dialogues and teaching sessions.' Among them one finds gems of practical wisdom:

> 'You can't just keep cutting and covering the furrows.'
> 'You've got to get your plow in the ground.'
> 'Don't have more harness than you have horse.'
> 'You can't grow a garden if you keep pulling up the roots to look at them.'
> 'The river only flows one way.'
> 'We believe in a good harvest, but we keep hoeing.'
> 'Don't buy blue sky.'
> 'Don't bury the horses with the Indian chiefs.'
> 'You could eat up your seed corn in a hurry.'
> 'This is biodegradable: it will dissolve itself.'
> 'Don't put too much green wood on the fire.'

J. Philip Hogan at Central Bible Institute (CBI)

The first description of Hogan as a young adult is his appearance as a student at Central Bible Institute (CBI) in Springfield, Missouri. (The school later changed its name to Central Bible College [CBC].) There, in the fall of 1933, he enrolled as a freshman student after having graduated from public high school near Kansas City. His contemporaries remember him as 'fine looking,' 'well liked,' 'devout,' 'a born leader.' His classmate Ruth Greve recalls that Hogan was one of a group of highly regarded students that included Cy Homer, whom Ruth later married, J. Bash Bishop and Roy Wead.[3] Each of the four would have a lengthy and rewarding career as a Pentecostal minister.[4]

The atmosphere of CBI in the 1930s was largely created by the imposing W. I. Evans, supported by several influential teachers, including Myer Pearlman, a British Jew who converted to Pentecostalism as an adult, local pastor Ralph M. Riggs, Roland Burns and A. L. Hoy, none of whom, despite their personal strengths, had much formal preparation. Also influential were CBI guest speakers Hattie Hammond, an engaging mystic, and Howard Osgood, a capable, inspiring former Presbyterian missionary in China.

For Ruth Greve, who had attended another college previously, academic expectations at CBI were disappointing. She found little intellectual challenge in the lockstep curriculum, where each student in the respective three years took the same courses. Rather than textbooks, students studied sets of mimeographed notes on which, typically, they were tested after the instructor handed out the answers to the anticipated questions.[5] The course content itself, given indiscriminately to both men

---

[3]   Ruth Homer, letter to author, 15 May 1995.

[4]   J. Bashford Bishop's father was a Dartmouth graduate and Columbia University PhD who had specialized in international relations. He met Bash's mother while the two were serving as Methodist missionaries in China, and gave their son, who was raised speaking Mandarin Chinese, a prep school education. After the family's return to the United States and the birth of a mentally impaired younger child, the Bishops began to attend a Pentecostal mission in Washington, D.C. Their Methodist Episcopal pastor, Dr Charles A. Shreve, meantime, had also come under the influence of Aimee Semple McPherson and left the Methodist Church to become a widely circulating Pentecostal evangelist. As a teenager, the sociable, athletic J. Bash Bishop was incapacitated by tuberculosis, from which he was healed in what became a dramatic turning point in his life. Bishop's wife Ruth, the daughter of a Presbyterian minister who became a Pentecostal, contributed importantly to his successful teaching and pastoral career. At his retirement in 1983, J. Bash Bishop had distinguished himself as a college teacher and author of Bible study materials. See Glen Gohr, 'J. Bashford Bishop,' *Assemblies of God Heritage* (spring 1993): 10–13; continued in (summer 1993): 27–29. Cy Homer attended seminary in the 1940s to qualify as a military chaplain and later served as president of Southeastern College of the Assemblies of God, Lakeland, Florida. Roy H. Wead became a prominent pastor and founder of Trinity Bible College, Ellendale, North Dakota; see Wayne Warner, 'Wead, Roy H.' in *DPCM*, 880.

and women, was either unduly practical (storytelling, blackboard drawing) or geared to public ministry (homiletics, prophecy). The redeeming feature of the time spent at CBI, beyond the firm structure it gave to students' personal growth in discipline, was the challenge to serve God wholeheartedly, to find their unique gifts and accede to the divinely appointed opportunities which made ministry as much an adventure in trusting God as it was a profession or even a solemn charge.

Campus regulations at CBI, like those at similar sectarian training schools at the time (Moody Bible Institute, Chicago, was the prototype) prohibited socializing between unmarried students, allowing dating only in the final semester of their final year, and then only once a month on Saturday afternoons, within the city limits and in the company of another couple. The dean of men was a 'snooper,' Ruth Greve recalls. 'Eleanor ("Mother") Bowie, the women's dean, was at least a little more understanding in overseeing the girl students in her charge.' Since Hogan lived at home with his parents until his third year, when he was deeply involved off campus in a local 'outstation' church, he had more freedom than most students.

Classmate Adele Flower Dalton remembers the impression Hogan made on her one morning as students were gathering in the cafeteria for breakfast. As he led the group in prayer, his intensity, the ease with which he expressed his feelings, his vision and sensitivity were arresting.[6] Reflection on Hogan's compelling convictions helps to explain why the socially marginal Pentecostal movement was able to attract and inspire some men and women of exceptionally great ability and dedication.

Hogan's early training

Hogan's earliest recollections were of a home in Colorado's Western Slope. His father's family had come from Rockingham County, Virginia, while his mother's, the Van Trumps, originated in Pennsylvania. After the Civil War, Hogan's paternal grandparents came west to St Louis by train, then proceeded up the Missouri River by barge, sculled and pulled by mules. They landed at Waverly, 56 miles east of Kansas City, and settled on the clay hills to the north of the Missouri River.

Hogan's parents remained in Missouri for several years after they married, but hearing reports of a reclamation project that would bring water from the Gunnison River on Colorado's Western Slope, they moved to the still developing region when World War I was becoming a watershed in the life of the nation. Olathe, where they made their home on the California Mesa, stood a mile high, more than a thousand feet above nearby Grand Junction, on a tributary of the Gunnison. The task

5 Ruth Homer, letter to author, 15 May 1995.
6 Adele Flower Dalton, letter to author, 12 February 1995.

confronting settlers was to subdue and cultivate the land, wresting from
it the wealth latent in its soil. Although in the beginning life in their
clapboard house was severe, conditions improved as under irrigation the
arid, sage-brush-covered land began to flourish. The couple's oldest son
David was just two years old when the family came from Missouri in
1909. Their daughter Helen was born in 1911. The next year the family
moved into a two-story house where Gene Hogan was born in 1913 and
J. Philip Hogan on 4 December 1915.[7]

By the time the youngest child Robert was born in 1925, Hogan was
attending a little country school, rising at 5 a.m. to help milk the cows
and clean the separator before breakfast. 'We survived by running cattle
in the hills, and raising sugar beets, corn and alfalfa,' he recalls. 'I had my
own pony and kept track of the livestock.' During these years he first
encountered people who spoke a different language and had different
customs, giving rise to his deep sense that all people, despite cultural
differences, are fundamentally the same. Referring to the Mexican
laborers hired to help with the beet harvest, he recalls having learned
enough Spanish to communicate basic information. Life was hard and
demanding, he confides. 'I grew up accepting things as they were, to live
life as it comes.' Given these rugged, leveling circumstances, it would be
difficult to find any stronger influence on J. Philip Hogan's personal values
than the hardy, self-sufficient life imposed by long workdays, responsibility to one's family, extremes of weather, and the impatience of the often
anxious tiller of the soil who plants, waters, and cultivates with an eye to
the sky, praying for a bountiful harvest.

The test of the man

Hogan's home on the north side of Springfield, Missouri, is filled with
reminders of his boyhood. The bookshelves are lined with the works of
western authors Zane Grey, Will James, and Louis L'Amour. Western
works of art, depicting cattle drives, campfire scenes, and horses, are the
representations that he guards of his own background, exuding nostalgia
for an era long past. 'When my parents took the Colorado homestead,
one of the few pieces of furniture that they took with them was an Edison
gramophone that played with a scratchy needle. One of the tunes I
remember hearing over and over again was "We'll build us a nest,
somewhere in the West, and let the rest of the world go by." '

Even if that tune failed to foresee his later globetrotting career, having
a Western emotional refuge remained important to Hogan. In mid-career
he began to train quarter horses and keep cattle, a diversion from the

---

[7] Information about the Hogan family is taken from interviews with J. Philip Hogan
and Virginia Hogan, printed materials in the Hogan Files, DFM archives, Springfield,
Missouri and a taped interview with David Hogan which is now in the Assemblies of God
Archives, Springfield, Missouri.

administrative pressures and a way to identify with the values and way of life of his youth.[8] For several years Hogan and a group of friends would take their annual vacations in Colorado, riding their mounts amid massive, sculpted landscapes, enjoying the fragrance of lofty, pine-scented trails. The Rockies for Phil Hogan were imposing, sometimes tranquil, often ruthless and unforgiving, but always impressive in nature's display of exuberance, sheer power, and unsurpassed beauty. 'I started going back to Colorado to hunt and ride some of that same high ridge country,' he comments. 'Twice I have ridden with a pack animal from central Colorado to the New Mexico state border.'

The message of Hogan's identification with frontier life and his attachment to books by cowboy authors, some of whose stories he read repeatedly, is unavoidable: the unrelenting demands of life soon determine the mettle of the man. This was the determination, the resilience, the strength of character that lay beneath Hogan's Pentecostal faith. There is no escaping the tests of courage and the need to be self-sufficient for men and women who must work out of doors, subject to fickle changes of weather, easily frightened animals, and the unpredictable hazards and brute power of nature. Ultimately, here Hogan had to face himself, his weaknesses, his fears, his mortality, his God. Character, for the person who sees nature as a constant adversary as well as a sometimes bountiful provider, is not so much conferred as it is forged, tempered in adversity, by facing with equanimity the worst that circumstances can bring. Pointing out a selection from a Louis L'Amour short story, Hogan identifies in the protagonist's doggedness his own unyielding tenacity.

> There is a time when human nature seems able to stand no more. There is a time when every iota of strength seems burned away. The thought of how easy it would be to quit came to him. He considered the thought. But he did not consider quitting. Life was ahead, and he had to live. The man with the greatest urge to live would be the one to survive.[9]

How such a philosophy relates to the rise of Pentecostalism has perhaps rarely been considered, but the process of plumbing the foundations of confidence, finding greater reliance on God's provision, and developing ever greater sensitivity to divine leading comes closer to an understanding of Pentecostal spirituality than does the alleged escapism, emotional opiates, and flights of hysteria attributed to the 'tongues people.'

---

[8] An anecdote found among the letters of congratulation presented to J. Philip Hogan at the time of his retirement in 1990 recalls how a pastor visiting Springfield from out-of-state was introduced to Phil Hogan at the home of a mutual friend. Hogan, coming directly from working at his ranch and wearing Levis and dusty boots, had dropped by to attend to some matter of business. 'I knew then,' recalled his new acquaintance, 'that Phil Hogan was my kind of man.'

[9] Louis L'Amour, *Law of the Desert Born* (New York: Bantam Books, 1983), 13, 14.

While Hogan knew the affection of loving parents, he also knew severity, discipline, and emotional control. At moments of greatest tragedy he handled his own personal anguish with stoic impassivity. Virginia Hogan recalls the evening in 1957 when she received a call from the deputy sheriff to inform her that their eighteen-year-old son Richard had been involved in a fatal automobile accident. The terrible confirmation followed as Virginia's father, Gayle Lewis, went to the hospital to identify Richard's body and learn the details of how a motorist under the influence of alcohol had come across the center divider to collide head-on with the Hogans' car, filled with young people and driven by their son.

Hogan, out of town at the time, returned immediately to confront the most difficult moments of his life. Why was Richard taken? The fact that he had been a model Christian young person – capable, well-liked, serious about life, and eager to serve God – made accepting his loss even more difficult. The kindness of the Hogans' colleagues and friends and the vitality of the young people, who affirmed what his parents believed about Richard in the moving memorial service, were not enough to assuage the couple's pain. 'Phil Hogan took Richard's death so hard that he couldn't talk about it,' observed a close friend. 'He carried within himself the crushing grief. Probably the wound never healed.' While Hogan, on the face of it, closed the door on that part of his life and moved on, determined not to allow his personal tragedy to dampen his conviction that God's ways were above his own, the awful event remained to shape his attitudes and his perspective on life. Other personal disappointments equally were buried deep in his own reflections, not allowed to intrude into what increasingly he believed to be his divinely appointed course.

The process of realizing his calling had begun early in Hogan's life. 'Most of my training was given to me by my mother,' he reflects. His older brother David explains that their mother was very religious, a Methodist. 'At the birth of each child she solemnly dedicated each of her children to the Lord.' Hogan remembers her as the most stabilizing influence in his early development.

> She taught me a love of reading, of learning. She would say, 'Find something to improve your mind.' She would keep things for us to read on the long winter evenings. I developed the habit of reading profusely. I have always loved books.

When Hogan and his brother were about 6 and 8 years old, their mother found the boys trying to roll cigarettes in the cabin occasionally occupied by hired hands. Hogan's brother remembers how their mother, with the help of a leather strap, taught her sons a memorable lesson on the wages of sin.

Pentecostalism comes to Olathe

A major turning point in the family's experience occurred one day in 1920 when the Full Gospel message reached the remote valleys and mesas of the Western Slope. 'No single person stands out, but, one by one, different individuals appeared on the scene to cultivate the fledgling revival,' Hogan recalls. 'They came by bicycle, by bus – and since by this time our family had become a sort of custodian of the new spiritual fervor – these visiting evangelists ended up in our house.'

One day, after some of the seekers had begun to meet in the local school, the little group arrived to find the door padlocked. The pastor of a local denominational congregation had prevailed on members of the Ku Klux Klan to stop the growing influence of the 'Holy Rollers.' Hogan's father, while not at the time a committed believer, nevertheless would brook no intimidation. He stopped at the local store and asked the proprietor for a box of shells for his 12-gauge shotgun. Asked why he wanted buckshot at that time of the year Hogan's father made his position unambiguous: 'Elmer, I hear that the Klan is planning to pay a visit to our meeting, and I just want to be prepared.'

The Klan never came, though they reached their zenith nationally in 1925, just before revelations of a scandal sent their membership into sharp decline. But the Pentecostal meetings continued to grow. When the Morton sisters, an evangelistic team from Florence, Colorado, arrived to emphasize 'tarrying' for the baptism, the group gained even more adherents. 'A substantial number of young people, several of whom later became ministers, came under the evangelists' influence,' noted David Hogan. Eight years Phil's senior and a high school student at the time, David Hogan recalled the town's negative reaction to the meetings in Olathe. 'The persecution in the community was pretty hard on a young person,' he confessed in later years. 'I just couldn't take the heat. After high school I went to Grand Junction to attend college, just to get away.'[10]

Aimee Semple McPherson and Pentecostalism's spreading influence

The Hogans and the tiny community of Olathe were not alone in the religious ferment of the mid-1920s. Aimee Semple McPherson, a former missionary who was widowed while with her husband in China, several years earlier had travelled across America in a touring car to preach the message of salvation, healing and divine empowering in the tradition of earlier Holiness evangelists. She offered a clear-cut eschatology that presented disoriented lives with a picture of God's reliable, orderly working amidst an uncertain, distressed world. Her well-attended meetings, beyond their impact on major cities, stirred up local currents of

---

[10] David Hogan, taped interview with author.

spiritual renewal that swirled around thousands of men and women in small towns and rural settlements throughout the nation. Actor Anthony Quinn, who as a youth was for a time absorbed in McPherson's charms, remembers her as the woman with the 'most magnetic personality I was ever to encounter' in his career in Hollywood.[11]

Drawing the spiritually hungry from the various denominations, as well as numbers of the previously irreligious, McPherson's meetings produced hundreds of new churches. Despite good-natured – and sometimes malicious – mockery, ridicule and rejection the movement grew. For many tenacious men and women these usually small, spontaneous meetings in homes, storefronts, improvised tabernacles, warehouses, and abandoned churches became the source of animating spiritual strength. After years of disdain and rejection many such embryonic congregations, like the church in Olathe, Colorado, would emerge notably in tune with the times, gathering up on every continent men and women whose lives, set adrift by social upheaval, abrupt change and growing uncertainty, responded to the compelling reassurance and enthusiasm of Pentecostalism.

McPherson's meetings in northern California won over to her cause Dr William Keeny Towner, the pastor of a leading Baptist congregation in San José. His friend, Charles S. Price, pastor of the Congregational Church in nearby Lodi, ventured to attend the religious spectacle, even accepting an invitation to sit with the sponsoring ministers on the platform. Despite his reservations, Price was drawn into the vortex as the crowds gathered from the surrounding churches and eventually found the message and its accompanying experience irresistible. Returning to his congregation, Price, who never relinquished his credentials as a Congregational minister, announced his Pentecostalism and soon began to tour the United States and Canada as a proponent of the movement.[12]

In Winnipeg, Manitoba, Daniel Buntain, a Methodist pastor, reacted to the announcement of Dr Price's pending Canadian meetings by encouraging the local pastors to denounce the fraud. Failing in his efforts to stop the campaign, he began a preaching series dealing with the theological reasons why the Pentecostals' message was erroneous. On the third Sunday, while in the pulpit, he was unable to continue, confessing

---

[11] Anthony Quinn was briefly associated with Mrs McPherson through the influence of his grandmother. His autobiography tells about his grandmother's healing and the impression that the Pentecostals' kindness made on him. He says of his first meeting with Mrs McPherson, 'I was fourteen when I met the most magnetic personality I was ever to encounter. Years later, when I saw the great actresses at work I would compare them to her. As magnificent as I could find Anna Magnani, Ingrid Bergman, Laurette Taylor, Katharine Hepburn, Greta Garbo and Ethel Barrymore, they all fell short of that first electric shock Aimee Semple McPherson produced in me.' Anthony Quinn, *The Original Sin*, (Boston, Little, Brown & Company, 1972), 121.

[12] Price published an autobiography, *The Story of My Life*, 3rd. ed. (1944). A profile of his career is found by R.M. Riss, 'Price, Charles Sydney' in *DPCM*, 726, 727.

to his congregation that his attacks on the Pentecostals were motivated primarily by his own arrogance. In contrition he experienced a personal confirmation that transformed his ministry – and resulted in his being relieved of his pastoral position. Buntain soon emerged as a leading figure in what became the Pentecostal Assemblies of Canada. His two sons and daughter, Mark, Fulton, and Alice, after similar personal struggles, would later abandon their professional aspirations to enter the ranks of the Pentecostals.[13]

Pentecostals as 'Holy Rollers'

In 1921 Robert and Marie Brown, former Holiness ministers who for several years had operated a Pentecostal mission in New York City, acquired a former Baptist Church building which as late as the 1950s continued to be the hub of Pentecostal activity in the Northeast. By the late 1920s the church supported a weekly radio broadcast, hosted well-attended evangelistic rallies, and placed special emphasis on sending the congregation's young people abroad as missionaries. During its prime, the church was cited regularly for contributing more than any other single congregation to the Assemblies of God missionary effort.[14]

In 1925 The *Forum*, a general interest magazine, ran an article by sociologist Jules Bois who, in analyzing the Pentecostal phenomenon, chose examples from New York City, including, apparently, the Browns' Glad Tidings Tabernacle. In the author's opinion the 'Holy Rollers,' though famous, were in reality unknown.

> To tell the truth this denomination is still without a name. They are casually spoken of as 'Pentecostal Movement,' 'Glad Tidings Tabernacles,' 'Assemblies of God,' 'Light House,' etc. The passer-by witnessing in the street or in campmeetings or in improvised temples their clamors, gesticulations, and oddities, calls them sarcastically, 'Holy Howlers,' 'Holy Yowlers;' but without outrage and with a mild irony they have been most often christened 'Holy Rollers' or 'Happy Weepers.'
>
> Testimonials and individual prayers are interrupted by congratulations and thanks to the Lord. Poverty saturates the atmosphere, but not sadness; these parishioners are rich with faith. Even in their worn clothing, with shoes down at heel, the neediest show an unshaken behavior pleasant to see. They hold a secret. They have found something and they are kind enough to offer to share it with you.
>
> [At testimony time] each one speaks in his turn, praising and blessing the Lord with lyric optimism for the various graces received. In three months in

---

[13] Ron Hembree, *Mark*, 45–48; see also R.A.N. Kydd, 'Buntain, Daniel' in *DPCM*, 102.

[14] R.M. Anderson, 'Brown, Robert and Marie' in *DPCM*, 99, 100; and Edith Blumhofer, 'Marie Burgess Brown,' *Paraclete* (Summer 1987): 5–9.

Pentecost, he, a failure with the Methodists, succeeds now in everything. 'Hallelujah! Glory!' punctuates the crowd. A true miracle! Those people are happy with the happiness of their neighbor.

In spite of regrettable eccentricities, there are, it seems to me, torrents of sincere tears shed in the 'Assemblies of God.' Though to our eyes their method be as vain as it is pathetic, these people long to reach God; and it is faith, abundant faith, which prostrates them in these halls, bare of adornments, without altars, without beauty, without even the atmosphere of piety, in front of a wood rail or a nondescript platform – Faith! It exists, it overflows, and lacks only true apostles and true saints to purify and guide it.[15]

If Jules Bois's assessment lacked comprehension, he at least captured something of the deep feeling and spiritual aspiration characteristic of these groups. But whereas Bois looked at the phenomenon as an outsider, Phil Hogan knew it from the inside.

Spiritual foundations

Hogan was 9 years old when his family and various of their neighbors were swept into the Pentecostal revival. The congregation, in a community which even in the 1950s had grown to a population of only 800 persons, later became the Olathe Assembly of God. As the little congregation grew it took over a former Presbyterian church that had been used for several years for crop storage. In the euphoria that filled the family's home, Hogan's conversion followed almost immediately.

> My mother was the spiritually stronger of my parents. My father was supportive, but he let my mother take leadership in our devotional life. Mother would gather us together on Sunday afternoons for a little service, Bible reading and devotions. Under the cottonwood trees which bound our homestead, mother would read Sunday school literature.

If among Hogan's earliest recollections is the vague sensation of a pastor's damp fingers on his head when he was baptized by sprinkling in the local Methodist church, he can clearly remember at the time of the Pentecostal revival going to the altar for four consecutive nights.

> We had tarrying meetings that lasted into the early hours. The people saw my tears and struggle. They said that I didn't need to pray so intensely. But at the conclusion of that experience I felt that God had saved my soul. I felt a release. Walking to school I felt light of heart.

Later the Hogan family found a small group that met in Montrose, Colorado – the beginnings of still another Assemblies of God church – where they sometimes attended meetings. 'We would stay and pray till early in the morning, it seemed,' Hogan recalls. 'We boys would sleep in the

---

[15]   Bois, 'The New Religions of America,' 155.

Dodge touring car during the drive home. We went to bed as light came up, then slept a little before getting up to begin chores and go to school.'

'Back in those days most Pentecostal ministers were independents,' recalls David Hogan. 'Stories circulated about harassment of Pentecostal meetings, broken windows and disruptive noise. There was little organization at that time. The first Assemblies of God churches in the area were in Grand Junction and, to the northeast, in Paonia. That was about all we knew about the Assemblies of God.'

The Hogans encounter the Assemblies of God

In 1928 the Hogans sold their holdings in Colorado and returned to Kansas City where other members of the family had remained. There Gene and Phil Hogan finished high school. Then in 1933 another turning point occurred in the family's spiritual life. The senior Hogans left their farm in the care of their sons and made the trip to Alexandria, Minnesota, to hear evangelists Charles S. Price and J.N. Hoover, who at the time were touring the country to preach the baptism in the Holy Spirit. J.N. Hoover, a former Baptist, was cited as being a preacher who saw clearly the futility of 'pouring this new wine into old bottles.' In a manner befitting any number of fundamentalist preachers, Hoover stated his position unequivocally in a message of which the content still survives. 'Too many of our churches are becoming an ethical society instead of a "soul-saving station," ' Hoover pronounced. 'Modern theology is a religious infection, centered in the heart of organized Christianity. Modern theology, while retaining an outward appearance of Christianity, not only rejects everything supernatural, but casts the Bible aside as the infallible word of authority. You are taking atheism in small doses when you accept the doctrine of modern theology.'[16]

Ironically, within three years the leading figures in American fundamentalism would meet in Chicago and pass a resolution repudiating the Pentecostals.

> Whereas, the present wave of modern Pentecostalism, often referred to as the 'tongues movement,' and the present wave of fanatical and unscriptural healing which is sweeping over the country today, has become a menace in many churches and a real injury to the sane testimony of Fundamental Christians, Be it Resolved, That this convention go on record as unreservedly opposed to Modern Pentecostalism, including the speaking with unknown tongues, and the fanatical healing known as general healing in the atonement, and the perpetuation of the miraculous sign-healings of Jesus and His apostles, wherein they claim the only reason the church cannot perform these miracles is because of unbelief.[17]

---

[16] Cited in Everett A. Wilson, *Seventy-five Years*, 156. Hoover's sermon, recorded stenographically, was preached in Glad Tidings Temple, San Francisco, on 19 June 1927.
[17] Cited in Edith L. Blumhofer, *Assemblies of God*, vol. 2, 17.

Responding to this rejection, British-born Stanley H. Frodsham, editor of the Assemblies of God official paper, the *Pentecostal Evangel*, insisted on the Pentecostals' commitment to the biblical faith. He noted that the fundamentalists had by their action 'disfellowshiped' a great company of men and women who accepted the historical Christian doctrines just as they did.

> We prefer not to quarrel with those who do not interpret the passage quoted in Matthew 8 from the 53rd chapter of Isaiah. For many years some of us were blind to this glorious truth, but today we are grateful that the Lord has graciously opened our eyes to it. Although we Pentecostal people have to be without the camp, we cannot afford to be bitter against those who do not see as we do. Our business is to love these Fundamentalists and to unitedly pray, 'Lord bless them all.'[18]

Thrilled with what they had seen and heard at the Alexandria meetings, Hogan's parents returned home convinced of the reality of their experience and prepared to invest their remaining years in support of the emerging movement. When the Hogans learned about the Central Bible Institute through articles in the *Pentecostal Evangel*, they moved to Springfield in 1933 to enroll their sons in CBI. 'We had not been members of an Assemblies of God congregation,' Hogan recalls. 'In looking back it was a marvel that my parents made the move to be near the Bible Institute.'[19]

As a student Hogan's ambition to become an effective preacher was evident. He devoted all available time to study and soon found opportunity to work in a small outstation. 'CBC changed my life,' he later disclosed. 'I was raw, except for what I had received from laypeople like my mother. The single individual to establish me in spiritual matters and give me a thirst for the Word of God and preaching was William I. Evans. It was his desire to work in the harvest fields to preach the gospel which soon seized me at CBI and which grew increasingly stronger all through my time of training.'

It was this influence that Hogan used on occasion to explain his – and other students' – missionary callings. He recounted Evans's example of a typical American boy who abhorred soap and water and saw no need for regular haircuts, freshly laundered clothes and polished shoes. Then, when the boy's parents had just about reached the point of complete exasperation, he suddenly started combing his hair and scrubbing his neck and ears. They soon discovered that the source of this new motivation was a girl about their son's age whose family had moved to the neighborhood. Her appearance in his life completely transformed him. 'What the boy's

---

[18] Stanley Frodsham, 'Disfellowshiped!' *Pentecostal Evangel* (18 August 1928): 7.
[19] In Springfield Hogan's parents attended the Central Assembly of God. His mother died at age ninety-four while living in the Assemblies of God retirement home. 'Until the day of her death she read everything I could give her,' her son recalls. 'When I visited her she could intelligently discuss the news of the church in the lands I had visited.'

parents could not do by laws and discipline,' recounts Phil Hogan, 'the girl next door did by her presence. This is what Brother Evans called "The compulsive power of a new affection." I can't say that at a given moment I received a call,' Hogan confesses. 'Mine was simply a developing burden, and I knew that somehow I would find myself in a harvest field.'[20]

The novice preacher sought opportunities to develop his ministerial skills, including serving as the pastor of a student mission, which later developed into an Assemblies of God church in the Springfield area. Then, after graduating from CBI, he itinerated as an evangelist in churches in the Midwest. He remained close to the school, however, where Virginia Lewis, daughter of an Ohio pastor who later served as the superintendent of the denomination's Central District, had arrived at the beginning of Hogan's second year. Virginia had spent a year in missionary work in Lexington, Kentucky. From her second year at CBI, Virginia's name was linked with Phil Hogan's, despite the school's efforts to discourage student romances.

Phil and Virginia Hogan and missions

China? The idea of becoming missionaries, much less missionaries to China, came only gradually to Phil and Virginia Hogan. During their days at Central Bible College, missionary services were a regular feature, with organized prayer groups, a succession of missionary speakers and frequent appeals for students to offer themselves for overseas service. A classmate remembers that Virginia Hogan felt inclined to volunteer for service in China.[21] Since Phil Hogan had already indicated his interest in her, would her inclination to missionary work affect their relationship? Prohibitions against direct contact between men and women students could have left everyone guessing. But couples communicated between themselves in their own creative ways, giving encouragement, holding off suitors, and giving reassurance when it was desired. At the time Hogan was deeply affected, praying long and intensely, believing, some classmates speculated, that he would lose his sweetheart to her missionary calling. Later, as Phil and Virginia made plans, they concluded that they should stay together. If China was to be in Virginia's future, they would both hear further from the Lord.

When the couple married in December 1937 their parents were supportive of their career plans, which for the time kept them circulating from church to church as itinerant evangelists. Their son, James Richard,

---

[20]   JPH, 'It's What's Inside that Counts,' *Pentecostal Evangel* (n.d.): 16, an address given by J. Philip Hogan at the School of Missions commissioning service, July 1971. A notion that found considerable affirmation among early Pentecostals, 'the compulsive power of a new affection' is a phrase that previously circulated in Holiness circles.
[21]   Ruth Homer, letter to author, 15 May 1995.

was born in 1939, and their daughter, Phyllis Lynne, arrived two years later. After Lynne's birth, the couple spent Christmas with Hogan's parents in Springfield. At that time Bert Webb, Pastor of Central Assembly, encouraged Hogan to accept the pastorate of East Side Assembly, a dependent congregation that had grown sufficiently to become an autonomous church. The Hogans remained at the pastorate for little more than a year, before moving to Painesville, Ohio, to pastor a church there. In the next pastorate at River Rouge, Michigan, Phil Hogan helped the church move to a more desirable location, part of the urban flight of many socially mobile congregations in the years during and immediately following World War II. At that time, as his ministry gained recognition, Hogan was asked also to serve as the denomination's youth leader for the Detroit area.

During their time at River Rouge the Hogans invited a missionary to China, Leonard Bolton, for a series of missionary services. Having Bolton as a guest in their home gave the couple an opportunity to question him about missionary work. The last night of the meetings, Virginia Hogan recalls, as she was busy caring for their infant daughter, someone came and took the baby from her so that she was free to go and pray at the altar. Deep in contemplation she had a strong sense that her future would be in China. She remonstrated with the Lord that her husband would have to share her calling. Since they had married, in fact, there had been no mention between them about missionary service. She would say nothing about it for the time, she thought. But as the couple returned to their home that evening, with Virginia and the children riding in the back seat, Hogan kept up a conversation with Bolton seated beside him in the front. Virginia could only listen in amazement to her husband's probing questions.

Around the kitchen table at home the conversation continued as Hogan asked about missionary work in China and about the procedures for appointment. Then, before conferring with Virginia, he addressed Bolton, 'Brother, if you will recommend me to the missions department, I'll go to China to work with you.'

Leonard Bolton responded bluntly, 'If God wants you in China, you will get there without my recommendation.'

During the following weeks Hogan read everything about China that he could find in the public library. Then, as Christmas approached, he suggested to Virginia that they travel to Springfield to spend Christmas with his parents, whom they had not seen for three years. Hogan used the occasion to make an appointment with the missionary director Noel Perkin, and Virginia readily consented. As they were seated in Noel Perkin's office, Hogan came directly to the point. 'My wife feels a call to China. I, personally, have always been interested in Latin America.' His next comment brought a laugh from each of them. 'But wherever we go, we'll go together.' Then, in a more serious tone, he volunteered to go wherever workers were needed.

Noel Perkin identified a greater need in China. A mission begun some years earlier in Ningpo, near Shanghai, had been in need of a missionary since the death of its founder, Nettie Nichols. A Chinese pastor, Joshua Bang (pronounced Bong), was overseeing the congregation, helped by a North American woman who was serving without missionary appointment.

In the exhilaration of the moment Virginia dashed out of the meeting to call her parents, knowing that information might pass rapidly to her father, Gayle Lewis, at the time superintendent of the Central District. At home, Virginia's mother was troubled by the possibility of her children serving abroad. 'China is such a dangerous place,' she insisted. But Virginia's response was firm. 'You know that your grandchildren will be just as safe there as here. They could be killed in one of the race riots we are having here in Detroit or die of polio,' she remembers arguing.

Just before the River Rouge congregation moved to their new church location, Hogan resigned in order to raise support for their overseas venture. Since two other prospective missionary couples had just itinerated through the churches of the area to raise support, solicitation was difficult. The Hogans' missionary 'outfit' consisted of their personal possessions and the gifts given to them at a farewell shower by their former congregation as they boarded the train for the Pacific Coast, where, with other recruits from various denominations, they would study Mandarin and Chinese culture at the University of California, Berkeley. Having had scarcely more than an orientation in the language, the Hogans, along with a large contingent of missionaries *en route* to the Orient, left San Francisco aboard the troop ship *Marine Lynx* in February 1947.[22] With ports of call at Pearl Harbor and Hawaii, they were bound for Shanghai.

Phil and Virginia Hogan could only speculate about what the future would hold. The frustrations and dangers of the next three years would test their commitment. But the experience would enable the young missionaries to witness the clash of ideologies, the grandeur of the great cultures of the East, the explosive forces of social revolution, the impatience of the young people of Asia for change, and the frustrations of missionary life. The family would experience the mental suffering of separation and uncertainty. For J. Philip Hogan it would be a time of wrestling with his own doubts, fears, ambitions, and faith. As the days at sea and the uncertainty of an unknown future took them ever farther from the emotional support of life at home, the couple found themselves increasingly in need of reassurance. Although eager to get started in their work, they felt inadequate, increasingly dependent on divine resources.

---

[22]   On board with the Hogans was the young George O. Wood, later the Assemblies of God general secretary, whose family were then returning to China for a second term of service. A group of students from Glad Tidings Bible Institute, where Leland R. Keys was the pastor and J. Narver Gortner was the director, sang encouragement as the ship pulled away from the San Francisco pier.

[3]

The Making of a Missionary

Strong forces have been at work and all of a sudden the harvest is ready. Such has been the experience of many of us who have labored in the Far East. Wars and mass movements of men on a national or international scale are but God's plow and harrow in the fields of the world.

J. Philip Hogan[1]

China's challenge

Ningpo, the Hogans' destination in 1947, was at that time a peaceful, prosperous city in the tiny Chekiang province of east China. The port had been one of only five depots opened to the West for foreign residents and trade at the time of the infamous Opium War of the 1850s. With an economy based on massive sales of fish, Ningpo also attracted thousands of tourists as the birthplace of Generalissimo Chiang Kai-shek, China's strongman at the time. Although Ningpo, like the rest of China, was to change radically after the Communist revolution, in the years just prior to the arrival of the Hogans the city proudly boasted of newly installed trains, electric lights and telephones.

While Ningpo's substantial buildings and bustling commerce reflected its prosperity and the connections its business community had throughout China, it still retained a traditional flavor. The streets were twisting and winding so that, according to ancient custom, the evil spirits would lose their way. The largest of several Buddhist temples covered a hundred acres and housed a thousand monks. Ningpo was also the site of the first Protestant mission school in China, dating back a century. When the Hogan family arrived, about 30 missionaries from six different denominations were already at work there, maintaining among them two mission high schools and a large, well-equipped hospital. The largest Protestant church in Ningpo, which seated two thousand worshippers, was filled during the periodic revival campaigns.

---

[1] 'The Second Coming and Missions,' *Missionary Challenge* (January 1951).

Nettie Nichols's mission

The Assemblies of God presence in Ningpo began with the efforts of Nettie Nichols, later affectionately known as 'Mother' Nichols. She started caring for four orphans shortly after her arrival in 1910. By 1914 she had acquired responsibility for a family of 40 children. Despite her round-the-clock responsibilities she also began working with local adults. Once, at a low ebb in her physical and spiritual resources, she prayed earnestly for divine assistance and was rewarded with a vision of angelic helpers. Although at the time she had not heard about Pentecostal teachings and practices, she experienced baptism in the Holy Spirit in 1917 and soon thereafter became associated with the Assemblies of God.

Twelve years after her arrival in Ningpo, Mother Nichols still did not own the land occupied by her mission. Like many ministries to the very poor, her mission struggled financially. In 1925 she wrote, 'God has never failed us. At times our rice bin has been empty, but we have never missed a meal. One night while I was praying for help, the Lord assured me of victory. That night, a Chinese friend was awakened by a white-robed visitor who told him to bring us rice. Early that morning, he obeyed.'[2]

Undeterred by her lack of financial resources Nettie Nichols believed that God would provide her orphanage with a permanent home. In 1922 she was able to purchase land. She started by enclosing the property with a wall and building several cottages. Then she began praying for a central administration building. Within three years the Chinese congregation had raised the funds for its construction. In time Mother Nichols added a chapel, dormitories, and classrooms. From 1928 onwards the mission became a place of continuing spiritual revival. The sweeping renewal revival attracted many people from the community, often entire families, many of whom experienced the baptism in the Holy Spirit. In the years that followed the annual Bible conferences at the mission station drew increasingly larger crowds.

Joshua Bang

One of the persons whose life was changed as a result of this revival was Joshua Bang, who was to become a guide and an inspiration to the Hogan family when they arrived as missionaries in Ningpo 15 years later. Well educated and socially secure, Joshua Bang was hardly a promising spiritual leader prior to the Ningpo revival. Although he had been a nominal Christian for 20 years, he had never abandoned the common vices of his social position – smoking, gambling and excessive drinking. Unable to explain how it had happened, he found his way to

---

[2] Nichols and Bang, *God's Faithfulness in Ningpo*, 14; see also JPH, 'Ningpo Enjoys Blessings in Spite of Hardships,' *Pentecostal Evangel* (26 April 1947).

Mother Nichols's mission one night in 1931. There the dean of the orphanage high school found Joshua weeping at the altar, oblivious to everything around him.

Bang testified that he had received forgiveness of his sins. 'Praying earnestly in the Spirit,' he later explained, 'I saw Jesus with white garments coming down with clouds.'

> As I saw His beauty and His glory, I wanted to go to Him. I touched His garment, and I saw a glorious light like the light of the noonday sun. His glory went through me like an electric current with mighty power. With praise to His name I shouted, 'Hallelujah.' My arms were uplifted and held up until I yielded to His call, when He said: 'Go and preach the gospel. Tell sinners everywhere to accept Christ and be saved as you have been saved.' Since Jesus is so real to me, I cannot disobey the heavenly vision.[3]

Enthusiastic to dedicate his efforts to the work of the mission, Bang joined Nettie Nichols in founding the Bethel Bible School in 1932. They envisioned training a generation of Chinese evangelists and pastors who would carry the gospel to their own countrymen. Bethel's first four students graduated in 1935.

By 1938 the Bible School registered 96 students – 50 men and 46 women. As plans were made to begin an extension school in the city of Ma Yaio, Bang grew uneasy, feeling that he needed more preparation. That year he accompanied Nettie Nichols to the United States, where for a brief time he attended Central Bible Institute in Springfield, Missouri, the school where Phil Hogan had only recently completed his own studies.

When Nettie Nichols died not long after her return to China, Bang, along with American volunteer Lily Ganz, assumed the administration of the orphanage, the church, and the Bible school. Concerned about the school's future, Noel Perkin published an account of the work, urging his Pentecostal readers to 'help our Chinese friends and brethren in every way possible,' adding, 'One of the most effective ways to help is to pray and give for the training of the young men and women of China who possess the zeal to evangelize their own people.'[4]

The Hogans in Ningpo

The initial stirrings of Communist sentiments had not indicated the thorough upheaval that would later follow in China. In Ningpo the missionaries were warmly welcomed. A group of several hundred Christians from the Bethel community set off fireworks in an exuberant greeting at sunrise the day after their arrival. Surrounded by this friendly

---

[3]   Nichols and Bang, *God's Faithfulness in Ningpo*, 32.
[4]   Cited in ibid., 48.

mob, the missionaries were treated as honored guests in a rickshaw parade, at the end of which they were formally welcomed by Daniel Lee, the local magistrate and a member of the Bethel community.

Hogan was thrilled by the work being done at Ningpo, especially the training of students who were enthusiastic about ministry. His letters in the *Pentecostal Evangel* shared how the school had enrolled its largest class ever – nearly one hundred students. 'The spiritual tide among the students is high. They pray night and day – only in the deep hours of the night is the compound silent. Many of the students are undersized from lack of nourishment and some are older from having been prevented from attending school during the war years. There is no doubt that this is a vine of God's own planting and Mother Nichols was a mighty woman of faith.'[5]

The Hogans lived in the unheated Bible School compound, barely surviving the bitter winter. 'Virginia wears more clothes when we go to bed than in the daytime,' Hogan joked to friends.[6] Although their rooms had electricity, there was no indoor plumbing. There were other challenges too. The Hogans had to learn a different language, since the Mandarin Chinese they had studied at Berkeley was incomprehensible to the local people. Causing most concern, however, was the foreboding news of the advance of the Communists in the northern provinces. The inflammatory statements made about missionaries and other foreigners gave the Hogans good reason to feel uneasy. Garland and Florence Benintendi, who had accompanied the Hogans since their time at Berkeley and had planned to take up work in the north, soon learned that leaving Shanghai would be impossible. Howard Osgood, the field secretary for Asia, at the time also in Shanghai, had to change his plans for visiting other areas. Then Hogan began to suspect that he was under surveillance. Communist operatives had begun to infiltrate the south, waiting for their opportunity to seize control and avenge the injustices that had long fed smoldering hatred for the social and political establishment. Hogan wrote home that the situation was growing tense. Local business people, hit hard by inflation, were in panic at the Communist advance.

Even more horrifying was the violent reaction of the local government to suspected Communists. One afternoon Hogan witnessed the merciless execution of dozens of young people who were presumed to be Communist sympathizers. He saw young men and women led from trucks and shot by the side of the road, the soldiers firing their carbines into the still writhing bodies, splattering blood on the intense green of the rice paddies. Shocked at what he saw, Hogan wondered if these young people were really Communists, and if so, what powerful forces compelled them to risk death. What inspired their devotion, determination and sacrifice for

5 JPH, 'Mother Nichols's Legacy,' *Mountain Movers* (April 1991): 8, 9.
6 Virginia Hogan, interview with author, 16 February 1995.

this radical cause? 'For a brief moment I had an inkling of the strength of the vast spiritual tides already loose in the world,' Hogan noted.[7]

Then Joshua Bang told the Hogans that he could no longer afford to be seen with them in public. Association with the Americans was a threat to both him and his family. The Hogans immediately evacuated to Shanghai, where the missionaries of north China had begun to congregate. The Hogans understood Bang's concern, but they did not then realize how much their friendship would cost him. When the Cultural Revolution swept China in the 1960s the entire nation exploded in fury against all symbols of foreign influence. Bang immediately became a target. When Red Guards found the small library of Hogan's books in Bang's possession they beat him to death while members of his family looked on.

Vision for Taiwan

J. Philip Hogan was shattered by the painful turn that his work had taken. He scarcely had arrived before he was forced to leave. He walked the streets of Shanghai unable to converse in the local language and distressed by his apparent failure.

When the Hogans came across a brochure that described conditions in the now liberated Taiwan, the formerly Japanese-occupied Formosa, they began to see a way to continue their ministry among the Chinese. At the same time, Howard Osgood received word from a pastor in the north who was considering going to Taiwan to work among Christians in need of pastoral care. When Osgood brought the matter up for the Hogan's consideration, he found them willing to go. Excited by the prospect of getting on with their work, the Benintendis joined the Hogans in moving to Taiwan.

As soon as they could arrange the trip the three men took a ship to Keelung, a port about 25 miles from Taipei, to scout out the possibilities for a Pentecostal mission, the first on the island. They pooled their resources and put a downpayment on a house. Finally, it seemed, the Hogans could get on with sustained missionary work. But they had scarcely settled on Taiwan when Virginia was advised by her doctor to return to Shanghai for medical attention before political conditions there deteriorated further.

Virginia Hogan's ordeal

It had seemed relatively safe and easy for Virginia to fly alone to Shanghai, but shortly after her arrival she fell and injured her back. The missionary

[7] JPH, 'I Visited the United Nations,' *United Evangelical Action* (14 January 1951): 4.

doctors operated on her the next day, but the accident and the surgery left Virginia sedated and almost immobile. When he heard about the accident, Hogan rushed to Shanghai to be with her. But the hospital directors, concerned about the worsening political conditions, urged him to return to Taipei immediately. The Protestant chaplain of the US Seventh Fleet, then anchored off Shanghai, assured Hogan that he would be available to help Virginia and would put her on a plane as soon as she was able to travel.

That same night, however, the Seventh Fleet came under fire in the Yangtse River near Nanking and withdrew immediately to international waters. The entire foreign community received notice to be ready for evacuation at any moment. Because the Hogan family traveled on a single passport – which Hogan had taken back with him to Taipei – Virginia had no documents and, as well, no airline ticket. When Virginia, in her painful physical condition, attempted to make arrangements to leave, she found that the telephones were out of commission and the chaplain of the Seventh Fleet was one hundred miles at sea.

Alone and in a rapidly deteriorating political situation, Virginia knew that she was in grave danger. Anxious hours followed; she had to place her life entirely in God's care. The only call in two days to come through to the missionary home was a message for Virginia. 'Mrs. Hogan,' said a voice she did not recognize, 'be at the airport at 6:30 tomorrow morning.'[8]

Traffic clogged the narrow road to the airport early the next day. The American teacher who was driving began to worry that he would be stranded, unable to get back to Shanghai. Near the airport a man whom Virginia recognized as the Canadian consular attaché stopped their car and told her to get out. The two men half-carried Virginia to the ticket counter, where the attaché presented Virginia with her passport – the one she knew her husband had taken with him – and a ticket which had been issued to the attaché. Although the agent insisted that Virginia could not use the attaché's ticket, the two men left after having placed her beside the counter with her suitcase and an official-looking box covered with government stamps and embassy seals.

Once again Virginia felt dreadfully alone and frightened. The ticket agent insisted that her ticket was invalid and refused to give her any consideration. In too much pain to be concerned about her appearance she simply lay on a pile of luggage and watched as other passengers sought frantically to board flights.

At some point a man demanded that Virginia give him her money and the package from the embassy, telling her that he would take care of them for her. Later, an English-speaking Chinese girl came and urged her to return to Shanghai, as no flights would be either arriving or departing.

8   Virginia Hogan, 'Fleeing Shanghai: A Miraculous Escape from War-torn China in 1948,' *Assemblies of God Heritage* (spring 1989): 8.

Virginia had no money for food or for a cab – even if one were available – so she simply lay down on the luggage of a man sitting nearby and slept, intermittently drifting in and out of consciousness. In her feverish, bewildered state, Virginia prayed, 'Lord, You are the only one who knows I'm here. If this is the end, I don't want to suffer anymore. Just let me die.'[9]

Toward evening Virginia was awakened by a man who motioned her to follow him. She rolled off the pile of luggage and gradually eased herself into a standing position. She did not know her guide, but she followed him into a large, high-ceilinged room. The cement floor and walls were bare except for some small windows near the ceiling. The man locked the door behind them and, without saying anything further, crossed the room to another door, locked it from the other side, and left her entirely alone. Virginia recalls leaning against the wall, gripped by fear but determined somehow to survive.

Possibly an hour later, a door opened, and a figure motioned Virginia to enter the adjacent room. There she found a group of Chinese. Their somber expressions reflected the seriousness of the situation. Although all of them appeared to have been searched, no one made any demands of her. Then a man appeared at an outside door and instructed the group in Chinese, adding a command in English for Virginia's benefit, 'Run!'

Virginia had undergone surgery just two days before. She could barely walk. Yet the words of the verse from Isaiah filled her mind, 'They shall run and not be weary, they shall walk and not be faint.' She found herself running toward the waiting plane, reaching it ahead of some of the other refugees. Aboard the aircraft she sat on the low bench that lined the side of the plane. As the plane began to taxi down the runway, the last of the passengers just pulled through the door.

A girl eyed Virginia with curiosity and asked in English, 'How did you get here?'

'I don't know,' she murmured.

'Where do you want to go?' the girl asked softly.

'Taiwan,' Virginia uttered weakly.[10]

The girl smiled and moved away. Although Virginia still did not know it, the plane was *en route* to Taipei, her bag and the embassy box on board.

It was with joyous relief that Virginia found her husband waiting for her when the plane landed. He had spent hours there on previous days, meeting every incoming flight to find someone who would deliver the couple's passport to her. A crew from an American military plane *en route* from Hong Kong to Japan had finally agreed to help him. The crew had not planned a mainland stop, but had gone out of their way to hazard an unscheduled landing to deliver the indispensable passport in Shanghai.

[9]   Ibid., 15.
[10] Ibid.

Dutifully the Hogan's delivered the official-appearing box that had impressed the Chinese authorities and which had apparently guaranteed Virginia's safe passage. It contained, they learned from the attaché's wife, nothing more than a souvenir, a carved horse that her husband wanted to send to Taiwan without the inconvenience of carrying it himself.

At work in Taipei

After the Hogans' experiences on the mainland, getting settled in a home in Taipei was exciting. But the future remained unclear. Taipei in 1948 was a quiet little city surrounded by rice paddies. The Japanese occupation of 50 years had left the island modernized, with electricity, a railway system, improved port facilities, paved roads, and schools. The missionaries soon found a storefront in the commercial center where they could hold gospel meetings.

Each night either Hogan or Garland Benintendi stood on the street passing out tracts and inviting passers-by to the services, while indoors the other missionary preached. Soon a group of 50 – most of them young people – showed an interest to learn about Christ and were being discipled in the church. 'We do not call them converts,' said Hogan. 'They are inquirers, but in view of the fact that they have never read the Bible nor heard the gospel preached they have taken a great step.'[11]

Altogether the community of Canadians, Americans, and Europeans on Taiwan consisted of about 50 people, among whom the Hogans soon fitted in. The four Benintendi children and Richard and Lynne Hogan made up six of the only eight foreign children on Taiwan. The missionaries were invited to conduct services for English-speaking foreigners in the YMCA building. The American missionaries also spent time with the chaplain of the Seventh Fleet, with whom they had already become acquainted, and were invited to the various receptions for high-ranking military officers and other notables who arrived in Taipei. Virginia Hogan assisted the Presbyterian missionaries in their work with lepers.

A growing number of Chinese families fleeing from the mainland now had an experience similar to Virginia Hogan's abrupt flight from Shanghai to Taiwan. Increasingly, Chinese who had wealth, owned property, traveled outside China, or had extensive association with foreigners were in danger. Wealthy refugees began to arrive at a rate of five thousand per day. As they began investing in buildable property, real estate prices skyrocketed.

---

[11] JPH, 'Opening a New Field,' *Missionary Challenge* (May 1949): 12.

Evacuation

Since the Communist shelling of Quemoy and threats to take the Pescadores Islands in the Formosa Strait seemed to be the prelude to an invasion of Taiwan, the missionaries were soon ordered to evacuate. The captain of a merchant ship agreed to provide two staterooms for them, provided that they could leave immediately. Hogan felt constrained to remain, if at all possible. He obtained permission from the embassy to stay, with the understanding that the rest of the group would leave. He could be evacuated along with the embassy staff when the invasion began. 'If I thought that I had six months before the Communists take Taiwan, I would stay,' he told Virginia.

That night neither of them slept well. But in the morning Virginia told her husband that she would be willing for him to stay while she took Richard and Lynne home. That same day, in November 1949, Virginia Hogan, the Hogan children, and the Benintendi family left aboard the ship to arrive at a US port after 21 stormy days on the high seas.

Hogan placed his belongings into two suitcases and moved to a room in the Presbyterian seminary. He sold the house they had occupied and arranged oversight of the Benintendi's home in the hope that eventually missionaries could return to Taiwan. Hogan devoted his time to the little chapel and trained the secretary of the YMCA as his successor.

Hogan had become acquainted with James Dickson, the head of the Presbyterian seminary, at the time the only other American Protestant mission on Taiwan. On one occasion he accompanied Professor Dickson and his wife Lillian to the mountains of the interior to visit the Christian groups among the mountain people. At an improvised clinic Phil Hogan was given the task of administering worm medicine to the adults. Years later, when *Reader's Digest* published an account of Lillian Dickson's work among the mountain Taiwanese, Hogan wrote to congratulate her on the recognition her work had received.

I have just finished reading the excellent article in the July (1962) *Reader's Digest* concerning your work in Formosa. Besides the thrill of having someone whose life and work you know about so marvelously headlined, it also brought back many wonderful memories. Somewhere in my mementos I retain a certificate that was given to me by the members of the team that I accompanied on one of these first worm-exterminating missions into the mountains. If you remember, you had a special dinner for me at your house where you presented me with a worm exterminator's license, with a special seal – the top of a Nescafé coffee can! I further remember my place in the first clinic line. You assigned me to give large black capsules to the tribesmen. These looked awfully large to me, and most of the people had difficulty swallowing them. When I went back to the box to replenish my supply, I was horrified to see on the label these directions, 'For veterinary use only!' But as far as I know, we never lost a patient.[12]

Having observed the beauty of the island and its well-designed systems of schools, roads, trains, telephones and electricity supply, Hogan was distressed by the impact of the increasing political tensions and by the many refugees crowding into the city.

> This land of the bluest skies in the world sees those skies crossed every hour of the day by warplanes, and at night by searchlights. This land of emerald seas and white, palm-lined beaches now tragically broken by barbed wire and defenses knows no security. This land of green jungle and purple mountains where every nook and cove hides the ugly snout of a howitzer or a cannon has not known peace since the Japanese invaded China. A land of beautiful modern cities and fine schools, of leaping power lines and good railroads and paved highways, a land that is now given over to carpet-bagging politicians who have ruined, pillaged, and made themselves rich. Before the War Formosa enjoyed a 96 per cent literacy rate, but now most of her schools are occupied by soldiers who have sold the glass windows, the brass door knobs, and all the movable valuables, and then have used the school furniture for firewood to cook their rice on the porches and balconies, and the children of Formosa roam the streets without schooling. In this land you hear Tommy-gun fire almost every night and the people are pushed around by sullen, crude, illiterate coolie-boy soldiers with American weapons. It is a land of spies – of Russian spies, of Chinese Communist spies, of Nationalist spies. Almost every time you step outside someone walks up to you and says, 'Say, what do you think about the Koumintang?' or 'When do you think there will be a third World War?' You soon learn to answer, 'Friend, I don't go in for politics; I am just a missionary.' Formosa is a classic example of the futility of man and the inability of his international organizations and treaties to bring about peaceful settlements among nations.[13]

Transition

As invasion seemed imminent, President Harry S. Truman ordered the US Seventh Fleet into the Formosa Strait, and the Americans were evacuated to Hong Kong. Just before the Americans left Taiwan, Hogan took his little group of converts to the river for a baptismal service, the first of its kind for the Formosan Chinese, since the Presbyterians did not baptize by immersion. He felt that despite the brief time he had had with the group, the work would continue without him.

---

[12] JPH letter to Lillian Dickson, Presbyterian Mission, Taipei, 11 July 1962. Lillian Dickson's story is told in C.W. Hall, 'Littlest Lady with the Biggest Heart,' *Readers Digest* 88 (July 1962): 159–64.

[13] JPH, 'Whither Formosa?' *Pentecostal Evangel* (29 July 1950, 5): 10f.

In Hong Kong Hogan wrote to the Division of Foreign Missions requesting instructions. Noel Perkin responded that he should return home, adding facetiously, 'so that his furlough in the future would correspond to Virginia's.' There Hogan was introduced to Christian leaders who had fled the mainland. A pastor from Shantung province reported that the church no longer could meet openly, only in secret. The pastors and church leadership had been scattered to earn their living as best they could. No pastor under the new regime could take offerings from the people: that would make him a parasite and all such were quickly liquidated. Church buildings were quickly confiscated to be used for 'productive' purposes.[14]

Back home, settled in a cottage at the DFM Mission Village in Springfield, Missouri, Virginia Hogan had attempted to create a normal life for their children. Reunited with her parents, she had emotional support during the frequent times when the newspaper accounts drew a frightening picture of Communist brutality and the chaos that resulted from the advancing forces. Richard, 11 years old, settled in quickly. Lynne, eight and a half, seemed to have more need for her father. The family was overjoyed when Hogan, having sailed from Hong Kong aboard a Dutch vessel, telephoned them on his arrival in San Francisco. Within a few days he was with them and could talk about his experiences in Taiwan after they and the Benintendis had gone.

For J. Philip and Virginia Hogan, however, the elation of being reunited soon gave way to an uncomfortable sense that their life together as a family might never be normal. The first Sunday after arriving from the West Coast, having been absent from his family for eight months, Hogan was booked for missionary services, and the schedule of meetings never slowed down. He devoted almost the entire following year to criss-crossing the country and giving account of what had occurred in China with the advance of the Communist forces and the influx of refugees into Taiwan. Virginia and the children stayed behind. 'J. Philip Hogan, who returned just recently from the political-football island, Taiwan (Formosa),' began the press release sent to the churches in advance of his coming, 'traveled extensively in areas held by Communist guerrillas and saw something of the impact of Communism upon the church while in China.' Missionary colleague Harold Lehmann, who participated with Hogan in services at the time, remembers a press conference at which the several invited speakers were introduced. After brief introductory comments the entire remainder of the session consisted of questions directed at Hogan, who skillfully handled the reporters' probing questions about Chiang Kai-shek, the Communist advance, and conditions in the Far East[15]

---

[14] Ibid.

[15] Harold Lehmann, letter to JPH, February 1990.

After almost a year the disruption to their family grew unbearable. The Hogans decided that they must provide a more conventional home for their children. When a congregation Hogan had visited in Florence, South Carolina, invited him to become their pastor, the opportunity seemed to be providential. Though well-established, the church lacked adequate buildings. Hogan helped the congregation to acquire a desirable building site and construct a Georgian colonial-style sanctuary seating 350 worshippers. With educational rooms in the basement the facility also boasted a soundproof nursery and a balcony that provided additional seating for 50 people. After dedication of the buildings, however, Hogan once again agreed to serve with the Division of Foreign Missions and resigned his pastoral position. The pastoral experience, as in the past, had many rewards, but the missionary calling had become Hogan's life calling.

China revisited

Years later, Hogan, who always considered himself primarily a missionary to China, returned to examine the work that had been left behind. In 1982, as restrictions on travel in China began to relax, he received word that a charter trip was being organized for one of the first groups to be admitted to the country. Obtaining bookings for himself, Virginia and a pastor friend and his wife, they were able to travel extensively and include a visit to the city of Ningpo. There they learned what had become of Joshua Bang and the work of the mission and were reunited with several Chinese believers whom they had known during the days at Nettie Nichols's mission. Through these and other contacts, Hogan made additional trips into the country and had opportunity to follow the course of the house church movement and the revival that has been reported in many of the provinces.

At the time of his initial experience in China in the 1940s Hogan had opportunity to observe the growth of indigenous groups. This taught him to appreciate how important it was that their Christian faith derived from the outlook, concerns, and cultures of the people themselves.

> My first mission station in China was near a region where Chinese Communist guerrillas had set up an autonomous regime fully two years before the main Red armies crossed the Yangtze. One day an elderly Chinese mountaineer came to my door, asking for me. He stood there with a little bamboo stick on his back. A few belongings, which gave evidence that he had traveled some distance, were tied to the end of the stick. He told me that he had come from a section where God had poured out His Spirit, and he wanted me to pay a visit to the Christians.
>
> I responded to the man's request, taking some of the local Christians with me. The believers were located about thirty miles away where there were

riots, lootings, and killings every day. I was not prepared for what I found. Before I was to return to my station it was my privilege to dedicate nine new churches. Not one of them had ever had one penny of foreign money. I saw hundreds, even thousands, of persons who had been baptized in the Holy Spirit, but who hardly knew what had happened to them. They were without any outstanding leaders, but had just built churches and were gathering together, happy for what the Spirit, their teacher, was doing for them.[16]

Thereafter Hogan's concept of missionary work was deeply influenced by what he had witnessed. With apparently no missionary who featured prominently, the movement appeared to be flourishing. 'I asked numbers of times,' he later recalled, 'Where did all this come from?' He was told that the movement had been influenced from Shanghai, but the members seemed vague about its origins. 'I can assure you that those people are going on today. They smuggled letters to me until the time I left Formosa, and if they knew where to contact me now they would no doubt still be reaching me.' Given the uncertainty of the times throughout Asia, Hogan realized that the church appeared to be on the retreat on many fronts. Hogan later wrote:

> Doors are closing as fast as they are opening, it seems, but we can pray down on those closed areas a mighty Holy Ghost indigenous movement that will evangelize whether missionaries are there or not. I think there are few places in the world where at least some seed of God's Word has not fallen. It is your privilege and mine, and our responsibility as well, to pray that God will send the reviving showers on that seed. The Holy Ghost can work behind iron and bamboo curtains. All the ideologies that the devil would seek to turn loose on the world could not hinder the Holy Spirit.[17]

Later he wrote, 'though China as a whole may not be experiencing the results we saw in Ningpo, the incorruptible seed, the Word of God, still lives and abides in the hearts of these people. In God's timing, the

---

[16]   JPH, 'The Second Coming and Missions.' The course of Christianity in Communist China is traced in David H. Adeney, *China*; and idem, 'Inside China's Churches,' *Christianity Today* (10 February 1992): 21–23. See also Daniel H. Bays, 'Christian Revival in China, 1900–1937' in *Modern Revivalism*, ed. Blumhofer and Balmer; and Anthony P. B. Lambert, 'The Church in China Today,' *Chinese Around the World* 136 (January 1995): 2–6.
[17]   'How Good Is The Seed?' *Pentecostal Evangel* (12 February 1967); James Dickson's description of indigenous churches on Taiwan corroborates J. Philip Hogan's accounts. 'The writer has sometimes gone to villages in the mountains, where no missionary or Chinese pastor has ever gone, to dedicate church buildings and examine candidates for baptism. Almost invariably the work was found to be started by lay Christians from other villages.' James Dickson, 'A Miracle of Modern Missions,' *Christianity Today* (5 January 1959): 27. The church on Taiwan is treated thoroughly by Murray A. Rubenstein, *The Protestant Community on Modern Taiwan*.

wind of the Spirit blew on the coals that missionaries had kindled in human souls, and the church in China has now burst into flames.'[18]

Through the years that followed his missionary experience, Hogan's commitment to the establishment of the indigenous church was based on more than simply an inherited policy or an abstract theory. The essence of Christian faith – a changed life and personal trust in God – he learned, had to originate with the impulse of the Holy Spirit. And the method of church growth also proceeded from the dynamics of the Spirit, as leaders and associations formed an organic unity based on their simple confidence in God's empowerment.

---

[18] 'The Church in China,' *Mountain Movers* (September 1987): 12–13. Hogan was aware throughout his subsequent missionary career that a high price had been paid by Assemblies of God personnel who remained in China. In JPH, 'The Dust of Shansi,' *Pentecostal Evangel* (24 July 1994): 20, 21, he tells of attempting to contact Anna Zeise, who carried a German passport and had elected to remain behind at the time of the Japanese Occupation. Free to operate because she was legally a citizen of the German Democratic Republic, a Communist bloc country, Anna Zeise died in Shansi in 1969. A similar case of devotion to one's calling is that of Marie Stephany, who remained through the Japanese occupation until she was repatriated in 1942. See 'Mother Peace,' *Assemblies of God Heritage* 7 (winter 1977–78): 3–5, 18.

[4]

Forging a Philosophy

The crucible of experience teaches these days that the final and only really successful unit for world evangelism is the church – the local unit of the mystical Body of Christ. Squarely on the shoulders of the church rests the commission and the responsibility for world evangelism. This clearly establishes the priority for all Christian activity. Any expenditure that does not have as its final objective the building of a witnessing church cannot be God's best for this hour.

J. Philip Hogan[1]

Protestant missions in transition

When J. Philip Hogan resigned his South Carolina pastorate late in 1952 to join the newly created promotional division of the DFM, he became part of a team that was to structure the denomination's developing missionary program. The most important consequence of their effort was the formulation of a distinctly Pentecostal approach to global evangelization. At first tentative, leaning heavily on other people's ideas, and aiming to promote rather than to analyze missionary endeavour, the missionary perspective that emerged in the process came to characterize Hogan's mature thinking during his lengthy leadership.

.The progress the DFM made toward the development of these policies can hardly be appreciated without reference to the social, political, and economic upheaval occurring simultaneously on the world scene. Indeed, it would be difficult to find in the almost two hundred years of previous Protestant missionary experience a period of greater disruptive change. It was an era of crisis which, for that reason, was exquisitely opportune for retooling evangelical missionary approaches. 'Tremendous advances have been made in human welfare,' wrote J.O. Percy of the Evangelical Foreign Missions Association in 1961, 'yet an even greater price has been paid in human suffering, death and destruction. This is our world of seething upheaval.'[2] The same year Eric Fife and Arthur Glasser observed that since 1945 'changes of colossal magnitude [had] transformed the very nature of the world in which we live in undreamed of ways.' 'Today,'

---

[1] 'Harvest Hints,' *World Challenge* (January 1957): n.p.
[2] J.O. Percy, *Facing the Unfinished Task*, 8.

they warned, 'there is the very real possibility that our missionary leadership may find itself at the head of a missionary arm that is "admirably organized and equipped" to evangelize the world as it was prior to 1939, or at best 1945, but totally out of touch and unprepared to minister realistically and effectively to the world as we find it today.'[3]

While many Protestant missionary assumptions were undermined as early as World War I, the missionary system that had been in place for more than a century came crashing down with the expulsion of most Christian missionaries from Asia during World War II and the cessation of foreign missionary activity in China after 1950. For both Roman Catholics and Protestants, who had concentrated a great deal of effort in that field, its loss was disheartening. Then followed the growing tensions of the Cold War and the apocalyptic 'balance of terror' once the Soviet Union had acquired nuclear weapons. These changes in geopolitics in turn gave rise to the bloc of nonaligned nations that included or affected virtually all of the missionary-receiving countries. Added to these staggering setbacks were growing concerns about the world demographic explosion, increasing poverty, and the rise of massive, sprawling cities in the developing nations. In the wake of these developments came the break-up of colonial empires and the rise of nationalism almost everywhere missionaries were at work.

Moreover, apart from these destabilizing conditions, the missionary movement itself experienced wrenching internal changes. Whereas a few decades earlier European Protestants were important partners in the overseas effort, increasingly missions to developing nations fell to North American agencies. Also, while most missionaries as late as the 1930s were sent under the auspices of the mainline denominations, missions after 1945 increasingly became the concern of the younger evangelical groups, including the Holiness and Pentecostal denominations and nondenominational agencies. And, while global evangelization had once been primarily an undertaking of career missionaries sent out by denominational boards, overseas evangelism increasingly was undertaken by short-term, occasional, and 'tent-making' personnel working under the auspices of 'faith' or parachurch organizations.[4] Ironically, however, while the

---

[3] Fife and Glasser, *Missions in Crisis*, 241. Similarly, Ralph D. Winter treats these massive changes in his *Twenty-five Unbelievable Years*.

[4] In addition to the foregoing study by Ralph D. Winter, for treatments of the revolution in Protestant missionary approaches see Hutchinson, *Errand to the World*; Harold Lindsell, 'The Eloquence of Missionary Statistics,' *Bibliotheca Sacra* 113 (July 1956): 239–247; idem, 'Faith Missions – Their Growth and Outreach,' *Bibliotheca Sacra* 115 (April 1958): 143–152; J.O. Percy, 'The Independent Movement As It Relates to Faith Missions,' *Missions Annual, 1959* (New York: Interdenominational Foreign Mission Association, 1959): 14–22; Olan Hendrix, 'Too Many Missions?' *EMQ* 2 (summer 1966): 227–230; Ralph D. Winter, 'Protestant Mission Societies and the "Protestant Schism," ' in *American Denominational Organization*, ed. Scherer, 194–224; and Chapter 18, 'New Methods and Strategies,' in Ruth Tucker, *From Jerusalem to Irian Jaya*, 461–486.

composition, objectives, and methods of missions changed drastically, resulting in new programs scarcely related to much of the work undertaken in the past, the general appearance of the enterprise, including its promotional rhetoric and representations of missionaries and their work, remained largely unchanged.

Against this backdrop of unsettled conditions and changing missionary approaches, the Assemblies of God DFM remained remarkably consistent in its focus and policies, relying primarily on personal initiative and subjective promptings rather than on well-organized institutional campaigns for the recruitment and deployment of personnel and solicitation of funds.[5] But as new crises and opportunities appeared and new strategies were advanced, J. Philip Hogan grappled with the thinking of several prominent missionary theorists. Without either abruptly abandoning time-honored approaches or ignoring innovative concepts, Hogan developed a missionary philosophy that was faithful to Pentecostal emphases as well as to his own missionary experience. The result was a program that, while remarkably in step with the times, would appear increasingly unique.

The indigenous church legacy

Respect for the emergent overseas Pentecostal community, the DFM policy of 'indigenous missions,' had long been a pillar of Assemblies of God policy. National autonomy had been strongly advocated by Noel Perkin, the soft-spoken Englishman who had already been at the helm of the DFM for 32 years before relinquishing its direction to J. Philip Hogan.[6] Perkin, in turn, had been influenced by J. Roswell Flower, the first Assemblies of God

---

[5] J. Philip Hogan referred to the concerns of Evangelical Foreign Missions Association (EFMA) leader Clyde Taylor, which included the need for greater numbers of volunteers. 'Immediately after the war there were thousands of ex-GIs who had caught the missionary vision from their experience overseas,' he noted. 'This surplus is now gone. So boards actually find difficulty in securing applications for missionary service'. 'Happily', commented Hogan, 'this condition does not exist among us of the Assemblies of God. We have constantly more applications than we can process.' JPH, 'Five Fronts,' *Missionary Challenge* (April 1958). n.p.

[6] Noel Perkin represents some of the best features of the early Assemblies of God. Reared in a Wesleyan holiness home, Perkin was working in a Toronto bank when he came into contact with the Christian and Missionary Alliance. In 1918, influenced by a Pentecostal group, he was ordained and served as a missionary in Argentina. Perkin returned in 1921 to attend the Elim Bible Training School in Rochester, New York, and pastored Assemblies of God churches in western New York briefly before joining the Assemblies of God missionary staff as a bookkeeper in Springfield, Missouri, in 1926. The following year he was named the missionary secretary of the DFM, a position he held until 1959. A kindly, understanding man, Noel Perkin was personally acquainted with all of the overseas personnel in his charge, visiting 73 countries on four round-the-world tours during his tenure. 'He always took personal interest in the missionary staff, kindly overlooking persons who disappointed him,' recalled Adele Dalton. 'Don't put

missionary secretary.[7] In formulating a coherent philosophy Hogan referred to his predecessor as his 'mentor in missions leadership.'

> Noel Perkin was the guiding force in establishing our commitment to the indigenous church principle as a basic missions philosophy. Long before other missions leaders grasped this concept, he saw self-governing, self-supporting, self-propagating national churches in every country as the key to world evangelization.[8]

The publication in 1953 of *The Indigenous Church*, a series of lectures by Melvin Hodges, the field secretary for Latin America and the Caribbean, reinforced the concept of national responsibility.[9] Beyond mere lip service to local initiative and leadership in each of the Assemblies of God fields, the DFM gave priority to training programs, especially the development of Bible institutes. By 1960 there were 61 of them, more than those of any other Protestant mission agency at the time, an achievement that on occasion brought the DFM rare recognition from outside the movement.[10] As the years passed an increasing proportion of

---

missionaries on pedestals,' Perkin pleaded. 'They are just ordinary people working under trying circumstances.' Historian Gary McGee has summarized the achievement of Perkin's tenure of office as having 'turned the department from an agency that largely distributed funds to one that provided leadership and planning to the enterprise.' Moreover, Perkin's 'fervor and gentle demeanor assured the supporting constituency that the spiritual objectives of the effort remained at the forefront.' By the time of his retirement in 1959, Noel Perkin had become a venerable figure among evangelical missions leaders, serving as president of the Evangelical Foreign Mission Association, the first Pentecostal to hold the office. Gary McGee, *This Gospel*, vol. 1, chapter 8; idem, 'Perkin, Noel' in *DPCM* 710.

[7] J. Roswell Flower served in that position when the Foreign Missions Department was formed in 1919 to oversee the 196 missionaries already working within the group's loose administrative structure. It should be noted that Flower and Perkin were both influenced by Alice Luce, a former Anglican missionary in India, who after receiving the Pentecostal experience came to Canada and then worked in Mexico briefly during that country's revolution. Committed to the thinking of Roland Allen and persuasive as a writer and teacher, Luce made a strong case for the 'indigenous' church policies in the early movement. See Gary B. McGee, 'Luce, Alice Eveline,' *DPCM*, 543, 544; and idem, *This Gospel*, 2:33.

[8] JPH, letter sent to DFM missionaries after Perkin's death in 1979. The eulogy went on to read: 'His vision for reaching the lost was matched by his care and concern for the welfare of the missionaries who looked to him for leadership. A man of devotion and prayer, a gentleman who was always courteous, a leader whose gentleness was that of a father dealing with his children – Noel Perkin gave his life to the cause he loved.'

[9] Hodges, *The Indigenous Church*.

[10] Winehouse, *Assemblies of God*, 194; Gary McGee points out that the DFM was not aware of this distinctiveness until a Southern Baptist missions leader pointed out the achievement; McGee, *This Gospel*, 2:36. In his initial sweep through the Assemblies of God missions fields after becoming the executive director, Hogan identified foreign Bible schools as one of three cornerstones of the DFM effort; JPH, 'Fifty Thousand Miles of Missions,' *Global Conquest* (December 1960): n.p.

US Assemblies of God missionaries were engaged in leadership training. In the 1970s it was estimated that half of all DFM missionaries were teaching at least part-time in a national Bible institute, in addition to their other leadership preparation functions. The wisdom of the policy became evident in the annual reports: by 1961 the 11,300 national Assemblies of God pastors overseas compared favorably with the 8,000 pastors serving congregations in the United States at the time.

Geared to crises

Strong precedents for strategic planning and a ready response to crisis were also part of the legacy that accrued to J. Philip Hogan. When World War II presented the visionary denomination with new opportunities to proclaim its message, General Superintendent Ernest S. Williams called for spiritual readiness. At the Nineteenth General Council held in Minneapolis in August 1941, he reminded ministers and delegates that the world had passed through a serious crisis during World War I. 'Now the world faces a crisis which gives promise of becoming more severe. God has placed us in the midst of this hour. We have a place to fill.' In response Texas pastor Raymond T. Richey urged for the adoption of a program that would especially target service personnel. And, following World War II, it was observed that thousands of men and women in uniform had been converted, some of them returning to become Pentecostal pastors and others to become missionaries in the country where they had served.[11]

This same aggressive response to the world's needs was applied directly to the overseas missions program during and after World War II. 'World War II curtailed some missionary activities, notably those in Europe and the Far East,' explains historian Gary McGee, and 'as a result, the missions department gave more of its attention to regions still available for evangelism.' Although Assemblies of God missionaries opened three fields in Africa – Nyasaland, Tanganyika, and Basutoland – Latin America presented the most accessible opportunities for expansion. During this period, the Assemblies of God began work in Costa Rica, Paraguay, Colombia, Jamaica, and the Bahamas. In response

---

[11] 'The Assemblies of God and World War II,' *Assemblies of God Heritage* 10 (summer 1990): 6. While many local ministries to service personnel came into being, the most extensive evangelistic effort during World War II was a nationally sponsored project, the publication of *Reveille*, a nondenominational publication prepared for mass distribution to men and women in the armed forces. With Myer Pearlman, Hogan's Central Bible Institute teacher, as editor and evangelical cartoonist Charles Ramsey as illustrator, the paper found such a welcome reception that it was reportedly the only nongovernmental publication that was given free postage to any war zone. Altogether, nearly one million copies of each of the 15 issues were produced during the 52-month life of the publication.

28 new missionaries went overseas in 1942, 24 heading for Latin America or the Caribbean.[12]

The DFM experienced a burst of growth during the final years of World War II; 150 missionaries were added to the rolls, bringing the total personnel to 538 by 1945, although many of them were prevented from leaving immediately for their fields of service. By 1946 there were 600 Assemblies of God appointed missionaries, and the annual budget grew from $1.5 million in 1946 to nearly $3 million in 1953.[13]

World War II thus stands in McGee's analysis as a watershed in the development of Assemblies of God mission strategizing and goal setting. In 1945, in the first of several planning meetings, Noel Perkin entertained ambitious objectives, including literature production in national languages and overseas radio evangelism.[14] Through subsequent discussions these proposals were reduced to several strategic goals as the members of the staff agreed: that more emphasis should be placed on evangelistic efforts in large population centers; that efforts should be stepped up to reach remote and inaccessible peoples; and that aid should be provided to the sick, hungry, and homeless, as resources permitted. Members of the staff further urged that ties between Pentecostal churches around the world should be strengthened, 'thereby realizing, to a greater extent in actual experience, the real unity of the body of Christ.'[15] As virtually the final undertaking of Perkin's administration in 1959, the department launched 'Global Conquest,' essentially a distillation of the various proposals, presented to Assemblies of God constituents as strategic objectives.

J. Philip Hogan's missiology

Beyond affirming these previously adopted approaches, however, J. Philip Hogan supported other emphases that emerged from his own experience in Asia and the surge of new concerns that affected all missionary work during the 1950s. His personal missionary philosophy was invariably strategic, concentrating efforts on major, critical targets. Here one can best see his strength of character, self-reliance, clear perception, and single-mindedness – his stubborn arbitrariness, some critics would say – set against frequent pressures to accommodate alternative approaches that Hogan believed to be less effective and less worthy of DFM support. When a missionary complained that 'It is our glorious Pentecostal heritage to be free, to go where we please and develop our work as we individually

---

[12]   McGee, *This Gospel*, 1:165, 166.

[13]   Roger Culbertson, 'A Glimpse of the Old Central District,' *Assemblies of God Heritage* 6 (spring 1988): 16. In 1959 the DFM reported 753 missionaries and a budget of $6,734,780.

[14]   McGee, *This Gospel*, 1:166.

[15]   Ibid., 168.

see fit and are led,' Hogan questioned whether such an attitude was 'practical, successful, or Pentecostal.'[16]

The Global Conquest program adopted in 1959 reflected this stance, an aggressive response in the face of the then current ideological and demographic challenges. Along with an affirmative 'backing for our already superb and worldwide program for training national leadership,' as the existing philosophy was described in a contemporary publication, the mission would concentrate on specific needs and opportunities – notably the megacities all over the world that were swelling with immigrants from the countryside were targeted – and production of printed material for an increasingly literate world population. The price of these new opportunities, Hogan pointed out, however, was a world of perpetual crisis. 'Let us not waste any time looking for a missionary status quo; there is none,' he wrote in 1955.

> Such a procedure would suggest a return to normality – that is a forlorn hope. You have likely lived through the last normal days you will ever see. All the former standards are obsolete. Christianity cannot grow, no, it cannot even exist as a religion of averages. It has made its best progress when it had to speak over the death rattle of a dying world order. The crisis, the 'now or never' note you have detected in the ministry of real missionaries, is the very hallmark of God.[17]

The unreasonable personal cost of missions

The placement of qualified personnel in the field was also an integral part of Hogan's view of missions. While he supported the use of every available tool, including the latest technological advances, he saw missionary work as being essentially a personal undertaking of highly motivated, focused men and women compelled by a divine calling. The enterprise in this sense was 'labor intensive.' While the tendency in missionary effort increasingly was to rely on mass media, short-term workers, and other labor-saving innovations, Hogan from experience rejected reliance solely or primarily on impersonal, mechanical, and short-term approaches. 'The most important factor in missions is not money, but men,' he argued. 'Where God can find dedicated, yielded men, there will be success.'[18]

As part of his concern with placing missionaries on-site at certain phases of a church's development, Hogan knew that to do so would sometimes require sending personnel into situations of considerable inconvenience and even risk. Although loneliness and deprivation had always been taken for granted in missionary service, the experience of wartime disruption, the concerns of the Cold War, and growing nationalistic and ideological

---

[16]   Idem, *This Gospel*, 2:105.

[17]   JPH, 'A Sense of Urgency,' *Pentecostal Evangel* (24 February 1974): n.p.

[18]   JPH, 'The Most Important Factor in Missions,' *Pentecostal Evangel* (31 July 1960): n.p.

tensions made him sensitive to these hazards. The need for dedicated, motivated volunteers was clear; the task could not be completed without men and women who responded wholeheartedly to the calling and who were willing to accept the sacrifices, obstacles, and danger their work entailed. Flesh and blood missionaries, convinced and convincing men and women, were indispensable to the undertaking. 'In Colombia, Spain, Greece, Ethiopia, India, and in all Communist-dominated lands opposition is open and fierce,' wrote Hogan. 'However, God still honors His Word and in spite of the organized efforts to hinder, there is a constant note of victory.'[19]

> Jesus did not say, 'Send missionaries until there is political turmoil or danger,' but 'till I come.' Everything about the missionary program must bear the trademark of the expendable. 'For whosoever will save his life shall lose it; and whosoever will lose his life for my sake shall find it.' Let me mention the continuing need for men, women and families that are willing to go abroad and stay, even though danger threatens. There is a tendency in these days to indicate that there are better methods than sending missionaries. I am convinced more than ever before that there is no adequate substitute for persons whose hearts are on fire and who will put forth the effort to learn a language, identify themselves with a foreign culture, and live among the lost in order to establish a witness for Jesus Christ.[20]

For the evangelical world, the deaths of five young missionaries in Ecuador in 1956 demonstrated the potential price of persistence in mission. Hogan referred to Elisabeth Elliot's *Through Gates of Splendor* as 'one of the most spiritual, and deeply moving pieces of literature that has fallen into my hands in many years. It will doubtless rank with the greatest of published works on the subject of missionary heroism and enterprise.' Most believers will never have to pay such a price, he continued, but those who are not exposed to such danger nevertheless are required to demonstrate their commitment.[21]

Already, however, a long list of Assemblies of God missionaries had given their lives during their terms of service. A slender volume published in 1955 in promotion of the Assemblies of God work in Africa identified more than a hundred missionaries, from all fields, who had died while at their overseas posts during the brief 40 years of the operation of the DFM, a statistical average of more than one couple per year. While many of these casualties resulted from natural causes and mishaps that might have

[19] JPH, 'Five Fronts:' n.p. 'Different from many other missionary societies, we have no significant shortage of candidates – despite the fact that we do not have a recruitment program.' See also Wesley R. Hurst, 'What's New Statistically?' *Missionary Forum* (January–March 1965): 8,9.

[20] JPH, 'Till I Come,' *Pentecostal Evangel* (29 January 1961): n.p.

[21] Elliot, *Through Gates of Splendor* ; JPH, 'Missionary Potentials,' *Missionary Challenge* (September 1957): 22; Editorial, 'Reflections on the Auca Tragedy,' *Practical Anthropology* 3 (January–February 1956): 1–4.

occurred regardless of the location, most of these missionaries had died in accidents resulting from precarious means of transportation or because they lacked adequate health safeguards and medical attention. Several had died violently by intrigue, assaults, or in other circumstances provoked by their missionary service.[22]

Hogan's response to danger and risk revealed his strongly held belief about the missionary calling and its 'unreasonable' demands on leaving one's home, security, and creature comforts to identify closely with a given people. Beyond merely tolerating a new culture, Hogan advocated as complete an identification with a missionary's adoptive people as possible, a cultural assimilation only possible to career missionaries who are willing to forgo indefinitely the benefits of life at home. Not only had Hogan himself known separation, personal loss, and sacrifice, but also he worked daily with people whose lives were governed by a sacrificial higher calling.

> All of us, left to our natural human impulses, would seek the easiest course, like a river. We would always avoid a crisis. [But] nowhere in God's dealing with the human race is there even the mildest dose of anesthesia. The religion of Jesus Christ has always faced competitive demands.[23]

These emphases on the priority of obedience and service, faithfulness to one's calling and trust in God for the means to accomplish the task, if they had long been central to Pentecostal missionary emphases, were given new impetus by J. Philip Hogan.

While these approaches were consistent with Assemblies of God past policies, they were not unique among evangelical missionaries. The annals were filled with similar examples of dedication and sacrificial service. Much of the missionary theory that lay behind the policies of the various missionary agencies corresponded to the same opportunities and challenges of the post-World War II era. Yet, as time passed, it was increasingly clear that the DFM, responding directly to the influence and vision of J. Philip Hogan, developed a program that was philosophically distinct and especially appropriate to the Pentecostals' experience and perspectives.

Why churches grow

Virtually all evangelical missionary theory then and since has begun with the question framed by Dr Donald McGavran in 1955: 'What makes churches grow?' J. Philip Hogan's ideas corresponded closely to those of

---

[22]   Sanders, *Meet the Mossi*, appendix; Gary McGee, 'Historical Perspectives on Pentecostal Missionaries in Situations of Conflict and Violence,' *Missiology* 20 (January 1992): 33–43.

[23]   JPH, 'Bequeathed a Crisis,' *Missionary Challenge* (July 1959): n.p; reprinted in *Pentecostal Evangel* (16 November 1969): n.p.

Donald McGavran, whose critique of missions was only then developing into what would eventually become the church growth movement. In *The Bridges of God*, McGavran developed the idea of 'people movements,' spontaneous or at least broadly based responses to the Christian faith, of which there were good examples found in McGavran's own field of India, as well as elsewhere. McGavran noted that churches most often grew almost indiscriminately among members of a given ethnic group. He observed that when a 'revival' occurred, 'The church did not spread out like ink in water; it usually grew along family lines, or at least within societal boundaries.'[24] The missionary's failure to recognize the social and cultural dynamics of conversion, McGavran argued, tended to inhibit growth.

Conversely, recognition of how people respond to the gospel ensures that evangelistic efforts will take best advantage of a population's spiritual readiness. McGavran reasoned, for instance, that missions operations should be as mobile as possible, seizing opportunities as they develop. His views helped to explain why the indigenous church emphasis should be observed even when other expedients tended to make it appear unwieldy and in some situations better set aside. 'Non-Christian nations,' he warned, 'are impatient with foreign tutelage.'

> A new pattern is demanded. A new pattern is at hand, which, while new, is as old as the Church itself. It is a God-designed pattern by which not ones but thousands will acknowledge Christ as Lord, and grow into full discipleship as people after people, clan after clan, tribe after tribe and community after community are claimed for and nurtured in the Christian faith. Christward movements of peoples are the supreme goal of missionary effort. Yet we not only affirm it, but go further and claim that the vast stirrings of the Spirit which occur in People Movements are God-given. We dare not think of People Movements to Christ as merely social phenomena. But there is so much that is mysterious and beyond anything we can ask or think, so much that is a product of religious faith, and so much evident working of divine power, that we must confess that People Movements are gifts of God.[25]

---

[24] McGavran, *The Bridges of God*, 53.

[25] Ibid., 81. The alternative, McGavran saw, is what missionaries at work in Asia had long witnessed – the slow, tedious proselytism of individuals who, after their conversion to Christianity, were so alienated from their own culture, family connections and community that they retained no influence. 'Gathered colonies, rather than vital churches,' he concluded, tend to form on missions fields. A contemporary review of McGavran's book by missionary-anthropologist William A. Smalley supports McGavran's philosophy by emphasizing the need to direct resources and effort into responsive groups that need discipling. The result, he contends, would be 'a turning to Christ on a scale analogous to that of the early church.' He continues: 'Is it possible for missionaries to give up their ideas of "forming" churches and instead light a spark which will spread among these peoples, sweeping many thousands into the Kingdom of God, and which will give me an opportunity to teach and to foster and to strengthen a church which the Holy Spirit has founded?' William A. Smalley, 'The Bridges of God,' *Practical Anthropology* 5 (January–February 1958): 24, 26.

McGavran's explanation of people movements was notably compatible with the thinking found in the historic statements of the indigenous church concept and with the thinking that lay behind Assemblies of God policies. McGavran saw the church as putting down roots in 'the soil of hundreds of thousands of villages,' with an implied priority of the local church, no matter how humble, rather than the flow of support, administration and initiative coming from a foreign mission. In such congregations the 'indigenous' culture would prevail, avoiding the problem of foreignness in, for example, music and styles of worship that often were imposed on the formative church. Moreover, the focus was on conserving and cultivating the initial, often spontaneous, response of peoples to the gospel, encouraging them to come to full discipleship. 'People after people, clan after clan, tribe after tribe and community after community,' he envisioned, would be 'claimed for and nurtured in the Christian faith.' Even McGavran's way of stating these principles was compatible with Pentecostal sensibilities.

> Spontaneous expansion involves a full trust in the Holy Spirit and a recognition that the ecclesiastical traditions of the older churches are not necessarily useful to the young churches arising out of the missions from the West. New groups of converts are expected to multiply themselves in the same way as did the new groups of converts in the early church.[26]

Eugene Nida and Pentecostal missions

J. Philip Hogan also was aware of the writings of Eugene Nida of the American Bible Society, a linguist and Bible translator who, on the basis of ethnology, formulated approaches similar to the ones the Pentecostals seemed to adopt intuitively. Nida saw earlier than most missionary writers the special relevance of Pentecostalism for evangelism. Where Donald McGavran explained the dynamics of social movements, Eugene Nida explored the world view, values, and aspirations of emerging peoples. He observed that Pentecostalism (which he often referred to as 'indigenous Christianity') was especially suitable for peoples in transition because it permits them to appropriate the Christian faith in familiar cultural terms. 'Pentecostal ministers are not as concerned with teaching the Bible as with teaching *people*,' observed Nida. Taking most of his examples from the peasant and indigenous (in this sense 'native') peoples of Latin America, he explained even before most Pentecostals were aware of their movement's extraordinary overseas effectiveness why their message was so appropriate.

> [In these groups] there is great emphasis upon group participation in prayer and singing, and the sermons are generally on the level of the people, with

---

[26] McGavran, *The Bridges of God*, 88.

plenty of opportunity for men and women to respond, not only verbally but by signs of the filling of the Spirit. In contrast, the average evangelical meeting is so often colorless, tasteless and boring. [Pentecostal] sermons in Latin America are theologically thin, but often they are more effectively direct to the needs of the people than many sermons delivered in more traditional churches. [In these] the sermon too often deals not with religious expression and life, but with the 'grammar of religion,' namely the doctrines which are not infrequently a verbal substitute for the real life experience. The utter lack of pageantry, drama, and group participation make [some] evangelical services seem more like a session in a lecture hall than a corporate worship of the Most High.[27]

J. Philip Hogan and Arthur Glasser

J. Philip Hogan was especially close to fellow China missionary Arthur Glasser, whose China Inland Mission was then recoiling from the sudden loss to Communism of virtually its entire field. Glasser saw the need for nationally sustained churches that displayed maturity and initiative. 'One notable exception to this failure of the [missionary] church,' wrote Eric Fife and Arthur Glasser in reference to the work undertaken in El Salvador, 'has been the Pentecostal group.' 'As in any human work, there are weaknesses. It is true that the ministry of the Assemblies of God has been very largely limited to the very poor classes. But whether or not we agree with our Pentecostal friends on every detail, we have much to learn from them.'[28] The authors went on to identify three features of Pentecostal missions that set them apart: their emphasis upon the work of the Holy Spirit led to 'unusual' expectations that went beyond merely human resources; they adhered to 'indigenous' church principles; and they tended to empower the laity. These missions leaders called for imagination and adaptability in the missionary enterprise, warning that 'there is only one strategist in the Church of Jesus Christ, and He is the Holy Spirit of God.'

---

[27] Eugene Nida, 'The Communication of the Gospel to Latin Americans,' *Practical Anthropology* 7 (1960): 633. 'There are practical similarities between all Pentecostals despite organizational differences,' wrote Nida, 'such as the preparation of leaders through an apprenticeship, the full participation of almost everyone, and gradation of respect within the congregation on the basis of function rather than social status. They consistently and repeatedly emphasize the key points of the Christian faith, [and] beyond rehearsing the cardinal doctrines they emphasize the need for becoming part of the church as a witnessing member. Despite the "hubbub" which seems to characterize the Pentecostal-type meetings, there is nevertheless a great deal of genuine feeling of the presence of God and a sense of group participation which is the life blood of a congregation. One can only thank God that these churches have been able to reach so many of the economically and socially dispossessed, and have become the "third force" of religion in Latin America.' Idem, *Understanding Latin Americans*, 145.

[28] Fife and Glasser, *Missions in Crisis*, 185.

It is imperative that we use every scrap of information we are able to obtain, and that we mobilize our finest resources in the cause of world evangelization. But when we have done this we need to recognize that there is only One who 'searches everything, even the depths of God.' It behooves us to cultivate deep humility of mind and action as we consider the work of the Lord throughout the world and Christ's purpose for His church. By human standards it may be relatively simple for us to determine what are the 'important' and the 'unimportant' types of missionary work, but our ways are not His ways. In the final analysis a man or women goes to a particular mission field, not because he likes that particular type of work, nor because he fits in with an imaginative man-made strategy, but because he receives his marching orders from the Commander-in-Chief of the Army.[29]

Church growth: design or dynamics?

From a fund of seminal ideas for restructuring the evangelistic enterprise, however, missionary thinking in the next decades tended to be captured by a specific blueprint, the church growth school of missionary theory. Adopting an engineering model, a great many students of missionary work took up the tools of sociology, emphasizing demographic analysis, the growth rates of particular churches, and the rationalization of missionary methods. Their primary concern was to assess the numbers and locations of the 'unreached.' Following such assessment, missions directors and missionary volunteers attempted in good faith to identify neglected populations and to deploy their available resources accordingly.

Church growth thinking, increasingly applied also to evangelism in the United States, reached a climax in the publication of David Barrett's *World Christian Encyclopedia* (1982), a beautifully conceived and executed profile of the religious world, its needs, and the progress of evangelism to date.[30] Presented in informative tables, precise definitions, tabulated growth rates, and projected church sizes, this comprehensive volume was a delight. Armed with such tools, mission executives and personnel committees could tactically select objectives and deploy personnel. Missionary volunteers were matched with suitable agencies, programs, and positions, converting some missions agencies into little more than overseas personnel placement services. After 40 years of unflagging support and sustained interest in what may be the most extensive and influential modern missionary program, there can be no doubt that the church growth movement has been one of the most successful efforts ever for promoting missionary activity.[31]

---

[29]   Ibid., 241

[30]   Barrett, *World Christian Encyclopedia* (New York: Oxford University Press, 1982).

[31]   Some favorable assessments of the impact of the church growth movement include Donald G. Hill, 'Apostle of Church Growth,' *World Vision* 12 (September 1968): 10, 11; Ralph Winter, 'An Unlikely Revolutionary,' *Christianity Today* (7 September 1984): 14–18; Tim Stafford, 'The Father of Church Growth,' *Christianity Today* (21 February

But despite its important motivational contribution, and while it provided missionary effort with a much needed focus – assessment of a mission's success or failure to achieve its purposes – church growth theory for J. Philip Hogan had limitations. The rush to reduce overseas evangelism to a science of missiology with a systematized body of information and supportive theory, he believed, was accomplished at the price of ignoring many of the field-tested, analytically incisive and personal – if not biblical and spiritual – insights of McGavran, Nida, and Glasser. The emphasis of much church growth literature on resistant, remote, or inaccessible populations, for example, he saw too often interpreted as a romantic excuse for not undertaking what was immediately at hand – and contrary to McGavran's emphasis on making the best use of missionary personnel by placing them among peoples who were already responsive to evangelistic efforts and who stood in need of discipling. Focusing on the world's cities, Hogan argued that it was not a matter of reaching tribes, it was a matter of reaching people! And to reach people we must go where they are – into the cities.

'Reaching a soul,' is it throwing a tract from an airplane, conducting a mass evangelism outreach, preaching on a radio broadcast, or personally leading a man to Christ? 'Reaching a soul' can have many interpretations. We are cautious about claiming results that are only known to the Lord of the harvest. The only results we announce are those which are obvious. We count our gains in churches, not endeavors. There are many superficial kinds of missionary activity that may be good in themselves, but do not result in the emergence of the local body of Christ. We must not be blinded by small successes. We seek to gather converts into a local church for the discipling and maturing process which is the goal of the Great Commission.[32]

Some missions agencies, in the nature of their precise focus, appeared to neglect the formation of new congregations altogether. Others, rather than the judicious reinforcement of spiritually responsive sectors in a given society as advocated by McGavran, made their objective the establishment of evangelical beachheads by the imposition, if necessary, of foreign agencies backed up with massive resources and sophisticated methods. Attention especially seemed to be given to approaches that favored daring and confrontation, use of the electronic mass media, and clandestine schemes to penetrate difficult-to-reach populations, even, Hogan concluded, where more prosaic, constructive efforts might have been available or might have produced greater long term results.

While Hogan felt strong personal affection for the founders of the church growth movement, most of whom as personal friends he invited to lecture at the DFM annual training sessions throughout the 1960s, and

1986): 19–23; Editorial, 'Church Growth Fine Tunes its Formulas,' *Christianity Today* (24 June 1991): 44–45.
[32] JPH, 'Missionary Priorities,' *Pentecostal Evangel* (30 September 1962): n.p.

while he seriously weighed the theory these writers produced, his own focus was often considerably different. He especially parted company with what he believed to be a reductionist view of missions as mechanics. Some extremes of church growth theory, he protested, made the guiding principles of missionary deployment into mere abstract coefficients of need – the relative per capita Christian population of a given country or the proportion of the total missionary force allocated to a given field.

In Hogan's view, the Holy Spirit already knew the world's needs, had prepared the soil of lost humanity for the message of the gospel, and was primarily concerned with directing spiritually sensitive laborers into strategic harvest opportunities.[33]

While the church growth movement was concerned largely with the meticulous assessment of need, the systematic proclamation of the message, and the rational deployment of resources, J. Philip Hogan, without neglecting these concerns, urged his colleagues to keep the end of the missionary task in view. The sowing of the spiritual seed, although a logical priority, was a wasted effort if a church did not eventually emerge. He believed that wherever the good seed of the gospel was sown in fertile soil, the normal process of germination would result in the emergence of at least some tender plants.[34]

> Our experience has reaffirmed what we long have believed that the Bible teaches – that the church of Jesus Christ has its seed in itself, and that it can reproduce itself under amazingly difficult conditions. Political and social ferment are the hallmark of this generation but it is our business to seek to evangelize, build churches, and witness so that the Holy Spirit may perform the task ascribed to Him in Acts 15:14 – to 'visit the Gentiles, to take out of them a people for his name.'[35]

Reaping a harvest thus entailed the entire process: sowing, cultivating, watering, and whatever else was needed to produce a crop. 'The missionary must determine whether it is May or September,' Hogan insisted, 'whether the workers should take up the hoe or the sickle.'[36]

---

[33] JPH, 'We Are Taught to Teach,' *Sunday School Counselor* (October 1952): 11.

[34] More than a decade after he assumed his executive responsibilities, Hogan wrote: 'It is important to discern where God is moving and to react quickly and decisively. In recent years the Assemblies of God has entered a number of new mission fields, not as a result of long-range planning of men, but as a result of a spontaneous, sovereign move of God's Holy Spirit. Sensing His will, we have followed. Such a move of the Spirit is now taking place in many of the distant islands of the Pacific. The Spirit of God is brooding and moving over the face of this great and widely scattered population.' JPH, 'Leaders Are Good Followers,' *Pentecostal Evangel* (26 December 1971): n.p.

[35] JPH, 'If This Were 1776,' *Pentecostal Evangel* (29 July 1962): n.p.

[36] Printed message by JPH delivered to the twenty-fifth anniversary conference of the Assemblies of God of Malaysia. Hogan further emphasized the need for a pneumatological missiology based on the local church. 'Please know that no significant work in the Kingdom is ever accomplished that does not have its anchor in this unit of the body of

For Phil Hogan, accordingly, proclamation of the gospel was only the initial – not the final – step in the missionary enterprise. He was concerned with what came next, what occurred in the spiritual growth of the handful of believers who made up the nucleus of the emergent church. Would they mature personally and collectively into the functioning body that could in turn reproduce itself? In contrast with the cerebral positivism of much missions theory, Hogan saw missionary effort as being extremely contingent – as the unpredictable, timely, and ongoing work of the Holy Spirit based on the individual, sacrificial effort of sensitive, amenable, and dedicated men and women. Monitoring the development of a church; nurturing, encouraging, and supporting its spiritual health; and discerning its needs at various states of its development – in other words, providing pastoral care – were his primary concerns.

What J. Philip Hogan actually saw overseas might have given some observers little reason for delight or pride. The churches were sometimes fragile, shallow, and poorly formed. All too often they were congregations of the poor, the marginalized, the powerless, and the deprived. But for Hogan, the issue was not the external attractiveness or conformity of the emergent national church, but the fact that it was made up of men and women whose lives had been changed and whose hope had been placed in the power of the gospel. An association of such believers by definition was a church. These believers had roots in their own culture, exhibited the metabolic, self-renewing, developmental functions of a vital organism; and from the beginning were reproductive, enthusiastically sharing their faith with relatives and friends. While Hogan learned a great deal cognitively about church growth processes from the prevailing rational model of missions, he placed his confidence rather in the personal, motivational, organic emphases implicit in his Pentecostal convictions.

> In our foreign missions program we are not only concerned with evangelism, but with church maturity. The initial thrust is not enough. Every evangelistic thrust must be followed through until there appears on the scene a local unit of the Body of Jesus Christ. Only in this way can the fruits of evangelism be conserved. The church so born may not have a building; it may meet under the trees. It may have only the weakest of leadership; it may know nothing of Western forms of worship. But if it is a community-identified testimony of Jesus Christ, it is worth everything. Training will be a premier role of foreign missionaries in the coming years, should Jesus tarry. No activity on the part of the Western church and its thrust abroad – no matter how well received in the homeland – can really be God's best unless it has strong overtones not only of evangelism but also of maturing and training believers.[37]

Christ. Statistics and glamorous reports notwithstanding, if the work of God grows, it must grow at the local level. Provision must be made for it there. Leadership and laborers must be provided for there, and all the superstructure that is necessary must have its base there.'

[37] JPH, 'Beyond Evangelism,' *Pentecostal Evangel* (18 April 1965): n.p.

The marks of a Pentecostal missiology

Two aspects of Pentecostal missionary philosophy were especially per-
tinent to Hogan's thinking. First, missionaries in his organic way of
looking at evangelism were viewed not merely as impersonal soldiers,
the rank and file who indiscriminately carried out the assignments. They
were extremely human representatives, often as notable for their weaknesses as for their strengths. They were, however, differentiated by their
personal gifts and callings, by their vision, tenacity, and responsiveness
to divine leadings. Their effectiveness was based only in part on their
qualifications and preparation. Primarily they were effective because they
were God's representatives, the right man or woman in the right place
at the right time. In missionary ministry the opportunities as well as the
achievements were often unforeseen and unexpected. Moreover, since
these missionaries recognized their own inadequacy, they left room for
– and persistently sought – divine help to realize the goals they felt God
had given them. Far from demeaning missionaries by pointing out their
human inadequacies, their participation in the process of evangelism was
enhanced.

In addition, Hogan's concept of missionary work looked beyond
immediate, palpable achievements to the potential the church displayed
for future development and productivity. The yield in his thinking was
not primarily the initial group of believers who responded to the gospel,
but the continuing impact these founding members of congregations
could have as they continued to function as a spiritually mature community. The harvest would not really result until the church, however small
and humble, demonstrated its spiritual maturity by reproducing itself.
Successive 'generations' of converts, the compounded growth of converts
who in turn made converts, when incorporated into a healthy association
of believers, had the potential for exponential, not simply incremental,
increases. '[A] goal in our efforts to establish the church abroad is to
mother, not smother,' he wrote in the 1980s. 'This is the acid test of
missions – to plant a church that reproduces itself and emerges to a position
of solidarity and independence with its own leaders.'[38] Missionaries who
restricted church growth by inadequate resources, paternalism, their
foreignness and, sometimes, inappropriate approaches to evangelism were
well advised to make national churches productive rather than hoping to
accomplish the evangelistic task themselves. Hogan, referring to biblical
metaphors of productivity, believed that an expectation of high returns
on missionary investment was well founded.[39]

Nor is there, Hogan believed, sufficient information, wisdom, and
prescience to determine where best to invest missionary resources.
Rather, 'the Spirit blows where it wills.' Missions cannot be reduced

---

[38] JPH, 'Moving Mountains,' *Mountain Movers* (September 1981): 3–5.
[39] JPH, 'It's Harvesttime,' *Missionary Challenge* (November 1951): 6.

entirely to rational strategies, priorities, and techniques, no matter how astute the planners or how comprehensive the information. 'There just isn't enough human motivation. There is not enough human love, not enough human wisdom. Sum up the best of it, and some have more than others, but there still isn't enough!'[40] Furthermore, for the spiritual health of the overseas church, should the sending countries even assume this kind of oversight and responsibility? Consequently, for Hogan missionary activity became not so much a way in which systematically to complete a finite task, but the beginning of an infinite process of spiritual growth.

These missiological distinctives of J. Philip Hogan were not merely semantic and theoretical; they had immediate application in planning and policies. While missions theorists had long talked about 'pre-evangelism' – conditions in the order of human affairs that by their nature prepared men and women to comprehend and receive the gospel – Hogan, in keeping with the Pentecostal eschatological emphases, argued that God directly initiates and supervises the process of evangelization among a given group of people at a given time. The church thus works in tandem with divine preparation of the 'soil' of humanity through historical events, using even the secular, the tragic, and the revolutionary in order to prepare entire populations for the presentation of the gospel. Hogan had observed just such preparation in Asia.

> Strong forces have been at work and all of a sudden the harvest is ready. Such has been the experience of many of us who have labored in the Far East. Wars and mass movements of men on a national or international scale are but God's plow and harrow in the fields of the world. Whole areas of the Japanese Empire were brought to fruition with the blinding flashes of Hiroshima and Nagasaki. Millions of men, whose minds have been bound and channeled into [emperor worship] were suddenly set free. Their too long throttled desires for reality in worship were unleashed in the mightiest cataclysm of history.[41]

Hogan also noted that the processes of sowing and reaping happened practically simultaneously in Taiwan and in other fields.

> When we opened in the city of Taipei we thought that it would be necessary to go through a long series of sowing-the-seed meetings, that it would be necessary to move into the vacuum left in the minds of the people with a build-up of the great truths of the Christian religion. How surprised we were after a very short time to sense that the folk were ready to be saved. That first altar call will remain in my mind as a great spiritual triumph. Almost the entire congregation moved forward to be saved. The harvest was not four months away, but right then. But, alas, the forces that cause doors to open quickly may cause the same doors to close just as quickly. A harvest is a fleeting matter.[42]

---

[40] JPH, 'The Fuelless Flame,' *The Pentecostal Evangel* (22 October 1972): 8.
[41] JPH, 'It's Harvesttime:' 6.
[42] JPH, 'We Are Taught to Teach:' *Pentecostal Evangel*, n.d. 11.

Emphasizing that the task was to establish a reproductive church, Hogan noted that having first called disciples, Jesus then sent apostles. The commission given the apostles was specific: the establishment of the church – a spiritual but identifiable, durable, and developing body of believers. 'The criterion for measuring the strength of the church (whether at home or overseas) is not merely the number of indiscriminate professed followers of Christ, but the proportion of whom become part of the vital process of extension.' Ultimately, he concluded, the 'spirit of the church is missions.'[43]

The priority of the local church

Accordingly, J. Philip Hogan's missionary philosophy reflected his highest priorities when he described an organic concept of the church. The church emerged as the criterion by which everything else missionaries undertook would be evaluated. The central, strategic role of the individual congregation in the establishment of the kingdom, understood to be a myriad of local expressions of the body of Christ, was Hogan's greatest concern. Writing in the late 1950s, he noted that he had before him an interesting article describing a very successful effort overseas, with up-wards of 40,000 in attendance and hundreds reporting conversion.

> [A] question that faces one immediately, and it is an entirely legitimate question, is how many of these converts were finally integrated into a church, a local segment of the body of Christ, where they can be fed, led and developed into normal followers of the Lord Jesus? In America it is conceivable that a person could be converted and develop some kind of Christian maturity and never be affiliated with the local church. However, overseas where the atmosphere is laden with heathen opposition, where persecution is the rule rather than the exception, is it not unreasonable to expect that people, who raise their hands saying they accept Christ, can go on to spiritual development if they do not find a church home? For this reason churches overseas are doubly important. I am talking now of church buildings. Simple structures to house and localize the body of believers, and to identify them with their community as a group of Christians, are essential. The progress of the field is measured not by the crowds [of people] who gather for revivals or special meetings, but by the number who finally become identified with a local group of believers and meet together Sunday after Sunday to worship the Lord. Yes, church buildings on the mission field are of vital necessity.[44]

'One can hardly feature the work of God being successfully carried on without a definite locale, and this inevitably involves a building,' he wrote elsewhere. 'Somehow the work of the church demands a small plot of

---

[43]   Ibid.

[44]   JPH, 'The Fuelless Flame:' 8.

earth, four walls and a roof. These . . . stabilize the congregation and bear constant witness to the community that here worships a group of people whose religion is not a myth, but a way of life.'[45]

J. Philip Hogan's approaches were all the more remarkable in that at the time these were not the prevailing priorities of most missionary programs. While he was committed to strategic approaches like targeting cities and newly literate populations, he saw all efforts as having their justification in their contribution to the edification of the local congregation. In short, throughout the 1950s the DFM structured a missiology that placed it at the center rather than at the margins of a troubled world scene. As leaders rather than followers, the developers of Assemblies of God missionary policy understood that their Pentecostal emphases were more suited for aggressive encounter than for maintenance. In any event, Hogan and his colleagues placed their confidence more in the promise that 'these signs shall follow them that believe' than in the presumption that more rational uses of resources by itself would accomplish the overwhelming task of world evangelization.

These Pentecostal approaches, giving rise in the next several years to a growing number of overseas national churches, were still little recognized and generally unobserved. With not much more than their convictions and some encouraging past experiences, Hogan and the missionaries of the DFM set out to accomplish what on the face of it was humanly impossible, knowing that given their obvious inadequacy, success depended on divine vindication.

---

[45] JPH, 'A Permanent Witness,' *Pentecostal Evangel*, 25 September 1960, n.p.

[5]

Mobilizing a Mission

We of the Assemblies of God are dedicated to world evangelism. This is not just an incidental phase of our work, but is the main purpose for which we are associated together. Everything else is subsidiary to this commitment.

J. Philip Hogan[1]

The financing of missions in a denomination in transition

During the 30 years J. Philip Hogan stood at the helm of the DFM, the Assemblies of God developed a remarkably focused missionary program that, apart from its overseas impact, also contributed to the spiritual renewal of the denomination at home. A rough index of the members' growing vision for world evangelism can be inferred from their reported financial giving, which year after year exceeded the previous year's total. Offerings increased annually from just under $5 million in 1960 to $11 million in 1970. During the decade of the 1970s, however, annual giving increased to almost $40 million, and by 1989 it reached more than $80 million. By 1992, two years after Hogan left office, annual giving exceeded $100 million. 'We now receive weekly almost as we much as we once received annually [in the 1940s],' Hogan reported at the end of his tenure.[2]

Even with some disclaimers – undoubtedly a proportion of this increase was due simply to the movement's growth and affluence; moreover, no claim can be made for a direct relationship between funding and overseas effectiveness – this concern for world evangelization reveals much about these churches precisely at a time when growing social acceptance and affluence raised questions about the group's faithfulness to its revivalist roots. Between 1960 and 1990 the Assemblies of God 'inclusive membership' (full members and adherents) grew fourfold from 505,000 to 2,000,000. Over the same period of time missions giving increased twentyfold from $3,895,000 to $84,300,000.[3] Even allowing for inflation, giving had increased much more rapidly than had member-

---

[1] JPH, 'Seventy-five Years of Pentecostal Missions,' *The Council Today* (9 August 1989): 1.

[2] JPH, letter to author, 18 February 1995.

[3] DFM Annual Reports for 1960 and 1990.

ship. While both the composition and image of the Assemblies of God changed considerably over this period of three decades, their missionary vision appears to have intensified rather than diminished.

The patterns of denominational missionary giving during these years may indeed reveal a great deal about the spiritual condition of the denomination. In 1958 J. Philip Hogan in his capacity as director of promotions reported that per capita annual giving for the Christian and Missionary Alliance (CMA) was $55, while that of the Assemblies of God was only $10.32. 'This means,' he commented, 'that on a national scale our missionary giving is still in the petty-cash class.' The 1980 report, however, indicated Assemblies of God per capita missionary contributions of $28.67, while the amount for 1989 was $57.09 and for 1992 was $75.15, then virtually identical with CMA per capita giving and exceeded only by that of the Seventh-day Adventists ($111) among the American denominations.[4]

Given the tenuousness of the Assemblies of God organization, comprised as it was of clusters of often quite independent districts and congregations, such a coherent missionary vision would hardly have been possible without appropriate promotional and administrative structures. The task was more than formidable; it was presumptuous. Given the characteristically pragmatic nature of Assemblies of God members, the limits on available resources, and the tendency for strong-willed visionaries in a voluntary fellowship to take their respective programs and projects in a variety of sometimes conflicting directions, Hogan's achievement was extraordinary. When, ten years after the launching of Global Conquest, the 1970 listing of missions agencies placed the DFM eighth in personnel and sixth in giving, it was clear that missions had become a major focus of the movement. By 1989 the two-million-member Assemblies of God contributed annually more to its overseas program than did any other Protestant denomination except the fourteen-million-member Southern Baptist Convention.[5]

This record demonstrates Assemblies of God members' uncommon vision and sacrifice, even allowing for upward mobility, a burgeoning national economy during much of the period, and the assimilation of many new middle-class members that joined Assemblies of God congregations from other denominations. More than merely a tender-minded, sentimental indulgence, financial giving for a substantial proportion of Assemblies of God members fell into the category of a spiritual discipline.[6] Given their lack of confidence in the material value systems of the world in which they lived from day-to-day, they gladly supported a program which they believed to be nothing short of a

---

[4] DFM Annual Report for 1980; cf. G. Land, 'Seventh-day Adventists,' in *Dictionary of Christianity in America*, ed. Reid, 1076; and Siewert and Kenyon, eds., *Mission Handbook*.

[5] Siewert and Kenyon, *Mission Handbook*.

[6] JPH, 'The Missionary Dollar,' *Missionary Challenge* (October 1957): n.p.

divinely initiated effort to bring glory to God and salvation to desperately lost men and women.

Adopting the 'faith promise' approach that was then popular in evangelical circles – and was especially appropriate to Pentecostal theology and sentiments – missions became for many members a spiritual exercise, a covenant with God to submit their material resources to divine oversight. Acknowledging that Pentecostals often had an alternative perspective on world affairs, Hogan noted that 'In 1962 the words that caught our attention were: space, Cuba, Ecumenical Council and Nuclear War, but in spite of all this, believers scattered throughout the world went about their Father's business of telling a waiting world that Christ is the answer.'[7]

After three decades, however, the paper trail of receipts, reports and analyses indicated that while the Assemblies of God constituents were generous in their support of missionary effort, the overseas achievement of the DFM could not be accounted for simply by their financial contributions any more than by their having applied superior efforts and strategies. If giving was a spiritual ministry inspired by divine vision and enabling, it was also Pentecostal to expect that such sacrifices would be blessed and multiplied – as was apparently the case – with an effectiveness well beyond what could be considered within the range of normal achievement.

Missionary vision as institutional redemption

The backdrop for these material indications of spiritual vitality was the thoroughgoing transformation of the movement itself. From a marginal American sect the Assemblies of God underwent a metamorphosis to emerge within a generation as a recognized, institutional denomination. While the movement's modification may have been anticipated – change is inevitable – constant renewal, by definition, is required of any religious revival. The challenge was to retain its early fervor in the face of a social and cultural evolution that tended to dampen its intensity and threaten its effectiveness.

While the denomination was going through this process of meta-morphosis, socially, culturally, and institutionally, the feature that helped stave off self-serving interests and disruptive internal conflicts was the frequently reiterated commitment to global evangelization. While almost everything else was in flux, and while denominational executives were hard pressed to rein in some of the group's most vigorous and colorful figures, missions was an inspiring, unifying force that gave the movement a transcendent reason-for-being. Further, it may well have been that the denomination's overseas efforts – its sacrificial, collective vision for

---

[7] JPH, *Key* (second quarter 1964): 2.

reaching out to a needy world – was its principal stimulant to inspire its youth and mobilize an increasingly passive or even alienated laity. In any event, the argument is compelling that it's missionary focus has played an important role in keeping the denomination on course, resisting or forestalling drift and deterioration.

As time passed, the effects of generous missionary giving became evident. Most obvious was the curbing of many centrifugal tendencies by a united effort at global evangelization. Hogan's contribution in this sense to the formation of the movement, if immeasurable, was undoubtedly enormous. By the end of his tenure, the profiles of denominational giving clearly demonstrated that the entire movement had rallied around the missionary cause. Self-interest, rather than dominating motives and policies, tended to recede, fostering spiritual growth. Missions money did not provide the donors with new sanctuaries or self-serving programs; the purchasing power of their offerings was lost to them except for the sense that theirs was an investment that God could multiply indefinitely.

A strategy of the Spirit

Historian Gary McGee, in summarizing the impact of Global Conquest on Assemblies of God missions, points out that overseas efforts required a corresponding commitment at home. 'This new forward thrust for world evangelization, symbolized by the theme of Global Conquest, required enormous commitment and teamwork. Despite a tradition of undisciplined independence among many Pentecostals, the demonstrated benefits of teamwork and planning had convinced many that there could be no return to the earlier days when accountability for one's missionary work and expenditures hardly existed.'[8]

The events of this period indicate that their strategizing took place with spiritual sensitivity. According to Hogan: 'In these days we must be strategic in all we do. God is moving and pouring out His Spirit in many parts of the world. We must move in the direction God is working, meeting needs as they arise and as He supplies.'[9] Many of his fellow ministers shared this sentiment. Planning and spirituality could proceed together when they were directed by the Holy Spirit and were undertaken in harmony with divine objectives.

Melvin Hodges, Field Secretary [later Field Director] for Latin America and the Caribbean, encouraged his colleagues by saying, 'None of us is wise enough to chart the future course of missions. We don't have to be! The Holy Spirit will lead us on a better course than we could possibly plan. He is already doing so!'[10] For this reason, concludes Gary McGee, 'Assemblies of God growth concepts, particularly when compared with

[8]   Gary McGee, *This Gospel* 2:107.
[9]   JPH, 'Leaders Are Good Followers,' *Pentecostal Evangel* (26 December 1971): n.p.
[10]   McGee, *This Gospel*, 2:106, quoting Melvin Hodges.

those of other missions, exhibit a certain tentativeness: They reflect a uniquely Pentecostal concern for the guidance of the Spirit, going well beyond what can be gained from the study of social structures. So even though planning increased, concern for the guidance of the Holy Spirit remained an enduring cornerstone of Pentecostal thinking.[11]

Moreover, Pentecostals, who by nature believe in the divine empowering of any and all available human vessels, saw their efforts as divinely initiated. The authority, guidance, and provision of the Spirit necessarily worked in association with men and women placed at divine disposal. Paradoxically, the key to receiving apostolic power was relinquishment of all one's personal interests in the light of God's superior claims. Every Pentecostal activity, beginning with Spirit baptism, demands resignation of oneself and one's resources to divine Lordship. A Pentecostal theology necessarily implies faithful support of God's work in every way possible; in fact, Pentecostals were remarkably generous in support of missionary endeavor, motivated by gratitude and a vision for effecting God's work as well as compassion, loyalty, and a sense of obligation – not to mention tax deductible receipts.

In addition, DFM spokespersons revealed the expectation behind their approaches. If the Lord did not immediately return, 'nations that are now the recipients of missionary endeavor are themselves becoming sending organisms. Before the decade of the seventies is finished, it is quite likely that in many countries we will stand side by side with national missionaries from these lands who will have come at the behest of their Master.'[12]

The mission of the Assemblies of God is missions

In the 30 years of his executive administration, J. Philip Hogan repeatedly affirmed that missions were the mission of the Assemblies of God – the single most important reason for the denomination's existence and the most extensive and successful of its many undertakings. Apart from its achievements overseas, the Assemblies of God contributed to the unlikely fusing of a loose association of churches of widely disparate cultures and orientations into effective cooperation. 'We of the Assemblies of God are dedicated to world evangelism,' declared Hogan. 'This is not just an incidental phase of our work, but is the main purpose for which we are associated together. Everything else is subsidiary to this commitment.'[13]

The fact was that the Pentecostals early on had made foreign missions a priority. As assessed by Gary Burhart, the 'need for action in the world

---

[11] Ibid.

[12] JPH, *Key* (June 1964): 1.

[13] JPH, 'Seventy-five Years of Pentecostal Missions:' 1.

led the Assemblies of God to adopt a national structure in 1914, at the founding convention of this group. While some [members] thought that any structure would impede the free flowing of the Holy Spirit among individuals, those seeing a need to spread the message and to make converts triumphed.'[14] At the outset Pentecostals had even explained tongues, for some people the most fascinating and distinctive of their doctrines, as a divine means for obliterating linguistic barriers. Their further emphasis on divine callings and guidance, supernatural care and provision, confirming demonstrations of God's power, and their strong eschatological motivation – all characteristically Pentecostal emphases – tended to drive the members' efforts outward in pursuit of their conversionist mission. Overseas evangelization, one of the main reasons given by the founders of the Assemblies of God for the existence of their organization, had also contributed to perpetuating these emphases at home.

Assemblies of God overseas endeavors initially sprang from the missionaries who, having experienced Spirit baptism while at their overseas posts, sought to unite with other ministers of kindred faith. From the original handful of missionaries who joined the organization as charter members in 1914, the number increased to 196 by 1919. 'The very core of the founding of the Assemblies of God was the fervor to fulfill the Great Commission and to preach the gospel in all the world,' asserted Hogan. 'This missionary burden was the common denominator of the Fellowship. During this early period, John W. Welch, our third general superintendent, said, "The Assemblies of God was never meant to be an institution; it is just a missionary agency".'[15]

Challenging the membership

Given the rapid changes occurring within the movement, however, such claims of missionary purpose meant little without the leadership to convince the often independent-minded constituents of the priority of the church's mission. At this J. Philip Hogan appeared to be remarkably successful – challenging, cajoling, promoting, and daring the membership to respond to the vision of the movement's founders.

> For many years the Foreign Missions appeal has had priority over most other appeals made in our churches. Interest in missions continues to grow, thank God; however, there is also a growing interest in the development of many other phases of Assemblies of God life and ministry. For instance, the liberal arts colleges, Bible schools, and now, a projected seminary, all make their appeals to the one source of income in the denomination's life – the local

---

[14]   Gary P. Burhart, 'Patterns of Protestant Organization' in *American Denominational Organization*, ed. Scherer, 59.

[15]   JPH, 'Seventy-five Years of Pentecostal Missions:' 1.

church. Additional departments are developing nationwide interest, such as Men's Fellowship [later, Men's Ministries], Evangelism, Benevolence, Women's Missionary Council [later Women's Ministries], and others. Currently there is a widely accepted new responsibility for the development of home missions, particularly with respect to opening new churches and pioneering in some of the fast-growing suburban areas of America. The Home Missions Department is currently sponsoring a drive called 'Operation Breakthrough.' All of this is having its effect not only on the volume of receipts in foreign missions giving but also on the pattern of this giving.[16]

The substantial increase in resources depended on effective missionary publications as well as congregational and district commitment to the priority of the task. 'Everyone milks the same cow,' was the expression that circulated among denominational leaders. 'Support for any given program competes for funds with every other appeal.' But Hogan tended to get there first. Throughout his tenure regular publications kept the Assemblies of God membership informed, and for the most part enthusiastically supportive, of the DFM programs. 'We may not make every church and every pastor missionary-minded overnight,' vowed Hogan, 'but we do propose to make them uncomfortable in their neglect.'[17]

Hogan's approach was typically insistent. 'Worldwide conditions compel us to step up our missionary evangelism program,' he announced. 'We feel that further endeavor will help by placing special emphasis upon specific items. In the fields of literature, training of national workers and the invasion of population centers, we are scrapping all the old timetables. Objectives we dreamed of realizing in five years must be attempted now! Crash programs are not new in our generation.'[18]

A strategic approach

In keeping with his conviction of the priority of missionary effort, J. Philip Hogan early on rejected a policy of maintenance or of limited, incremental growth. He rejected growth limits imposed on the DFM out of respect for other programs in favor of an all-out, strategic assault. The Global Conquest effort introduced at the 1959 San Antonio General Council reflected his vision. The program embraced a three-pronged undertaking: the acceleration and increase of gospel literature production and distribution; increased efforts to train and commission trained workers; and intensive efforts to reach carefully selected, strategic population centers. By adopting metaphors appropriate to the Cold War atmosphere of the 1950s, the Global Conquest program as the main thrust of Assemblies of God overseas effort had been forming throughout the

---

16 JPH, 'Trends in Missions Giving,' *Missionary Forum* 1 (January–March 1962): 4, 5.
17 JPH, 'The Missionary Dollar:' n.p.
18 JPH, 'Call to Action,' *Pentecostal Evangel* (31 May 1959): n.p.

previous decade; invasion, extraordinary sacrifice, unconditional surrender, offensive and defensive tactics and strategies were more than mere
abstract notions. The program's belligerent name, however, produced
such reaction overseas that by 1967 it was changed from 'Global Conquest' to 'Good News Crusades.'[19]

Losing no time in promoting the program, Hogan portrayed Global
Conquest as both imperative and attainable. His presentation to promote
the program in February 1960 noted in an upbeat way that: 'Not one
discordant note has been sounded for the program to date. Hundreds upon
hundreds of enthusiastic communications have been received. Dare we
to believe that Global Conquest is the face of the future for missions?
Your support will . . . be an investment in what many friends believe to
be the best planned, best focused, and most strategic missionary program
we have ever launched.'[20]

Realizable objectives

In 1970 Hogan further raised expectations, based on the ease and extent
of global communications, that completion of the missionary task was
within reach.

> Stripped of its complex theological trappings, the primary business of the
> church in this dispensation is communicating an idea, and as long as the simple
> factor of communication is kept foremost, the secondary and ultimate results
> will follow. If our prophetic insight is true, the end cannot be far away. If the
> end is near, then the possibility of total world evangelism must also be near. I
> am prepared to make a categorical statement that the church now has at its
> disposal the tools to complete the task of worldwide communication of the
> gospel. The day has now dawned when news, if it is important enough, can
> reach every corner of this globe in a split second.[21]

Behind the solicitation of funds was the view that missionary effort is
urgent and indispensable. If Pentecostals were not the only evangelicals
to believe in the missionary task, they tended to justify and encourage
financial support on the grounds of divine directives and their belief that
supernatural means for accomplishing the work would be forthcoming.
'The world isn't going to be converted; it's going to be witnessed to,'
Hogan stated in 1969. 'Closed doors are no alibi, neither is political stress
an alibi; the world simply must be evangelized.'[22] Later he wrote that even

---

[19] The name 'Global Conquest,' according to some of his colleagues, was Hogan's only
really serious error of judgment during his tenure. Its aggressive, imperialistic tone was
offensive to some overseas churches.
[20] JPH, *Global Conquest* (February 1960): 9.
[21] JPH, 'World Communication,' *Advance* (October 1970): 4, 5.
[22] JPH, *Key* 2 (April–June 1969): 3.

if he had an accurate forecast of pending crises or of other indications that
the costs of undertaking work might be high, such information would
not deter him from his task. The dimensions of the task might lie beyond
our view, he acknowledged, but the Lord of the Harvest was unerring in
his control of circumstances; therefore immediate, decisive action should
not be deterred for that reason.

> The Great Commission cannot be obliterated by clouds on the world's
> horizon. The Lord of the Harvest has indicated that our mission would last
> until the end of the age, and His command is to occupy until He comes (Matt.
> 24). The truth of this prophecy is exemplified in our labor today. While Beirut
> slowly commits suicide, Egypt, through an odd turn of events, is more open
> and receptive than it has been in years. Vietnam closes and releases personnel
> and resources to Indonesia where the door is opened wider than at any other
> time this century. Man-made political barriers thrust themselves up overnight,
> but [the International Correspondence Institute] penetrates into previously
> unreached cultures. The granting of passports and visas slows ominously, but
> we join with other evangelical forces to sponsor the first gospel broadcast from
> satellite in early 1976.[23]

For Pentecostals who aspired to relive the age of the apostles, missionary effort was not just the premier task, it was the only real assignment.

> Had any less authority than the Lord Jesus Christ Himself uttered the
> commands to make disciples of all nations and to witness to the ends of the
> earth, we might feel that the orders were impossible of fulfillment. However,
> what seemed physically impossible in the year A.D. 30 is entirely possible in
> the year 1967. Under the stupendous intoxication of the Holy Spirit following
> Pentecost, and to the eternal credit of the early disciples, they certainly tried
> – and how they tried – to fulfill the Lord's command. They took sailing boats
> westward across the Mediterranean; they followed the Roman roads to their
> very end. Even the most secular of historians admits that by the end of the
> second century Christianity captured the Roman Empire and incidentally
> established the high-water mark for world evangelism for all time. Undoubt-
> edly the church of the first two centuries more completely obeyed the Lord's
> command than any church in any successive century. However, there were
> some places they could not go. The deadly Sahara without roads, only limitless
> sand, kept the witness of Christ from all sub-Saharan Africa. The people there
> did not hear until the eighteenth century. The impassable barrier of the
> Himalayas kept the gospel out of Asia. In the main, the people of this part of
> the world have not heard yet. The early church could and did go to their
> world, the Roman Empire. Our world is immeasurably more immense, but
> thank God, immeasurably more easily reached. The jet, the electronic
> microwave teamed up with the transistor, amazing developments in the field
> of graphic arts coupled with miraculous rise of literacy rates not only means

---

[23]   JPH, DFM Annual Report for 1976.

kaleidoscopic changes but gigantic responsibilities. When we do this we recognize that our Sahara and our Himalayas are not sand and mountains, but spiritual barriers which keep us from knowing that God's commands are always God's enablings.[24]

The key: everyone's participation

A major step in mobilizing the church for missions was to recognize the need for total involvement. A fairly small per capita annual missions contribution, Hogan recognized, was no so much a matter of the penury of the giving members as of the failure of a substantial proportion of the churches and members to give anything at all. Thus, the goal became 100 per cent participation. 'Believe it or not,' Hogan asserted in his annual report of 1971, 'foreign missions boards and societies will never, as such, evangelize the world.'

> Chiefly the reason is that the Great Commission has not been committed to them. The most that they can do is organize the work, examine the candidates, send the money and supplies, and maintain liaisons between the missionaries and the home base. The Great Commission to witness this gospel to every creature has been given to the church, and to every individual Christian. Churches, then, are the real resources for world evangelism. What is our goal – a few wealthy men to give huge sums of money to a few large churches [that] are favorably situated to share their wealth with foreign missions? All of these are commendable, but they [by themselves] do not comprise the army of the Lord. Our goal is that every church, regardless of age or surroundings, will consistently share part of the responsibility for world evangelism.[25]

Hogan pointed out that new electronic data processing equipment had provided the DFM with a complete view of both the volume and the pattern of response. 'It is rather disconcerting,' he lamented, 'to note that there are still hundreds of Assemblies of God churches that give nothing to foreign missions and that there are several thousand more who have given only a token response.'[26]

'It might be said that dollars are not a complete criterion of missionary work,' Hogan explained. 'However, only by the amazing alchemy of money can it be possible for most folks to be two places at once. By means of your dollar you can stay at home and go into all the world at the same time. Your money is really you. It is your character coined and evaluated. It is the only medium of exchange for your time, talents and energy. Yes, the magic power of money eliminates any excuses for our failure to share in the Great Commission. Every church should know the joy of giving

---

[24] JPH, *Key* 2 (April–June 1969): 1.
[25] JPH, DFM Annual Report for 1971, 39.
[26] JPH, 'Promotions,' *World Challenge* (April 1955): n.p.

consistently to missions – the blessing of participating in the command of the Lord to extend the gospel to the ends of the earth.'[27]

Despite frequent references to comparative giving, Hogan advocated giving based on ability.

> Of great importance is the trend toward deeper involvement of districts and churches that previously were less committed to the cause of world evangelization. Foreign missions giving is becoming more evenly distributed over the country, and districts with little organization of their foreign mission resources are participating in a wider range of mission activities. Another related trend is the growing importance of the office of district missionary secretary. Each year the DMS gather in Springfield, Missouri, for the second week of the School of Missions, held annually on the campus of Central Bible College. In some cases, the DMS is the district superintendent, in others, he is the assistant superintendent, a missions-minded pastor, or even a layman. In more and more districts he is a man who dedicates himself and a major part of his time to the development of missions in his area.[28]

Designated giving

Unlike many denominational missionary programs, the Assemblies of God from its beginnings had used a program of candidate solicitation to raise funds rather than a system of budgets. Although technically all missionary funds are given without strings attached, the DFM encouraged the donor's identification with a given ministry to provide a sense of responsibility and ongoing support, making the program in effect based on designated giving. In the 1950s the Assemblies of God had adopted a World Missions Plan for proportioning all funds directed to the denomination's global evangelism efforts. According to the plan funds given to missions (exclusive of contributions directed to specific ministries) would be distributed according to a formula of 70 per cent for foreign missions, 20 per cent returned to the various districts (exclusive of foreign-language branches), 5 per cent for administration, and 5 per cent for national home missions. By 1960, however, almost all the contributions were targeted for specific purposes – in the terminology of the DFM, 'designated.'

Despite constant pressure from some quarters to revise the approach, Hogan vigorously defended the 'faith mission' model of designated giving, whereby missionaries themselves presented the spiritual needs of their respective fields, as well as their needs for financial support. This process required missionaries to visit scores of churches, not just to raise funds, but to personalize the missionary task by sharing their vision, becoming acquainted with their supporters, and relating the rewards and trials of missionary ministry. 'What a shame that missionaries have to travel

[27]   Ibid.
[28]   JPH, 'Sacrifice,' *World Challenge* (April 1957): n.p.

from church to church while at home,' the rhetorical question was asked in a DFM publication. 'A shame? No, it is not a shame but a privilege to share the excitement of missions with God's people!'[29]

Pressured by some missionaries, pastors, and members citing the example of other denominational groups, Hogan often found it necessary to defend this philosophy. Despite some limitations, such as a resultant lack of discretionary and emergency funds, he held to the system. 'The over-all trend away from undesignated giving continues,' it was reported in 1964.

> Yet we believe missionary support based in the will of the local church is the most scriptural system. And it has three meaningful results: First, it helps the missions education of our young people. Next, it helps ensure the personal prayers of the individual Christian who has become personally acquainted with you as a missionary. Third, it helps provide the faithful monthly support which keeps you on the field. Recently a missionary retiring after forty-four years of service testified that some churches had provided support throughout this entire period. What an evidence of the value of basing missions in the local church.[30]

Behind the concern for designated giving was the belief that visionary, dedicated missionaries, not impersonal efforts, were the key to missionary advance. As articulated by Wesley Hurst, Home Secretary in the 1960s:

> The thrust of missions may only continue its advance through dedicated missionaries. And those missionaries must depend on the prayers and financial support of Christians on the home front. Doomsayers have pointed to recession, unemployment, world inflation, and higher missionary budgets as reasons for cutting back. But supernatural provision is still ours! Just as Peter took the coin from the mouth of a fish to pay taxes, so our missionaries cast their lines into the waters of faith, and dedicated people here at home continue to make missions possible.[31]

Increases in 'real' giving

When the inflationary surge of the late 1970s devastated missionary budgets, J. Philip Hogan responded by facing the problem squarely.

> Inflation has eaten away a considerable part of the purchasing power of the missions dollar. And the cost of doing missionary work is soaring as a result. Skeptics openly question whether we can afford to continue sending missionaries overseas. Our answer is that the world's economic conditions do not render sterile and empty the command of Jesus. Worldwide inflation is the

---

[29]   DFM Annual Report for 1983.
[30]   JPH, Hogan Clippings File, DFM archives, Springfield, Missouri.
[31]   Wesley R. Hurst, 'What's New Statistically?' DFM Annual Report for 1980, 9.

most destructive economic factor of our times. As inflation skyrockets, the value of the dollar declines. The money we send our missionaries loses buying power while the cost of necessities increases drastically. The whole spectrum of missionary endeavor grows more costly by the moment in terms of the American dollar.[32]

If the rapid increase in gross giving to missions suggested a growing recognition of the denomination's priority to evangelism, Hogan's success in engaging the entire fellowship in the effort indicates that missions had a unifying, centripetal effect.

Programs to enlist broad participation

While congregational giving remained the primary source of giving, efforts to develop direct appeals played a strategic and increasingly important role. 'Since the founding of the Women's Ministries Department, its development, along with that of other support agencies in the General Council, has firmly tied lay involvement to the missions program.'[33] Indeed, by the 1970s many overseas endeavors would have been seriously impaired without the funds and volunteers of these agencies. Every age group, Hogan emphasized, can support missionary effort. Belief in the imperative of missions is essential. Every man and woman who prays and gives feels a keen sense of partnership with the missionary program.

Light for the Lost (LFTF)

In October 1959, the *Missionary Forum* reported the founding of Light for the Lost as the result of a merger between the Men's Fellowship program of the Assemblies of God and a regional effort, the Missionary Gospel Society. The latter had been formed by Sam Cochran, an insurance executive from Costa Mesa, California. Subsequently the program spread to the other West Coast districts, Northern California/Nevada, Oregon, and the Northwest District. The new agency, named Light for the Lost, would provide materials for distribution by Assemblies of God missionaries. The national operational expenses were paid by each of the men in local chapters and by a portion of the district funds. The district funds in turn were raised by the district LFTL on the basis of pledged support. Gospel teams began by holding services in local Assemblies of God churches, with the entirety of the offerings going for the purchase of printed materials.

---

[32] JPH, DFM Annual Report for 1980.
[33] JPH, *Missionary Forum* (December 1964): 8, 9.

Patterns of missionary giving

A sketchy but convincing display of the effectiveness of these efforts emerges in the patterns of missionary giving during this period. Participation in missionary support, true to the vision of J. Philip Hogan, spread increasingly downward into the ranks. If in 1960 the reports indicated that only one third of the districts reported the participation of 80 per cent or more of the churches in giving to missions, by 1990 only one district (exclusive of the ethnic districts and the recently created noncontiguous Hawaii and Alaska districts) gave less than 80 per cent, with two districts (Montana and North Dakota) reporting 100 per cent participation. The median and the mean averages of church participation for the mainland geographical districts (exclusive of Puerto Rico, Hawaii, and Alaska) was 92 per cent. Moreover, the proportion of giving by the largest one hundred churches slightly declined, from 22.8 per cent of the total budget in 1960 to 20 per cent in 1990, reflective of a broader base of support.

A comparison of regional missions giving in 1960 and 1990, respectively, shows that the Pacific Coast states of Washington (the Northwest District), Oregon, Northern California and Nevada, and Southern California alone accounted for almost $2 million ($1,928,924) of the entire missionary receipts of $6 million in the former year. By 1990, despite huge increases by these four districts (together totaling almost $19 million) their proportion had fallen from 32 per cent to 22 per cent of total national giving. In 1960 the proportion of the support provided by each of the country's eight regions had varied from 5.6 per cent of the national total given by the Southeast area 22.8 per cent of the total given by the Southwest area, a spread of 17.2 percentage points. In 1990 the spread had been reduced to 10.8 percentage points, from the North Central proportion of 8.4 per cent (virtually unchanged since 1960) to the Southwest proportion of 19.2 per cent.[34]

Although many of these increases may be attributable to regional demographic and economic changes (the growth of the 'Sun Belt'), as well as the general improvement in the national economy and the upward mobility or success in recruiting more affluent members, the argument that credits J. Phil Hogan's efforts at missionary mobilization with this unifying influence is compelling. In 1960 12 of the top 20 churches in missions giving (60 per cent) came from the West Coast, while in 1990 only 5 (25 per cent) were from that area. Meanwhile, during the same 30 years, the leading (top 20) churches went from 3 in the Southeast and Gulf areas (15 per cent) to 12 (60 per cent). Moreover, if missionaries tended to be supported by their own districts earlier on, the tendency for missionaries and missionary projects to draw their support from various districts was increasingly an indication of reciprocal missionary support from across the entire denomination.

---

[34] DFM Annual Reports for 1960 and 1990.

Of greater importance is the fact that missions activity – in a highly dynamic, constantly evolving association of churches – remained stable, inspiring the participation of a highly mobile membership. Given the constant erosion of the congregational base by a transient American population, generational and cultural changes, competing financial appeals, and pastoral changes, much of the task facing Hogan and the DFM was not expansion but simply maintenance. A comparison of the hundred leading missionary-giving churches in 1960 finds only a quarter of them still at the top of the list in 1990, while three-quarters of the major contributors reported in 1990 were new congregations, both in the sense of new to the ranks of generous giving and, in many cases, in the sense of having had only a brief congregational history. Given the shifting populations of Assemblies of God congregations, the foreign missions program served to unify these often disparate congregations in the interests of a single project, with its accompanying stabilizing effects.

A faith for the future

While the less tangible benefits of the Assemblies of God missionary program are difficult to document, they may after all be even more important than the quantifiable consequences. Instead of settling into a comfortable coexistence with the world about them or withdrawing into their own sectarian sanctuary, many Pentecostals were thrust into the world to identify with the dispossessed and their heart-rending need. Missionary interest was stimulated by activities designed for every age group – girls, boys, youth, women and men. Altruistic, transcendent, and often sacrificial, missionary commitment was the principle around which these groups organized their social and spiritual associations. The effect of these activities, besides the funds they generated, was the values, loyalty, and leadership that they generated. These intangible benefits may have even outdistanced the financial contribution various missionary programs produced for overseas work – and these programs resulted in a flow of volunteers for missionary service. Far from being men and women whose dedication exceeded their ability, many of these missionaries either left promising positions to enter missionary effort or returned from overseas service to re-enter ministry in the United States with distinction. These often capable, inspiring leaders demonstrate that the quality of personnel was high – individuals who inspired the movement's youth and gained respect for the missionary enterprise.

At still another level, the creation of a World Missions Board apparently also played an important part in the ongoing formation of the denomination. After a long tradition of active lay participation in the activities of the church, the professionalization of the clergy tended to drive a previously nonexistent wedge between clergy and laity. In the wake of the organization of the Full Gospel Business Men's Fellowship, laypersons found increasing opportunities in an interdenominational group to fulfill their desire for ministry, to associate with men of like interests and values, and to feel a sense of belonging. At the 1959 San Antonio General Council the issue came to the floor in the form of a resolution that would give voting privileges to accredited laypersons. Rejected out-of-hand by the movement's ministers after only perfunctory discussion, some prominent laypersons thereafter largely withdrew from national and district activities. Missionary effort, however, provided the primary corrective to this tendency. Already the World Missions Board and the Light for the Lost program had begun to function. The effectiveness and prestige of these agencies within the denomination provided many laypersons with the outlets and satisfaction that not only made them loyal, supportive participants, but brought their insights, skills, and financial resources into play within the movement. Whatever the implications of these lay efforts were for mission work overseas, they helped to attract and develop lay leadership within the still developing denomination.

A major weapon of missionary advance was created by the confidence that J. Philip Hogan and the DFM succeeded in instilling in an ever more diverse constituency of supporters through both the effectiveness of Hogan's public speaking ministry and the development of effective promotional publications. Only through astute maneuvering, constant effort and systematic coverage financial giving continued to be forthcoming. As in any promotional effort, however, ultimately the success depends on the quality of the product. While the DFM promoted the program at home, advances were far more effective overseas than the members supporting the program could have imagined. Missionary publications were largely positive reports of growth and extension and remarkable accounts of conversions, healings, provision, and protection. The 'widow's mite' contributions, in the aggregate, were producing one of the most effective missionary programs yet conceived, one that fared well in the rapidly changing, often hostile and treacherous circumstances facing the movement. In the end, not only did J. Philip Hogan succeed in making the Assemblies of God a major contributor to world missions, but his vision for missions, in turn, may well have fortuitously contributed even more, through a period of rapid, potentially destructive transformation, to the denomination's spiritual renewal.

An antidote for decline

The challenge was not to preserve the revival like a diorama by means of raising walls of cultural isolation or by adhering mindlessly to the forms and the formulas of the past. The process of spiritual atrophy can only be forestalled by each successive generation's experiencing – and each developmental phase generating – the same intensity, vision, and commitment to the task that had characterized the movement its prime. From its beginnings, modern Pentecostalism had been threatened by a range of debilitating tendencies that the participants had in some measure resisted, not only through faithfulness to their vision of a last-days revival, but also by sustained growth, recurrent renewal, and the incorporation of new, enthusiastic members. Failures were forgotten whenever fresh, vibrant, spiritual leaders emerged with the gifts to rekindle the revival.

Despite the tendency to find the key to ongoing Pentecostal vitality enshrined in Azusa Street, the focus of Pentecostal activity in the US for several years after 1906, or some other symbol of early Pentecostal transcendence, the record is far more checkered and prosaic. For more than half a century spiritual renewal had taken place in various ways, spurred by many different emphases. But intense currents of revival were often followed by slackening declines, and unanticipated, refreshing outpourings were often preceded by years of harrowing, unrewarded labor. Any number of distracting controversies, excesses, and cults of personality had threatened the sometimes gasping revival. As social change altered the functions of American religious bodies, as generational transitions made new demands on the leadership, and as success bred its own complexities and temptations, the movement had constantly to respond to new spiritual challenges or go into decline.

For most part these peaks and valleys, glorious moments of triumph and dark episodes of indifference, still remain to be analyzed. The history of how a century-long American Pentecostal movement struggled to define itself, realize its potential and make good its claims at this point of time can only be known by some of its most visible landmarks, beginning with the constitutional and doctrinal controversies and deep ethnic and regional fissures that early on profoundly divided the Pentecostals. Most Pentecostals, for example, had little to do with those from other racial backgrounds, and believers in the various sectarian fellowships seldom had contact with the vast proportion of their counterparts in other churches.

But throughout its existence the movement has rarely been without some creative moment, some new expression of its explosive dynamic that could penetrate the most hermetic sectarianism. After a three-decades-long tradition of revivalism that lasted through the 1930s, the most conspicuous forces in American Pentecostalism in the post-World War II era were its suburbanization and a succession of healing evangelists who for more than a decade gathered large followings and adapted revivalism to television audiences. The era began with the ministry of William Branham in 1946, about the time that the controversial Latter Rain movement appeared on the scene and shortly before the founding of Demos Shakarian's Full Gospel Business Men's Fellowship International in 1951. Then, even before these phenomena had peaked, David Wilkerson's Teen Challenge ministry, the Charismatic movement, the university-based Catholic Charismatic renewal, and the counter-culture 'Jesus Movement' appeared in rapid succession to change thoroughly the nature and expectations of Pentecostalism in the 1960s and 1970s.

Meantime, one can scarcely overstate the importance of explaining Pentecostalism to the religiously literate public of David Wilkerson's *The Cross and the Switchblade* (1963) and John Sherrill's *They Speak With Other Tongues* (1964). Soaring sales of these books demonstrated an increased interest in experiential religion which appealed to men and women at both extremes of the social spectrum. By the time Oral Roberts joined the Methodist Church, opened a Pentecostal university, and marched side by side with evangelist Billy Graham in a display of mutual respect and recognition at the school's inauguration in 1967, it was clear that Pentecostalism had broken out of its sectarian boundaries and belonged to anyone who was interested in what it had to offer.

The Assemblies of God and other previously established groups benefited materially from this new visibility and the broad acceptance of their once exclusive emphases. But traditional Pentecostals could only wonder at the future of their movement as Pentecostalism became the experience of people whose backgrounds and theologies were often quite different from their own – as seen when writer Doug Wead published *Father McCarthy Smokes a Pipe and Speaks in Tongues*, or when the high church Episcopalian Jean Stone, the image of corporate success, emerged as a leader of the 'charismatic renewal.' The price for a larger acceptance was accommodation to changing constituencies, emphases, and attitudes, both within and without the movement, a result not only of religious dynamics but of the extremely mobile and flexible character of American society.

This process of institutional evolution that recast the character of the Assemblies of God is illustrated by changing views of the movement's relationship to other Protestant groups. In 1960 Thomas F. Zimmerman, the newly elected general superintendent of the Assemblies of God, could describe most Pentecostal groups – including his own – as 'sects,' which he defined conventionally as renewal movements seeking a return to the primitive New Testament faith. These groups, he affirmed, were made up of adult members for whom religion was an absorbing 'way of life,' rejecting the formalities of infant baptism and purely intellectual assent to creeds. Acknowledging the modest origins of most Pentecostals, Zimmerman avowed that they should be credited with having reached 'social strata of the world's population never [before] touched by other forces in Christendom.'[35]

In contrast, a 1982 article in the *Saturday Evening Post* portrayed the Assemblies of God as a socially respectable, middle-class, evangelical denomination. According to these portrayals the fellowship in a brief interval had become a 'church,' a religious group that had come to terms with the larger society, according to the same definitions used earlier by Thomas Zimmerman. In 1989 Margaret M. Poloma sympathetically

---

[35]   Thomas F. Zimmerman, 'Where Is the Third Force Going?' *Christianity Today* (1 August 1960): 15ff.

discussed these changes in *The Assemblies of God at the Crossroads: Charisma and Institutional Dilemmas,* analyzing them to be an ongoing tension between spontaneity and bureaucratization, sociological constructs that resemble the theological distinction between the functions of a prophet and a priest.[36] Skirting the questions of whether these and other similar assessments in fact all used the same criteria or were fair in their comparisons, the challenge to the denomination was clearly not to preserve itself in mint condition, but rather to demonstrate the ongoing relevance and power of its original emphases in a radically different world a process of thoroughgoing change in its own composition. Only by recognizing the difficulty of stimulating the interest and harnessing the resources of such an internally disparate and kaleidoscopic religious amalgam can one begin to appreciate the importance of what J. Philip Hogan achieved during his lengthy tenure as Executive Director of the Division of Foreign Missions of the Assemblies of God.

---

[36] Margaret M. Poloma, *The Assemblies of God at the Crossroads: Charisma and Institutional Dilemmas* (Knoxville: University of Tennessee Press, 1989). A Charismatic Roman Catholic, Poloma pointed out the advancing problems that were natural to any revivalist group – the trends toward comfortableness, accommodation with the larger culture, and the difficulty of transferring religious zeal between generations. While the author's analysis and assessment treat the Assemblies of God kindly, she also points out the precariousness of revival movements. The Assemblies of God, like any revival movement, is constantly, inexorably, at the crossroads. The topic is treated also in Edith L. Blumhofer and Paul B. Tinlin, 'Decade of Decline or Harvest?: Dilemmas of the Assemblies of God,' *Christian Century* (10–17 July 1991).

6

The Indispensable Expendables

Wherever the cross of Jesus Christ has been planted on foreign soil, this has been accomplished not by clever hit-and-miss tactics, but by the solid, consistent stream of dedicated lives.

J. Philip Hogan.[1]

Men and women make the mission

J. Philip Hogan tossed around restlessly, unable to sleep during the early hours of a July morning in 1961. The previous evening, at the commissioning service for newly appointed missionaries, he had commented on the sense of responsibility that lay behind the consideration of every applicant. Just home from a grueling 40,000 mile trip that took him to West Africa, the Middle East, and most of the major capitals in Western Europe, Hogan had plunged into the administrative sessions conducted simultaneously with the school for new and experienced DFM personnel. Perhaps he was merely overweary, exhausted from the burdensome schedule, the long hours aboard cramped flights, changes in weather, food, and accommodation. There were also the pressing, sometimes overwhelming, problems of the missionary 'family' that he had dealt with overseas. He often reflected on his own responsibility by posing the rhetorical question: 'How would anyone like to be responsible for more than 2,000 persons spread all over the world, including every age from the elderly to tiny babies?'

Hogan could not get the commissioning service off his mind. Before him he could still see the serious, dedicated young people – often with small children in their arms or at their sides – preparing for demanding ministries that would routinely take them into unfamiliar, sometimes hazardous situations. Hogan was not just weary; he was anxious. Facing the issue squarely, he knew what was troubling him. 'What right have we as the Foreign Missions Department of the Assemblies of God to commit, or even encourage, these young lives to do missionary work in these days?'

Perhaps, in a small sense my burden was similar to that of a general who, on the eve of battle, realized he will commit troops, some of whom will become

---

[1] JPH, 'The Career Missionary,' *Pentecostal Evangel* (21 November 1965): n.p.

certain casualties. I went over the roster of these thirty-seven young people one by one. They had all been well-recommended by their respective districts. They had been led through the most complete reference system to which missionary candidates of the Assemblies of God have ever been subjected. In many respects they were the most mature and best-educated group we have ever had occasion to interview. They had been well briefed. They understood fully what the Foreign Missions Department expected of them. The majority of them have completed under-graduate degrees in their chosen fields. Some of them have successfully pastored churches. Yet no class of candidates has ever come forward for appointment in more critical times.[2]

Hogan had seen many of the fields where they were going. He knew that although these new missionaries would be working in many languages and cultures, there would be a common denominator that all of them would discover very quickly – they would all have to live with change and uncertainty. They were beginning their missionary work in a disintegrating world. Everywhere they would find upheaval and revolution. They would be surprised at the modernity of the great cities of the world and stand aghast at the poverty in those same cities. They would see modern living conditions surrounded by unimaginable filth and squalor. As Americans, they would likely be met with attitudes ranging from a mild welcome to outright animosity.

Hogan's comprehension of missionary work had been shaped by hard experience. He had observed a wide variety of approaches, most of which were well thought out. But some missionary ventures had bordered on the bizarre. Clearly the tactics of some missionary programs lacked logic, if not a biblical basis. The problem developed when instead of using technology as a tool, the impersonal tools took the place of human, Spirit-driven and sustained missionaries. Early on as DFM director, Hogan faced criticism from persons who, not sharing his vision for building indigenous national churches, wanted to promote relatively more 'efficient' methods of evangelism.

> There are people who believe that the way to evangelize the world is to fly over villages and kick out bundles of literature. There are others who believe we should bring the missionaries home and pay the nationals. Still others think the way to evangelize the world is to pass out literature in an every-home campaign. By following too many ideas we can divide our resources, dollars and manpower until we are going fifty ways at once and stand at the judgment condemned because we haven't done [what was] intended.[3]

The problem of depending on impersonal methods rather than flesh-and-blood people has been faced by groups other than the Assemblies of God. When in 1965 Roman Catholic Bishop Fulton J. Sheen congratulated Protestant foreign missions agencies for their high per capita missions

---

[2]   JPH, 'What Right Have We?' *Pentecostal Evangel* (20 August 1961): 3, 4.
[3]   JPH, 'Can the World Really Be Evangelized?' *Advance* (February 1968): 13.

giving – especially an Episcopal bishop who suspended all construction projects in his diocese to dedicate an entire annual budget to missions – an editor of *Christian Century* pointed out that it was the 'life offering' – not the financial support – of people that made the nineteenth century the 'great century' of Protestant missions.

> Some may attempt to justify this decline [in missionary volunteers] by the rise of the churches in the new nations: they are providing the leadership and the missionary is on the way out! This dreary and plausible argument provides a convenient alibi, and the outpouring of money only undergirds the alibi. Don't send me, send my check! If we equate missions with money, our mission in the world is doomed. Men still make the mission.[4]

Not that all foreign missionaries are perfect! The DFM was aware of the criticism of some of its overseas personnel when it presented recommendations for revising the missionary recruitment process at the San Antonio General Council in August 1959. The report stated that there was a need for more careful screening of missionary candidates and, accordingly, it recommended the adoption of new and enlarged application and reference forms to provide more detailed information about applicants.[5]

The issues that remained to be resolved for many people, however, concerned the role of the contemporary missionary and the recruitment of capable volunteers. The first question had been answered decisively in previous years: the primary role of any missionary is that they contribute to the formation of a national church. As Hogan stated the

---

[4]   Editorial, *Christian Century* (25 August 1965): n.p.

[5]   'It is normal in a missionary operation of the scope of the Assemblies of God,' the report concluded, 'that there will inevitably be found those who are ineffective on the foreign field. In such cases we recommend that the Foreign Missions Department take the initiative to return such workers to ministry in the home field.' Moreover, the 1959 San Antonio meeting approved an in-service training program that had recently been created for both new and experienced missionaries. The first School of Missionary Orientation (later called the School of Missions) was an intensive program conducted primarily for new candidates. In 1961 the sessions were extended to six weeks and held as classes in the seminary. The intention was to consider 'the whole spectrum of missions, including a complete appraisal of the missionary objectives with a fresh look at the difficulties and the opportunities.' Initially conducted only for DFM personnel, the district missionary secretaries and teachers of missions were later invited to attend. In the early years some of the nation's most respected missions leaders took part in the sessions, including Dr Clyde Taylor of the Evangelical Foreign Mission Association, Dr Henry Brandt, psychologist with the Inter-Mission candidate training program, and Eugene Nida, noted translator and executive of the American Bible Society. The speaker in 1964 was Arthur Glasser of the China Inland Mission (now Overseas Crusades). Others who contributed to the sessions included Eric Fife of InterVarsity, George Peters of Dallas Theological Seminary, and Donald McGavran of Fuller Theological Seminary.

matter succinctly, 'If what you do doesn't contribute to the local body of Jesus Christ it's not missionary work.'[6]

The second question, an important issue for most Protestant mission agencies, was never a problem for the DFM during Hogan's tenure. 'I believe there are two reasons for the constant flow of dedicated young people into missionary work,' wrote DFM home secretary Wesley Hurst in 1964.

> First, the Holy Spirit remains the greatest calling agent among our youth; the Pentecostal experience at its best impels them to witness to the world. Second, our system of designated missionary support requires missionaries to travel widely among our churches, thereby exposing our young people to both information and inspiration concerning missions. I know that missionaries' itineraries are often hard, wearying work, but we must not forget that one of the great benefits of this work is the spiritual preparation of those young people who will later take our places in missionary service.[7]

In 1991, when Hogan was invited to present the message for the 110 new candidates being commissioned, he assessed the current recruitment situation. A review of personnel policies, stated objectives, and the course of the growth of the church abroad illustrated the point clearly: 'The crux of the Assemblies of God missionary program is its people.'[8] Abstract, scientific, well-engineered concepts of missions tended to give way – no matter how ingenious and progressive the approach – to the concept that missionary work ultimately cannot be greater than the contribution of the individual missionaries.

J. Philip Hogan's interpretation of the missionary's role was clear. 'Great sacrifices still are involved in missionary ministry,' he asserted. 'Today they are less spectacular, though none the less vital. If Christianity could begin again its mission in the world, this time with a clean slate free of encumbrances, institutions, inherited ideas, and the whole clutter of human effort, missionary recruitment would be easier. However, we are the heirs of nearly two thousand irrevocable years of Christian expansion – two thousand years filled with glory and misery, with honor and shame. We cannot wipe the slate clean; we must begin where we are.'

> Missionaries must be students of history. They must [have] keen insight, and be extremely sensitive to the feelings of others. They must be patient and diplomatic because discerning nationals will test every inch of their spiritual armor. Missionaries must be willing to renounce a privileged position, and adjust to becoming equal with, or to being led by, nationals. Our Lord said, 'He that would be greatest among you, let him be the servant of all.' This verse was never more fitting than it is on current mission fields. Today, more

---

6   JPH, *Pentecostal Evangel* (29 September 1991).

7   Wesley R. Hurst, 'What's New Statistically?' *Missionary Forum* (first quarter 1965): 9. The mission had 891 missionaries at the time.

8   JPH, *Pentecostal Evangel* (29 September 1991).

than ever, the brand of men who are successful missionaries must be lowly, sacrificial, and humble in spirit.[9]

The directors of the DFM recognized that their personnel, formal qualifications aside, were frequently persons of considerable vision and dedication. In his regular column in the *Pentecostal Evangel* Hogan stated the DFM position in 1970: 'A critical analysis of our disbursement pattern continues to indicate that in the Assemblies of God we put most of our money on men. We still believe there is no substitute for a man whose heart is on fire and in whose life the call of God is compelling and real. However, the alchemy of world economics, organization, and communications makes it necessary that men be supported. This is where the parade of dollars begins.'[10]

Later, Hogan related dollars to people. 'Even the figures and columns accompanied by dollar signs are still reports about people, for by an amazing alchemy a man's dollar is really an extension of himself. All the world's problems are essentially people problems,' he insisted. 'The old cliché, that I have at times quoted myself, which says, "The missionary is working himself out of a job," really is not true. The reason for this is that the job gets bigger and bigger. Any young missionary feeling the call of God upon his life does not need to worry that the task of world evangelism will be completed before he can finish his training or reach the world.'[11] 'Wherever the cross of Jesus Christ has been planted on foreign soil,' he said on another occasion, 'this has been accomplished not by clever hit-and-miss tactics, but by the solid, consistent stream of dedicated lives.' He added: '[Nevertheless] the funds to supply their needs must be received from their sole means of support, [which is] the churches and individuals in the United States who have promised to give as God provides.'[12]

If the Assemblies of God missionary program grew substantially during the years of Hogan's tenure, the numerical growth of the missionary staff was not commensurate with the increased giving, the opening of new fields, and the growing responsibilities of overseas ministries. While the numbers of fields, the financial support, the overseas ministerial training institutes, and the number of congregations

---

[9] JPH, 'What Makes a Modern Missionary?' *Pentecostal Evangel* (28 July 1963): 6, 7. 'All that a missionary says and does is a testimony of stewardship,' Ray Brock advised his missionary colleagues shortly after Hogan took office. 'The incidental things we do, the accidental things we say, the innuendoes in the inflection of our voices are part of our testimony. The missionary who preaches one ethic and lives another only creates havoc in the lives of his [national] colleagues and trains them for inconsistent living. Ours is a sense of mission, a fulfillment of divine responsibility.' Ray T. Brock, 'Sense of Mission,' *Missionary Forum* (1963).

[10] JPH, 'A Review of the Sixties,' *Pentecostal Evangel*, 15.

[11] JPH, 'An Increasing Harvest,' *Key* (April 1969).

[12] JPH, 'The Career Missionary,' n.p.

and adherents all ballooned dramatically, the size of the missionary force grew much less rapidly. Many of the new personnel, in fact, were replacements for missionaries who had retired or resigned their appointments.[13]

Merely sustaining personnel overseas – the logistics of travel, housing, material support, schooling for families, health needs, language instruction, not to speak of providing the staff with the means for conducting their work and undertaking the projects like evangelistic campaigns, radio broadcasts and construction of facilities – made the entire missions operation increasingly complicated. While most missionaries engaged in training national workers, a large number still continued to perform the more traditional roles of church planting, evangelism, and literature preparation. But their efforts were different from those of past missionaries. Rather than ground-breaking and pioneering, with the objectives of 'systematic coverage' or 'reaching the most geographically or socially remote,' Pentecostal missionary effort was increasingly directed toward the strengthening of a specific national or regional church in view of the day when it would assume the entire responsibility for its own growth and development and contribute even greater resources for the task of evangelization of its own peoples.

'The Foreign Missions Department probes new candidates in an effort to find the deepest motivation for their professed call,' Hogan. 'Every person who comes to us for appointment is questioned in an effort to determine what really compels him. It is painful to discover that people are sometimes motivated by less than divine nature. Indeed, it is surprising how long some individuals can remain in God's work from purely human motivation. If Peter were publishing a book of sermons, he would probably call it, "It's What's Inside that Counts." The language of 1 Peter

---

[13]   An indication of the changing roles of Pentecostal missionaries is reflected in the breakdown of expenditures during the 30 years of J. Philip Hogan's tenure. From an emphasis primarily on personnel and travel, the focus was increasingly on select workers and support for their strategic efforts.

A/G Missionary Expenditures
Percentages Disbursed to Major Categories
(Showing decreased spending on personnel and increased on 'work' and capital projects)
1960–1990

	1960	1970	1980	1990
Missionary Support	47.5%	45.2%	44.2%	40.3%
Equipment	17.3%	14.6%	8.3%	8.1%
Work	16.5%	24.2%	26.0%	27.3%
Travel	18.6%	16.0%	11.1%	10.9%
Building	0.0%	0.0%	9.9%	13.4%

Source: DFM Annual Reports for the years cited.

1:13–16 is so emphatic that it can be paraphrased to say, "It's what's on the inside that compels".[14]

Having lived through difficult times overseas, Hogan was sensitive to the hazards involved in missionary work.

A problem to be met is the vast revolutionary tides which have swept the world in the last fifty years. These have had enormous side effects from which the church abroad has not escaped. In addition, while political and economic upheaval have come to many lands, the church has begun also to emerge in these lands and to assert itself through national leadership. Often this assertiveness has serious overtones of anti-Westernism. Political imperialism is dead and religious imperialism is passing also.[15]

The human cost of missions

No sooner had J. Philip Hogan come into office than he faced the distinct possibility that missionaries under his supervision might be called on to lay down their lives. Floyd Woodworth, a missionary to Cuba, had been involved in training Assemblies of God ministers in the Bible Institute in Manacas before Fidel Castro seized rule in January 1959. Show trials, rapidly deteriorating relations with the US government, and Castro's declaration that Cuba would be a Communist state soon followed. Floyd Woodworth continued his work, understanding the dangers of remaining but more concerned with leaving behind a group of well-qualified Cuban pastors.

The situation became serious by late July 1962 when intelligence reports confirmed the construction in Cuba of new military installations. By 14 October, U-2 overflights revealed not only a launching pad but also a ballistic missile in full view. After a tense stand-off, considered one of the most critical moments of the Cold War, the Soviet premier Nikita Kruschev and the American president John F. Kennedy came to terms: the Soviet Union would withdraw its ICBMs and the United States would agree not to invade Cuba. Although the settlement left Castro furious, there was little he could do to alter the agreement.

Meanwhile, the release of 1,179 Cuban exiles previously given long prison sentences after their part in the unsuccessful Bay of Pigs invasion was still to be negotiated. Castro demanded exorbitant amounts for their

---

[14] JPH, 'It's What's Inside that Counts,' 1971 School of Missions Commissioning Service, *Pentecostal Evangel*, n.d. 16. Concern for the missionary quite naturally extended to concerns for missionary families, which, on more than one occasion (possibly with a variety of nuances), referred to themselves as 'Hogan's Heroes.' A whole range of considerations were given early on to provide for missionary children's education, for the number of children with which new candidates would be appointed, housing, health, pensions, and much more.

[15] JPH, 'What Makes a Modern Missionary?' 6,7.

release. When talks between Castro and the State Department stalled, New York attorney James B. Donovan flew to Havana, conferred with Castro, and after weeks of negotiation persuaded him to accept a lesser sum in food and drugs instead of dollars. Hubert Herring, a respected Latin American scholar, called the settlement 'a miracle of tact, persuasion, and unflagging energy' – and unsparing credit went to Donovan.[16]

In the wake of his considerable success in humbling the United States, an elated Castro began to crack down on his critics, at first jailing and then expelling several hundred foreign-born Catholic priests. Then, on 13 March 1963, the anniversary of a university student martyred by the Batista government, Castro went on the air with a harangue against Americans during which he made a reference to the Assemblies of God Bible Institute in Manacas and its 'Yankee director.' Shortly thereafter the provincial police came to the Manacas school to arrest Floyd Woodworth. Though he was released after several hours, he was taken into custody again. The school was closed and the students were sent home on 16 March. Woodworth was placed under house arrest in a Havana hotel. Four days later his wife Millie and their two young daughters were also arrested, and he was removed to a military prison and placed in solitary confinement for the next 20 days.

During this tense time erroneous statements appeared in the American press, some of which implied that Woodworth had been or would be executed. In the meantime Hogan, on the advice of the Department of State, was in contact with James B. Donovan to effect Woodworth's release. Following Donovan's intervention, and certification by the US diplomats that Woodworth had never been in any way involved with the CIA or any other governmental agency, he was released on 5 April.

Floyd Woodworth reported that he had not been formally arraigned, threatened, or touched physically. 'I have no complaints of my treatment' was all he would disclose about his detainment, stressing that during his 12 years in Cuba he had carried out his work as a minister without any involvement in political activities. 'As a matter of fact,' he insisted, 'it is a policy of our missionary board that all of our missionaries in seventy-three countries of the world shall refrain from involving themselves in political matters of the foreign countries in which they serve.' He continued, 'The work of the Assemblies of God in Cuba is completely under the direction of national leadership.'[17]

While one is inclined to accept the words of a conscientious missionary of unimpugned reputation and transparent motives, there is good reason to believe that although Woodworth may not have been physically

---

[16]   Herring, *History of Latin America*, 416.

[17]   DFM news release, 12 April 1963, Springfield, Missouri. To the report that he had failed to fly the Cuban flag at the Manacas school, Woodworth replied that the flag was displayed in the Bible Institute chapel. Because of the unavailability of rope, it was not flown for several weeks previous to his detention.

harmed, he and his family were emotionally abused during their confinement, facts that Woodworth probably wished to conceal for fear of reprisals against his ministerial colleagues on the island and in the light of his continuing hope to return to Cuba himself.[18]

When Woodworth, dazed by his sudden freedom, joined Donovan on the Red Cross flight from Havana, Cuba, to the United States, he thanked the attorney for having obtained his release. Donovan congratulated the missionary but declined to take any credit. When he had brought the matter up, during negotiations, Castro had told him categorically that 'there would be no negotiating the freedom of that spy.' Nor did Woodworth ever learn why the special flight had been held up until he was on board, when, apparently, his release had not been planned.[19]

The high cost of serving in Zaire

The personal risk of missionary service, while seldom so costly, was poignantly illustrated in the case of the Assemblies of God missionaries engaged in literature preparation and distribution in support of the emergent national church in the former Belgian Congo. Gail Winters had worked in the Belgian Congo since 1941.[20] After being evacuated during the civil unrest that followed independence in 1961, Winters had returned to the Congo in April 1962 along with Lillian Hogan, her Canadian coworker. The two missionaries bought a Volkswagen Beetle in Europe before sailing across the Mediterranean to East Africa and disembarking in Dar es Salaam, Tanzania.

Armed with as much technical information as they could acquire for maintaining the printing operations that had been vital to the Assemblies of God leadership training ministry in the city of Paulis, eastern Congo, the two missionaries started off in their 'Beetle' through Tanzania, Kenya, Uganda, and into the Congo, a metal plate reinforcing the underside of the car to prevent the rocks of the unpaved roads from piercing the oil pan. 'We sometimes found ourselves holding our breath as we forded streams and pounded the boulders,' the missionaries later confessed.

Winters, who spoke French well and could communicate freely in Swahili, had been discouraged from returning to her work because of continuing political unrest. The missionaries' decision to return seemed

---

[18] Woodworth's condition upon his release, including weight loss and extreme nervousness, belie statements that he was not mistreated. Moreover, his oldest daughter appears to have been abused by the experience. Although her intellectual capability was demonstrated years later when she graduated from college with honors, she was withdrawn for several months after the family's release in Cuba, suggesting emotional abuse.

[19] Floyd Woodworth, letter to author, 7 July 1996.

[20] Winters, *It Is Your Affair, God*. The entire account of Gail Winters' ordeal is taken from her privately published memoirs. Winters, in 1996, attended the fiftieth anniversary of the founding of the Zaire Assemblies of God as one of the church's invited guests.

vindicated, however, when, shortly after arriving in Paulis, a stadium meeting conducted by evangelist Lorne Fox met with encouraging results. As the crowds grew to 8,000 persons nightly and reports of healings began to circulate, many provincial officials and other middle-class residents began to attend the meetings, often standing in the shadows some distance from the gathering in order not to be recognized. For months after conclusion of the campaign the missionaries were greeted with 'Hallelujah' or with words from the crusade's theme song about 'new life in the Holy Spirit.'

At about the same time news that rebel groups were training young men as terrorists had begun to spread. With support from Eastern Europe the rebels began to extend their hold on various parts of the country, eventually reaching Stanleyville, about 350 miles from Paulis. In view of the increasing anti-white sentiment, the national Assemblies of God leaders urged the missionaries to return home. The missionaries, however, felt that they should remain for the time being, but they carried on their work with suitcases packed and cars fueled.

Winters, seeking some sense of divine direction, was reminded of the verse she had appropriated on the occasion of her Bible institute graduation in 1937. 'Be strong and of good courage, neither be dismayed, for the Lord thy God is with thee whithersoever thou goest,' she had recited at Glad Tidings Temple in San Francisco on that evening 25 years earlier. As the tension mounted, Lillian Hogan felt that the Lord had also given her a verse of encouragement. 'Ye shall not go out with haste, nor go by flight, for the Lord will go before you, and the God of Israel will be your rear guard.' Although many foreigners in the business community left, others remained.

At the time the Jay Tucker family, on furlough in the United States, was wrestling with the decision of whether to return to a troubled Congo. Aware of the numerous difficulties they prayed that the Lord would remove these obstacles if it was his will that they should return. As obstacle after obstacle was moved the confirmation seemed clear and certain. The pledged financial support that they still lacked poured into the DFM office just before they had to make a decision about continuing their missionary service. Then, 24 hours before their return airline tickets were to expire, their visas were granted. With this reassurance, the family left for Leopoldville.

The Tuckers, however, soon found themselves in danger. On arriving in Leopoldville they learned that the rebel forces had taken Stanleyville, where the family were scheduled to take a connecting flight to Paulis. Word came the next day from Air Congo that a direct flight was scheduled from Leopoldville to Paulis. If they wished, they could board the next morning. Angeline Tucker was concerned. Her husband had asked whether the flights were essentially for the purpose of evacuation and had been assured that the new route was part of the regularly scheduled air service.

'Lord, is it right to take the children into possible danger? It is one thing for Jay and me to face danger, for we have the call of God, and it is our work, but is it right to take the children into danger for a work which they have not chosen and which is not theirs?' Angeline felt that God answered her prayer. 'I love them more than you do. And I will deliver you out of the den of lions.' During the flight to Paulis the pilot came to the back to tell Jay Tucker that his family was in danger. Their flight had been scheduled primarily to evacuate residents fleeing the city.

'The rest of us joyfully welcomed the Tuckers back,' noted Gail Winters. 'We thought that since the Lord had so divinely opened the doors for them to return, He surely did not intend for them and us to turn about and immediately leave.' The day after the Tuckers' return, however, rioting in the streets of Paulis convinced neighboring missionaries Melvin and Eleanor Jorguenson to leave Paulis with their two small children and return to their own remote post. Against advice, and forced by the local military commandant to take a wounded soldier with them, they started out, anxious and uncomfortable in their now overcrowded car. Only later did they realize that their lives were probably spared on account of their unwanted passenger, who managed to maneuver them through hostile troops – only one in a series of frightening experiences that nevertheless took them away from the nightmare experience that Gail Winters, Lillian Hogan, and Jay and Angeline Tucker and their children were to endure.

Critical conditions

By this time, the rebel Simba troops, who had been told that their rituals would make them impervious to bullets, had driven off the remaining units of the national army and had barricaded all routes out of Paulis. Within a few days Gail Winters and Lillian Hogan had their apartment searched and were threatened by rebel soldiers who swore to kill the employees of their print shop. Then late one night a group of drunken rebels arrived and demanded that the missionaries open their door. When the two Americans did not respond – they were harboring two Congolese – the group opened fire with automatic weapons; bullets penetrated to the inner rooms, breaking glass and leaving the rear part of the house in shambles. Inexplicably, however, they abruptly stopped firing and left. As the bullets continued to crash into the building, and the screaming below became more frenzied, Winters recalled, they prayed, 'Lord, we shouldn't be afraid, but we are. You said, "Perfect love casts out fear." We must not have perfect love. We are scared to death! But you have provided even for this in the verse, "What time I am afraid, I will trust in thee." ' The two women bolstered their courage with verses from the Psalms. 'The angel of the Lord encampeth round about them that fear him, and delivereth them.' Psalm 91 brought them special encouragement.

When the wife of one of the Congolese arrived the next morning she exclaimed, 'God does have power! He protected you through this horrible night even though they tried to kill you. God is good! The sights we have seen this morning are beyond telling! There are bodies everywhere, and blood is running in the streets.'

That afternoon the son of one of the printers arrived with a political registration card. Everyone on the street was required to produce one on demand. When he left, reluctantly, the woman refused to go. 'You are in great danger. I will be in danger with you. If you die, I will die with you. I have prayed that none of my missionary friends would be killed. Have you not come a long way to tell us of God's love?'

'But about half an hour later we heard some vehicles draw up outside the building,' Winters recalled. The rebels revved the motors while the men chanted, '*Simba! Simba!*' and called out the name of a rebel leader whose potions were believed to stop bullets. The rebels noisily vandalized the printing building, the bookstore, and the chapel, then crashed through the door of the apartment and stormed up the stairs to where the women had taken refuge. The Simbas were stripped to the waist and draped with animal skins, vines and leaves. Their eyes were dilated with drugs. 'Confronted by the rebels,' Winters recalled, 'we were given a perfect calm and peace. All fear left us.'

The two missionaries and their Congolese friend with them were herded out into the yard, knocked to the ground, and kicked. Various other neighbors were brought in, including a Greek merchant and their Belgian friend, Monsieur Louis. The Simbas argued about who should be killed and who was to do the killing. But the rebel officer who had witnessed the attack on their house suddenly appeared and put a stop to the threatened killings, ordering that the foreigners be taken to prison.

As they arrived they heard the band strike up the tune they had become accustomed to associate with executions. The 'Colonel,' accompanied by a woman sorcerer, cursed the missionaries and called them demeaning names. Then, unexpectedly, he ordered them to be returned to their house. The Simba guard who accompanied Gail Winters and Lillian Hogan advised them to secure the broken door. When the missionaries found a hammer and nails, their guard provided a wooden panel with which to make the repair. They were still concerned about their Congolese friend who had been taken into custody with them, but to their relief she appeared at their door the following Saturday, accompanied by two Simbas. When they thanked the soldiers for having brought their friend, the men were obviously pleased and replied, 'Did we not tell you we would care for her? Are not the both of us Christians? Are we not your brothers?'

The three women together went to find what had happened to the Tuckers. The family had suffered similar trauma, though with less damage to their house, and had been advised to keep their curtains open with a light burning at night. Jay had also been taken to the 'Colonel,' who, after shouting insults and threatening him with death, released him.

Conditions deteriorate further

But the reign of terror had just begun. The rebels had systematically killed the provincial officials as well as the village chiefs and almost everyone who belonged to the professional class. The country's provisional president, captured near the border with Sudan as he fled, was returned to Paulis, brutally tortured, and marched through the streets before the rebels killed him. Shortly thereafter, when some of the national soldiers who had been incorporated into the rebel forces assassinated a visiting Simba 'Colonel,' all remaining former government officers and men were summarily executed, the shooting lasting for several hours.

'The horror of the daily killings overwhelmed us,' wrote Winters. 'Our insides churned. When we saw people being beaten, or heard the blows and angry shouts we were left with an intense ache inside. We prayed daily at every sound of gunfire for those in danger. Often, I would whisper to myself, "When my heart is overwhelmed within me, lead me to a rock that is higher than I." '

During the first days of this bloodbath, Jay Tucker reminded the missionaries in Paulis of Isaiah 41:9, 10.

> Thou whom I have taken from the ends of the earth, and called thee from the chief men thereof, and said unto thee, Thou art my servant: I have chosen thee and not cast thee away. Fear thou not for I am with thee; be not dismayed, for I am thy God: I will strengthen thee; Yea I will help thee; yea I will uphold thee with the right hand of my righteousness. For I the Lord God will hold thy right hand, saying unto thee, Fear not: I will help thee.

Cricket Tucker, Jay and Angeline's 11-year-old son, openly confessed his fear. 'Sometimes I am so scared I can't sleep. But I have some good Bible verses I say to myself.'

'At first,' recalled Winters, 'we prayed much for our physical safety, but later felt we should be more concerned about spiritual values, about the needs of those around us, about the conditions of our churches, and the spiritual welfare of our Christians. The Lord led each of us to come to the place where we could thank Him *for* [emphasis hers] the situation, thank Him that we had been caught in the rebellion. For we felt we were where God wanted us. We couldn't believe the rebellion was of God, but we could give thanks that we were enabled to share the troubles with our African Christians. When we faced the possibility of death, I would say, "Lord, I am no hero and shrink from further suffering, or death. I would just as soon do without a martyr's crown. But my trust is in Thee. You will not ask more than we can bear. I know that your grace will be ample at the time I need it" .' Lillian Hogan once said, 'It is one thing to face death once or twice, but it is not so easy to keep committed when one faces death day after day, month in and month out.'

'We often discussed just how we should pray for those who had made themselves our enemies,' Winters later revealed. 'One man said he had no problem; he just prayed, "God, blast them!" But we wanted our prayers to be honest. We couldn't ask God to bless them in their wicked practices. We could ask that God bless them by turning them from their wicked ways. It was not difficult to pray for those who came to us telling us they had been forced into the movement and longed to get out. We could readily pray for those who had been true Christians that they might turn back to God. We often asked for guidance in our praying. It helped to take out our hymn book and sing songs such as "Great is Thy Faithfulness," "Under His Wings," and "All Hail the Power of Jesus' Name." I admit we usually avoided singing the verse of "Faith of Our Fathers" which speaks of dungeon, fire and sword – we thought that we were reminded of that possibility often enough.' Angeline Tucker added, 'I couldn't have lived through some of those days if I couldn't have sung.'

Lillian Hogan and Gail Winters went to the Tucker home for lunch twice each week. The Tuckers, in turn, were entertained by the single missionaries each Sunday after their French-language morning service, held in the chapel adjacent to the print shop. A service in the Bangala language was held in another location, but the Christians of other languages seemed to prefer the French service.

'Our African Christians frequently came to visit us, but we didn't go out to see them. As Americans we would have been too conspicuous. We felt that our presence in their homes would be a danger to them,' the missionaries later confided.

> Although food was scarce in the city, it was amazing how we always had something to eat and were frequently able to buy extra things for our employees. A Greek merchant across the street from our bookshop told us when the rebels first came in to order any cases of food we wanted and pay them when we could. Almost every week a certain Greek family brought us a basket of food containing fresh vegetables and sometimes a cake or some other delicacy. Often when we wondered what we could find for the next meal, some young boy would come to the door selling a few tomatoes, some native spinach, or even now and then an egg or two.

'We all lost weight,' Winters reported, 'Americans, Europeans, and Africans alike. The main reason was our lack of appetite because of the tension. The Africans told us that they sometimes let a head of bananas spoil right on the tree because everyone was so full of fear they had no hunger. Lillian and I usually took time to have a cup of tea in the afternoon or early evening.'

The conclusion

On 29 October 1964, the rebels imposed martial law. All the foreigners were required to register with the provisional administration. Jay Tucker, who was away inquiring about friends when rebel soldiers came to the house, was accused of trying to hide from the authorities. He was placed under house arrest, and a Simba 'observer' was placed in the Tucker home. Then on 4 November Jay Tucker and 72 other European men were detained in the Catholic mission compound. The Tucker's 18-year-old son John was among the men taken into custody, but he was soon released.

During Jay Tucker's imprisonment he was sometimes allowed to attend the chapel for Sunday services. When he was not present, one of the three missionary women took charge. Gail Winters recalls a Sunday when Jay repeatedly asked the congregation to sing the hymn, 'How Great Thou Art.' 'I felt that he was transmitting to us his – and our – overpowering need of assurance. I wondered what awful stress and experiences he had been enduring. He was singing from the depth of his being, expressing his confidence in the greatness of God. Never since have I been able to sing this song in any language without being deeply moved.'

The Tuckers – Angeline, Carol Lynne, and Cricket – were able to go and visit Jay once or twice and they talked to him on the telephone a few times. John didn't go and see his father because, the Tuckers did not want the Simba guards to see him. One night a group of Simbas went to the Catholic mission where the men were imprisoned and severely beat the prisoners.

As the national army moved toward Stanleyville and Prime Minister Tshombe broadcast appeals to the rebels to surrender, the Simbas in Paulis became alarmed. The sight of an American plane overhead, tremendously comforting for the besieged missionaries, made the Simbas wild with anxiety. More Belgians were imprisoned, along with many Congolese. One day a young Protestant clerk working with the rebel government telephoned the missionaries to say that Jay Tucker was in grave danger. The missionaries were advised not to go out on the streets, and the Congolese Assemblies of God pastor called his congregation to a day of prayer.

On the afternoon of 24 November 1964 Angeline Tucker called the Catholic mission to ask about her husband. The Mother Superior assured her that everything was calm. That evening, the missionaries received word that Belgian paratroopers, carried in by American Air Force planes, had reached Stanleyville, while a ground force of the Congo National Army had also reached the city. The retreating rebels, it was reported, had slaughtered men, women, and children.

J. Philip Hogan, who had attended Central Bible College with Angeline Tucker, remembers that he had slept fitfully the night of 25

November. All day long news updates were broadcast referring to
Stanleyville; the next day, however, the newscasts referred to Paulis.

> In our office we discussed the danger of these hours. We even used the
> intercom system at Headquarters to ask our 550 employees to pray. There had
> been months of unbroken silence. Our missionaries at Paulis were under house
> arrest – this we knew, but little else. The first news broadcasts of Thanksgiving
> morning reported that American missionary Joseph Tucker had been beaten
> to death. I wanted to believe it was not our man. We had never known him
> as Joseph, but always as Jay or J.W. However, there could hardly be two
> American missionaries by the name of Joseph Tucker in Paulis. This news was
> about *our* missionary. The silence of the months had been broken. In a few
> minutes my phone rang. It was the State Department, a voice that was friendly
> but firm. 'We can now confirm the death of missionary J.W. Tucker,' he said.
> There followed my sorrowful responsibility of notifying all the relatives. We
> want to believe that martyrdom, as far as Christians are concerned, belongs to
> earlier ages, forgetting that the Bible explicitly teaches that the contest between
> truth and error, between light and darkness, between life and death, will
> heighten in intensity as we approach the Second Advent.

Hogan, summarizing his sentiments about this tragedy that had touched
the lives of the entire missionary family, wrote Jay Tucker's epitaph:
'The greatest of honors has come to one of our fellow missionaries. We
salute our friend and brother, J. W. Tucker. He has reached love's
summit.'[21]

A reflection

Elsie Isensee, who lost her husband Frank in a truck accident in Peru
during the young couple's first term of missionary service, wrote an
appropriate comment on Jay Tucker's death.

> Through television, radio, and the press, millions around the world knew
> within a few hours the grim story of how this faithful servant of the Lord was
> cruelly tortured and then his body was thrown into a crocodile-infested river.
> Many and varied were the responses – outrage, horror, sympathy, anger. We
> as Christians, worrying deeply, could yet feel through it all a sense of triumph.
> J.W. Tucker loved a people not his own enough to go among those people,
> to raise his family, to give twenty-five of the best years of his life for their
> salvation. His life was dedicated to carrying out the Great Commission. Until
> his last breath he was proclaiming the message of eternal life to the Congolese.
> In speaking with those who knew Brother Tucker personally, I was impressed
> by the frequent mention of his determination to fulfill God's will and purpose
> for his life. Many spoke of him as a gracious, kindly person, always interested
> in others. His martyrdom, like that of Christ Himself, was at the hands of those

21   JPH, 'Love's Summit Reached,' *Global Conquest* (March 1965).

whom he would have helped. Mrs. Tucker and the children have lost a devoted husband and father. I know that kind of loss. The Assemblies of God has lost a consecrated missionary. But all of us have gained by a new challenge. We can be sure that Brother Tucker, who loved the Congolese people enough to give his life for them, would have us take up his unfinished task – working and praying with tenderness and love that those who caused his untimely death might yet receive the message of salvation.[22]

When the American missionaries returned to Congo the next year they learned that during the most violent months of the rebel occupation Christians were forced to withdraw deep into the jungle.[23]

The Sequel

Twenty-one years after Jay Tucker laid down his life in Zaire, one of his successors, Derrill Sturgeon, fully aware of the enormous and apparently futile price that Tucker and his family had paid to carry on their ministry, published an unexpected sequel to the account.

Yes, many thought his death was a waste, but now, twenty-one years later, the rest of the story must be told. The Mangbetu tribe in Nganga area had been resistant to the gospel. In the early days the Belgians had assigned this area to pioneer missionary C. T. Studd, who was never able to win even one convert. He eventually turned the area over to another mission, which through the decades never had converts among these Mangbetu. As the Congo rebellion subsided, the chief at Nganga persuaded a very competent policeman call 'the Brigadier' to move to Nganga and become the chief of his police department. The Brigadier had lived in the city of Isiro (formerly Paulis), where Jay Tucker had lived and was killed, and had accepted Christ under Tucker's ministry. An active witness, the Brigadier began sharing with the Mangbetus about the Savior he had found through the missionary whose body had been thrown into 'their' river and whose blood had flowed through 'their' waters. The Holy Spirit used this belief in the Mangbetu culture which considered the land and rivers where they live to be theirs personally. Now they must listen to the message of the one who had been thrown into their water. This proved to be the key to their hearts. Individuals began to accept that message and receive Christ. Soon the Brigadier was sending messages back to the national church in Isiro, requesting pastors and evangelists to come and minister to those who were saved and to witness to others. Today, Nganga has thirty Assemblies of God churches among the Mangbetu tribe, and thousands of people in this area have come to the Lord. Many of their young people have gone to Bible school and gone out to minister. A waste? Hardly!

---

[22] Elsie Isensee, 'Triumph Through Tragedy,' *Missionary Forum* (January–March 1965): 2.
[23] *Key* (April–June 1967): 1.

Commitment may appear to have a high price tag, but only eternity will tell the rest of the story.[24]

Throughout his tenure J. Philip Hogan never suggested that missionary work relied ultimately on anything but dedicated, committed men and women. The missionary, when all was said and done, was central to the program. Despite improvements in technology and the growing competition at home for the missionary dollar, everything else hinges on the men and women who play such strategic roles in assisting the national church, by their day-to-day influence, and by the models they present of commitment and service.

---

[24] Derrill Sturgeon, 'The Rest of the Story Must Be Told,' *Mountain Movers* (May 1986): 11.

7

The Greening of the Fields

The cities of the world will never be reached by a flood of foreign missionaries or by a tide of missionary dollars. They must be reached by a trained, Spirit-filled, national church encouraged in its earliest stages to be itself a missionary church.

J. Philip Hogan[1]

The rising tide

Not since the beginning of the modern Protestant missionary movement had any effort produced such an effect. Having received little serious attention when they first appeared, Pentecostal groups began to grow slowly, consistently, and then exponentially, decade after decade, without indications of peaking. In 1960, after 45 years of effort, the reported overseas missionary work of the Assemblies of God consisted of 62 fields, 10,400 pastors, 4,800 churches, and 600,000 adherents. In 1990, at the conclusion of J. Philip Hogan's 30 years of leadership, the number of overseas fields had doubled to 124, the number of credentialed ministers had multiplied thirteen-fold to 134,000, the number of churches had increased twenty-eight-fold to 137,000, and the total of members and adherents thirty-five-fold to 21,000,000.[2]

Although these national Pentecostal churches sometimes appeared tentative, made up of humble people and led often by pastors with little training, the trickles of new growth occurring almost everywhere began to accumulate. Pentecostal enthusiasm grew, from rivulets and brooks in the 1920s, '30s and '40s, to form streams that, while still modest in the 1950s, converged like tributaries to constitute increasingly noticeable national movements in the 1970s. These in turn spread so rapidly in the 1980s that they began to change the world's religious landscape. The

---

[1] JPH, 'The Bush or the Boulevard,' *United Evangelical Action* (11 February 1968): n.p. Address given at the Eighth InterVarsity Missionary Conference, Urbana, Illinois.

[2] Current (1997) estimates of Assemblies of God membership range from 30 to 40 million. In 1959 Brazil alone accounted for 52 per cent of all overseas Assemblies of God adherents. In 1990 that country's share of the DFM work still remained high – 29 per cent of the members. The number of overseas DFM personnel in the same period, however, only doubled, from 800 to 1600 missionaries.

phenomenon threatened to overflow the banks of traditional Protestant missionary effort and break out into entirely new channels. If Pentecostalism still evoked bizarre images for some people, the movement's growth overseas by its sheer numbers and continuity demanded attention.[3]

A people's church

Among the first academics to recognize the global spread and remarkable universality of Pentecostalism was Walter J. Hollenweger, a Swiss professor of mission at the University of Birmingham, England. Hollenweger's ten-volume doctoral dissertation at the University of Zurich, abridged and translated into English as *The Pentecostals*, for the first time gave a scholarly account (as opposed to previous popular, sympathetic treatments) of the Pentecostals as more than merely a religious aberration. Analyzing the movement from a social science perspective, Hollenweger saw it as a form of mass protest, an assertive statement by emergent peoples who demanded a place in modern life.

According to Hollenweger's analysis the key to understanding Pentecostalism was recognition of its effectiveness in communicating its message. Pentecostals transcended the barriers that restricted other proclamations of the Christian gospel. He believed that the Pentecostal churches in developing nations, unlike those in the United States generally, maintained the features that had characterized the initial twentieth-century revival.[4] Tracing Pentecostalism to African Holiness origins, Hollenweger saw the movement as the adoption by other ethnic and national-origin groups of 'the North American Negro's faculties for understanding and communicating by way of enthusiastic spiritual manifestations to build up a community and fellowship.'[5] Hollenweger believed that these means of communication – including hymns, speaking in tongues, dreams, and spontaneous forms of worship – are decisively important in developing nations, where information and impulses are exchanged by means of a kind of 'atmospheric communication.' Hollenweger asked, 'How can one describe in a book

---

[3]   In a recent treatment of world Pentecostalism, Harvey Cox cites the statistics compiled by researcher David Barrett that the movement is growing at a rate of 20 million new adherents per year to number presently more than 400 million members. Cox gives as his reason for the study the need to 'decipher Pentecostalism's inner meaning and discern the source of its enormous appeal . . . and what about it is so attractive to such a wide variety of people around the world.' Cox sees Pentecostalism as part of a much larger 'resurgence of religion' that includes as well the rebounding of the other major world religions. Cox, *Tongues of Fire*, xvii.

[4]   See David D. Bundy, 'Hollenweger, Walter Jacob' in *DPCM*, 409–410. Hollenweger believed that groups like the US Assemblies of God had come to believe that their 'reason-for-being was the perpetuation of their own organization and structures.'

[5]   Hollenweger, *The Pentecostals*, xvii.

a movement whose main characteristic is not verbal agreement but correspondence of sentiments?'

> For Africans and Asiatics, truth or untruth lies at a more profound level than for the white man. It is not the correspondence of the words which concerns him, but the interior correspondence of sentiments. The continuous spread of the Pentecostal movement in many countries must be interpreted as the discovery of new means of communication in a specific social field, which can be clearly defined for each Pentecostal group.[6]

Hollenweger took note of the great internal diversity of Pentecostalism, observing that 'there is no supreme international body in the Pentecostal movement.' Noting the movement's spread in such diverse 1960s societies as those of the Soviet Union, China, Africa, and Indonesia, Hollenweger concluded that in those parts of the world the 'older Protestant churches must either adopt a religious practice like that of the Pentecostals, including speaking in tongues, or else admit their inability to survive and disappear.'[7]

Long before Walter Hollenweger recognized Pentecostalism's relevance to the spiritual stirrings among the masses of the developing nations, the DFM appears to have understood what it took to grow a church. Recognizing 'fertile soil,' the spiritual hunger of emerging peoples, the Pentecostals often ignored the prevailing approaches to missions and devoted their efforts energetically to the Pentecostal message and its logically consequent methods. Without the restrictive features characteristic of many evangelical missions, such as incompatible liturgies, policies and traditions that only with difficulty could be adapted universally, the Christian faith seemed to spread unimpeded.

In most fields the national movements were intent on proclaiming a simple message that promised much and apparently often delivered even more. The modest, sometimes shaky beginnings nonetheless produced substantial institutional as well as spiritual growth during the period of J. Philip Hogan's leadership of the DFM.

The worst of times

Behind this spiritual insurgence was massive social upheaval, what could have been termed in Charles Dickens's words 'the best of times and the worst of times.' While the response to the evangelistic message was on the upswing, producing impressive growth statistics for the missions to advertise back home and for the missionaries' encouragement, the effect of the disruptive changes on the lives of hundreds of millions of men and women of the non-Western world were tragic and traumatic.

---

[6] Jacques Rossel, quoted in ibid.

[7] Ibid., 67. See also, idem, 'After Twenty Years' Research on Pentecostalism,' *International Review of Mission* 75 (January 1986): 3–11.

This social collapse began early in the twentieth century as a result of the changing political and economic structures that introduced new ways into traditional societies. Everywhere rural populations migrated to cities, with all the attendant adjustments and uncertainties. The earlier trickle of migrants grew after World War II into a torrent. Social turbulence brought distress and uncertainty never before experienced on such a scale. All over the developing world slum settlements appeared on the outskirts of large and rapidly growing cities, where country people found themselves poorly prepared to face the disappointments, exploitation, and cruel realities of everyday life. Nothing was as it was before. *Things Fall Apart*, Chinua Achebe's best seller describing social change in a Nigerian Ibo village, gave both scholars and general readers insight into the process of detribalization and the traumatic dissolution of traditional life.[8] So global was the experience that the book describes that readers in languages from virtually all cultures could commiserate with the bewildering sense of loss of Achebe's characters.

Novelist John Steinbeck similarly described things falling apart; new ideas arriving in a 'forgotten village' in rural Mexico, where the community was divided among traditionalists and progressives; the tensions between *curanderos* who used traditional forms of healing and doctors from the city who practiced scientific medicine.[9] Mexico City had a population of two million people when Hogan began working with the Division of Foreign Missions; this had grown to almost twenty million by the time he left his post. Anthropologist Oscar Lewis in *The Children of Sánchez* produced a day-by-day portrait, describing the lives of the common people recently arrived in the metropolis from the villages. It was so disturbingly graphic and unflattering that, while published in various foreign languages, its publication was resisted in Mexico.[10]

While the 'worst of times' brought uncertainty to missionary work, as when deep resentments were vented against Westerners, these conditions also provided missionaries access to previously inaccessible populations and new opportunities for evangelism. The aspirations for identity, recognition, and opportunity of people long suppressed made them disoriented and vulnerable to new influences. 'Everyone laments the decline of the traditional ways,' observed Guillermo Fuentes, the superintendent of the Mexican Assemblies of God, about the trauma his country was experiencing in the 1970s, 'but people from all social sectors here are desperate for solutions. They don't know where to turn. Now, for the first time they are listening to our message.'[11] Recurrently, the

8   Chinua Achebe, *Things Fall Apart* (New York: Faucett Crest Books, 1959).
9   John Steinbeck, *Forgotten Village* (New York: Viking Press, 1941).
10   Oscar Lewis, *The Children of Sánchez* (New York: Random House, 1961). Publication of a Spanish edition in Mexico provoked an outcry and deeply divided public opinion in 1965.
11   Guillermo Fuentes, Mexico City, Mexico, letter to author, July 1974.

Pentecostal emphases seemed expressly designed for people in crisis. Missions and missionaries that were sympathetic to local aspirations and sensibilities found new effectiveness. Overseas workers who could identify with the fears and hopes of the common people, whose message spoke to their deepest concerns, who believed that the gospel provided for physical healing, miracles, and deliverance from oppression – their message offered promise and hope.

But scarcely had this era of increased interest and opportunity begun than the independence movement threatened to disrupt missionary efforts. In Africa and Asia the break-up of the colonial system unleashed floods of resentment against outsiders and all those who collaborated with them, including foreign missionaries and national church leaders. Although the DFM had demonstrated its effectiveness over a period of 45 years, the systems, philosophies, and resolve of the US Assemblies of God would be thoroughly tested during the succeeding years of upheaval.

Discerning the times

Speaking at a meeting of the Urbana Missions Conference on the campus of the University of Illinois in 1968, J. Philip Hogan showed a clear understanding of the challenges and opportunities that changing times presented for missions.

> The city is often the place for the questing mind and the spiritual vacuum. Many of the young people are detribalized. They have forsaken the old culture of the villages and have escaped the control of the elders. The sights, the sounds, and the solicitation of the cities are all new. The stratified social and religious customs of the centuries are broken up, and souls and minds are like open fields welcoming any wind that blows and any seed that falls. Such is the posture of the twentieth century's greatest open door – the cities of the world.[12]

'The cities of the world will never be reached by a flood of foreign missionaries or by a tide of missionary dollars,' Hogan emphasized. 'They must be reached by a trained, Spirit-filled, national church encouraged in its earliest stages to be itself a missionary church. Cities, like individual souls, are subject to seasons.' He continued 'There is a time to sow and a time to reap. One of the greatest responsibilities of missionary statesmanship is to discover when the soil is ready.'[13]

Evangelistic effectiveness, however, could not be measured just by large meetings or the success of given evangelists. 'We have had the best-known Pentecostal evangelists here, some more than once, and there

---

[12] JPH, 'The Bush or the Boulevard:' n.p.

[13] Ibid.

has been no predicting their success or failure,' commented René Arrancibia, a pillar of the Assemblies of God in Chile. 'Some of them did well with their first meetings and then failed to attract much attention when they returned for succeeding campaigns. Others, who were successful elsewhere, failed to attract an audience here.'[14] While hundreds of thousands of people had attended meetings or heard an evangelical radio program or read a tract, many, perhaps most, of these listeners had not been incorporated into a local church for discipling and training.

As the Assemblies of God churches began to grow, it was apparent that the national churches were capable of providing both evangelism and integration of new converts into local congregations. In scores of countries national Assemblies of God churches emerged with minimal foreign assistance. In response to open-air evangelistic campaigns, healings, and the encouragement of friends and family members, the flow of conversions began to leave behind established congregations. From merely an academic theory, the concept of missionary work by local believers soon became the fundamental reality of the denomination's overseas effort.

Hogan was convinced that this was the correct approach. 'Nearly two decades ago many of our missionaries, moved by the Holy Spirit, began to gather around themselves a group of nationals to teach and instruct,' the DFM reported in 1961. 'This was seen as a means of multiplying the ministry of the missionary as well as preparation for the day when the missionary's influence would be greatly reduced.' He summarized the missionary philosophy of the DFM succinctly. 'Today, although this [effort] was not some master strategy of man, we can see that it was wisdom – God's wisdom. Our overseas adherents total virtually as many as our following at home.'[15]

The challenge, however, was overwhelming, reported Everett Philips, Field Director for Africa in the early 1960s. 'Political tides are volatile. Two British colonies, Nigeria, and Ghana are now in the throes of independence. The rule of the white man is being steadily thrown off. However, our work is flourishing with new churches and national organizations as well organized as many at home, with printing presses, Bible schools and all the other complements of an advancing mission.'[16]

Increasingly, it was clear that the gospel seed previously sown in country after country had fallen on fertile soil. The efforts of the pioneering missionaries, some of them hardly corresponding to the stereotypes of what a missionary should be, nevertheless established remarkably strong national churches. The biblical metaphors of the harvest were as applicable as ever to missionary work, but the greatest

---

[14]   René Arrancibia, Santiago de Chile, letter to author, July 1973.

[15]   'Indigenous Church,' *Key* 1961 report.

[16]   Everett Philips, 'Bon voyage,' *Key* (July 1957). In Africa, Philips observed, 'At present 228 missionaries are appointed working alongside 1,037 national workers in 1,467 churches and outstations to keep a constant and ever growing supply of national ministers in training.'

harvest was in most cases to be preceded by a time of development, the maturing of the fledgling church.

Put to the test

J. Philip Hogan viewed the developments in the 1980s as corresponding to what could be expected, given the principles of the autonomous overseas church and the harvest promised by the power of the gospel.

> The local Assembly remains the linchpin for our aggressively expanding missionary enterprise. Through the early 1970s we were doubling in overseas membership every seven years. As we finished the decade we were doubling at an incredible rate of every five years. This is indicative of the Pentecostal revival spreading around the globe to all nations, peoples, and languages. Ahead is a missions era fraught with both problems and possibilities.[17]

This self-reproductive emphasis emerged as the essence of the DFM's approach to overseas extension of the gospel. 'This issue of *Global Conquest* comes to you with the request that you help in this new "crash program,"' Hogan wrote at the beginning of his DFM leadership. The preacher is indispensable, he explained, but 'make no mistake in thinking that there will ever be enough "foreign-sent ones" to accomplish the task of world evangelization. As important as the missionary is, he must have the use of every modern means for the communication of an idea; he must turn his voice into a thousand separate channels, the national leadership that he trains.'[18] Reviewing the mathematical impossibility of reaching even the present population, he concluded that evangelism required every-member evangelism, with trained personnel, an organized and systematic effort, and the formation of local churches to guarantee converts' retention.

Referring to the rise of vigorous national leaders and the opening of previously closed doors, Hogan emphasized his conviction that in missions the task is to follow divine leadings. 'How could the church of Jesus Christ double its growth every [few] years in places like Colombia without simply accepting that forces beyond our control have presented us with an unsurpassed harvest field?'[19] The Global Conquest program launched

---

[17] JPH, DFM Annual Report for 1980, 3.

[18] JPH, 'Global Conquest Advances!' *Global Conquest* (May 1960).

[19] *Advance* (August 1969): 4. In comparison with other missions, the number of fields in which the Assemblies of God operated was significant. The Southern Baptist Convention in 1959 was engaged in 32 overseas fields. With 2,507 missionaries, that mission averaged 78 missionaries per field. Seventh-day Adventists in 1973 reported their work in 65 fields with an average of 20 missionaries in each field. The DFM in 1960 was in 65 countries with an average of 10 missionaries per field. Such extensive coverage scarcely permitted the luxury of maintaining foreign missionary 'compounds.' If DFM missionaries intended to be reasonably effective, they had to magnify their efforts through national evangelists, pastors and teachers.

an assault on the cities of the world, societies within themselves that became concentrations of hopelessness for hundreds of millions of men and women dislodged from traditional ways of life. Strategic efforts were made in dozens of cities. In Guayaquil, Ecuador, amongst others, there was an evangelistic center with three satellite churches in operation after 14 months. Similar efforts were made in Surinam, the Marshall Islands, and Bechuanaland. 'The national church with the largest outreach in the whole Assemblies of God family, however, is in Singapore,' Hogan reported.[20] This church showed the widespread tendency among Pentecostals to extend their message.

The Yoido Full Gospel Church

J. Philip Hogan repeatedly expressed his conviction about the divine nature of evangelism. 'It's not by accident that the largest [functioning] congregation the world has ever known was planted through the efforts of the Assemblies of God pastor David Yonggi Cho. The emergence of the Yoido Full Gospel Church is a fitting climax to an unbelievable story, the miraculous healing and raising up of a vigorous young leader.'[21] Hogan recalls how he first met the young Cho:

> I went to South Korea in the winter of 1961. Seoul had been chosen as the target city of our endeavour for that year. The city and the nation were still devastated from the Korean conflict. Refugees were everywhere, the economy in ruins. To add to this misery, there was no fuel for heat. South Korea has weather similar to North Dakota. By this time two or three families from our veteran Asia Pacific missionaries had moved to Seoul. We had been given property outside the city to start a small orphanage. The streets were full of orphans and waifs, the flotsam and jetsam of war. We could not ignore these children, so we opened a home for them. On a cold winter evening one of our missionaries and I had been out to the orphanage site. We started back to the main road to catch a bus to the city. As we walked through a narrow alley, we passed a makeshift building with cornstalks arranged around the outside, probably as insulation. My attention was drawn to two things. First, as we came near this building I heard the sounds of a prayer meeting. Second, I saw a shaky little chimney spitting out sparks close to the dry cornstalks. I remarked to the missionary with me that the leader of the prayer meeting was in danger of burning down his church! The missionary told me that a Bible school student by the name of Yonggi Cho was attempting to start a new church there. To my knowledge that was the first time I heard Cho's name.

---

[20]   *Advance* (August 1969): 4; McGee, *This Gospel*, 2:195.

[21]   JPH, 'Reflections on Cornstocks and Evangelistic Centers,' *Mountain Movers* (April 1994): 9.

Yonggi Cho was led to the Lord by a young lady while he was suffering of tuberculosis. After his recovery he almost immediately came into contact with our Assemblies of God missionaries. In the give and take of events, I made the decision to open the door for Yonggi Cho to become the pastor of that first downtown evangelistic center. We spent $25,000 of missionary funds to obtain the site and build a simple block building. So far as I know that is the first and last time that funds from overseas came to help this young pastor. His gifts, callings, energy, and personality asserted themselves in winning the lost and building a church in the city of Seoul.

As the church grew, Cho's congregation added three more floors to that building, including a media production studio. When the church reached capacity, having five services a day, Pastor Cho looked for a place to relocate. He found a sparse island in the Han River. I remember going there with him, seeing the willow trees and blowing sand, and saying to him, 'Are you sure you know what you are doing by building a new evangelistic center here?' At that time the island was accessible by only one small shaky iron bridge. Dr. Cho assured me that he and his elders had surveyed the area and that it would become the most enterprising section of Seoul. How right he was! Today Yoido Full Gospel Church stands near government buildings in a modern setting. It is the largest [Protestant] edifice that has ever graced the church of Jesus Christ on this planet. Its congregation, numbering some 700,000, meets in one continuous stream of worship services and prayer meetings. Their outreach is to the world. If you have not visited Yoido Full Gospel Church, it is nearly impossible to describe it. To tell about the church and its activities in candid terms will almost invariably lead to accusations of exaggeration. Yet the man whom I first met leading a prayer meeting in an improvised building surrounded by cornstalks today leads a mighty army of believers from a magnificent complex of facilities.[22]

Profile of a Pentecostal church

The emergence of national churches, subject as they were to local conditions, the quality of leadership, and the pressures that brought entire nations to reflect on the Christian message, cannot be understood in abstractions. Concretely, they are seen in the lives of determined men and women, a local body of believers that begins to take shape. At first they may show tentativeness, lack of commitment, and uncertainty. But as the individual members mature spiritually, the church appears increasingly rooted, developed, and strong enough to extend its own influence in the face of social pressures to conform to tradition or alternative patterns of change. The church from that point on might not grow or develop in a balanced manner, but whatever happens thereafter, like a plant, rooted and capable of further development, the church must

---

[22] Ibid., 10.

operate according to its own resources to grow into a responsible unit of the body of Christ.

The church, like an organism, not merely an association, must exercise its own metabolic and reproductive functions. The first generation of missionaries sows the seed of the gospel among a given people; but once a church emerges, that church, not the non-believing population becomes the focus of the missionaries' work. Evangelistic seed sowing becomes a supplemental service to the church, which, if it does not take responsibility for its own reproduction, will eventually wind down and deteriorate into just an institution.

This principle was articulated emphatically by Hogan at the end of his first decade in office as Director of the DFM.

> Ideally, the successful missionary is one who helps establish an indigenous church which shares the life of the country in which it is planted and finds within itself the ability to govern, support, and reproduce itself. These three principles are the core of the Foreign Missions Department's evangelism and education programs. It is understood that no fixed organizational patterns are applicable to every field. However, every effort should be made to plant an autonomous Assemblies of God fellowship composed of cooperating sovereign churches.[23]

Encouraged by the indigenous policies and self-energizing Pentecostal emphases, the church grew simultaneously in a remarkably broad range of cultures, social classes, and religious types. The church, ultimately the focus of the evangelization process, could readily adapt to a variety of environments and often quickly outgrow its need for continued assistance. As the church developed, it became clear that ministry gifts, in the form of qualified individuals, had emerged from within the new community to replace the artificially supported work of the missionaries. The work of the missionaries was not completed, but their initial tasks necessarily changed to accommodate the increasingly mature church.

Gary McGee points out that a major emphasis of the decade prior to Hogan's assumption of leadership was the elimination of assistance to foreign pastors. In the late 1950s the DFM resolved to support the growth of indigenous churches by slowly eliminating financial assistance for national ministers from the undesignated fund.[24] Referring to the solicitation of US funds for the support of foreign pastors, Hogan was adamant. No church at home or abroad 'can progress very far down the road toward being a stable, witnessing church until it assumes, sometimes at great sacrifice, the support of its own ministry and leadership.'[25]

---

[23] JPH, 'Goal: An Indigenous Church,' DFM Annual Report for 1971, 11.
[24] McGee, *This Gospel*, 1:199.
[25] Cited in ibid., 201.

We cannot evangelize the world until we realize that what the Lord of the harvest wants is the establishment of the local unit in the body of Christ. Jesus said, 'I will build my church,' not 'I will fill my churches' – not with statistics, not with a great organization, not with a magazine; but 'I will build my church.' Some of us believe we ought to count our gains in numbers of local churches. There is something to be done besides witnessing; there must be the discipling of the body of Christ. The Great Commission can only be fulfilled if we gather these people together in the body of Jesus Christ, let the Holy Spirit reign and lead, let the people feed on God's Word and let them develop spiritual strength. In my judgment the chief business of missionary statesmanship is to discover where God wants the harvest reaped and to be there with resources and men when God is ready. When we move this way, we will always have God's assistance and will fulfill our missionary commitment.[26]

Burkina Faso

Every mission field has its own story, an account of its own usually difficult, development. The account of the spread of Pentecostalism in the African country of Burkina Faso, a former French colony on the edge of the Sahara that suffers recurrent famines, is both unusual in the specifics and typical in its general outline. The population of ten million inhabitants, the vast majority of them subsistence farmers, reported one of the lowest per capita caloric intakes in the world and large proportions of children suffered from malnutrition. Half of all Burkinans are Muslims; one-third are animists; an eighth are Roman Catholics.

The Assemblies of God in Burkina Faso began in a typical manner in the early 1920s. When a party of missionaries arrived in Ouagadougou Naba Koom, having completed the trip by ship, train, canoe, and horseback, they were granted a concession of land for a mission station. By 1927, with an established church in the city, initial efforts were made to evangelize outside the capital. In the 1930s the northern territory was opened at considerable effort by missionary John Hall. With churches planted in each of the major language groups by 1950, a tentative national organization was created and a constitution adopted in 1955. At that time all church buildings were deeded to the national church and a Burkinan, A. Philippe Oudraogo, was elected to lead the movement.

After almost three decades of persistent effort the mission reported several dozen tiny churches with a combined total of 2,000 members. But since 1960 the national church has grown from a dozen recognized congregations and a hundred outstations to 1,500 churches with their

---

[26] JPH, 'The Fuelless Flame,' *Pentecostal Evangel* (22 October 1972): 8.

own buildings. The church that reported 5,000 members in 1960 presently has 400,000 members and adherents. With a missionary for each 500 members in 1959, there is now one missionary for each 50,000 adherents.

Clearly, the work of evangelizing their own people early on became the mission of the Burkinans themselves. Every year 150 young people enter the ministry, beginning with attendance one of several Bible institutes. In a country where per capita income was still only $310 in 1993, this mobilization of a national church movement cannot easily be explained apart from the inner resources the members have found in their own spiritual experience. Moreover, the Burkinan Pentecostals have followed their own tribal peoples into neighboring countries. More than 100 pastors are at work in the Ivory Coast, Ghana, Togo, Europe, and elsewhere, with four fully supported couples at work in Senegal, Mali, Benin, and Niger.

Malawi

The Assemblies of God work in Malawi (formerly Nyasaland) in the southeast of Africa dates from the mid-1930s when Laiton Kalambule, a Nyasa resident in Durban, South Africa, was converted and experienced baptism in the Holy Spirit. Despite the difficulties of returning to his homeland, he felt compelled to share his testimony with his own people, most of whom were peasant farmers living barely above subsistence level. On returning to Nyasaland he found considerable interest, and scores of people found impressive answers to prayer, healing, and freedom from spiritual oppression.

Hearing about missionary Fred Burke, who was then in South Africa, Kalambule urged Burke to come to Malawi to instruct him and his converts. When Burke returned for a second trip in 1942, after 8 years of absence, he found a fellowship of 600 believers with their own pastors and congregations, six of which had constructed their own church buildings.

In 1959, a quarter of a century later, the church had doubled its membership and had 26 congregations. A decade later the number of congregations had grown to 35, and by 1985 there were 85 church congregations with 10,000 believers. 'It can be very discouraging for a missionary to work year after year without seeing substantial progress in the work – especially when he hears repeated reports coming from many parts of the world telling how many people even from other denominations are receiving the Pentecostal experience,' wrote missionary Delmar Kingswriter as the church began to show signs of increasingly rapid growth. 'We have often asked, "Will we ever see such a move of the Spirit in Malawi?" ' But the day came, and the church, entirely under national leadership since the 1960s, began to grow spectacularly.[27] Presently the Malawian church consists of 1,200 established churches with 70,000 adherents.

Elsewhere in Africa the accounts are similar. Ghana, a West African country with a population the size of Texas, has an Assemblies of God community of 120,000, which represents 10 per cent of the active evangelical Christians, served by just two missionary couples in a total missionary force of 400 persons working with 58 missionary agencies. In Nigeria, Africa's largest nation, where both American and European missionaries have been at work for more than a century, the nominal Protestant population is a quarter of the country's 100 million people. There Assemblies of God groups report 1,300,000 adherents with the services of only one missionary couple, which represents 0.2 per cent of the total foreign missionary staff of 768 persons working with 76 different agencies.

For all of Africa the Assemblies of God membership was reported as 100,000 members in 2,050 churches in 1970; and 2 million in 11,000 churches in 1989. By 1994 the Assemblies of God had grown to 4 million members in 17,000 churches. Zaire alone has 600 churches and 200,000 adherents. To provide leadership for their work, the African Assemblies of God national organizations support several advanced training institutions, most notably the West Africa Advanced School of Theology (WAAST) the East Africa School of Theology (EAST) and the South Africa Advanced Training School (SAATS), as well as more than 70 resident ministerial schools.

The Philippines

In the Philippines the first Assemblies of God congregations were started by expatriate Filipinos who returned from San Francisco and other West Coast communities in the 1930s. Assisted in the post-World War II era by American missionaries, some of whom had served in the armed forces in the Pacific Theater of operations during the conflict, the work quickly took root. Despite discouraging political turmoil, natural disasters, economic deprivation, ethnic conflicts, and resistance to religious change, the work of the Assemblies of God in the Philippines nevertheless found an enthusiastic response. From 18,000 members in 146 congregations in 1960, the movement has grown at the time of writing to include 200,000 members in 1,250 congregations.

The dynamics of this growth may be viewed through the experience of Urias Ronquillo, the first Filipino worker to establish the movement in the Bicol region of southern Luzon, which, though only one of dozens

---

[27]   Quoted in Don Corbin, 'Africa – Great growth in a climate of crisis,' *Pentecostal Evangel* (13 March 1994): 20.

of administrative districts, accounts for about 10 per cent of the total Assemblies of God work in the country. Ronquillo's introduction to the Pentecostal movement came in 1954 when he was a construction con-tractor in Manila. Despite his stable family background and business success, Ronquillo was driven by a desire for spiritual satisfaction. At-tracted by the large neon sign that declared 'Christ is the Answer,' he entered Bethel Temple in Manila, one of the strategic projects to reach the world's burgeoning cities by the Global Conquest program. There he found what he had been seeking for and, after the spiritual experience of baptism in the Holy Spirit, he became a lay worker alongside several American missionaries, among them Lester Sumrall and Alfred Cawston.

A native of the Bicol region, Ronquillo served in Manila as a deacon, Sunday school superintendent, and men's leader for several years until he was urged to accompany missionary Ernest Schoberg for some initial meetings among his own people. Their team was granted permission to conduct a Sunday evening meeting in a non-Pentecostal church in Santiago. The testimonies and message of that service produced an immediate response. The ensuing revival continued until the new con-gregations in Bicol were eventually organized by the Philippine Assem-blies of God into a separate district in 1964. A Bible institute was built two years later. By 1989 the district had grown to include 66 established churches and many more dependent 'satellite' congregations.

South India

The DFM effort in India since its inception has been divided, according to the prevailing cultural and ethno-linguistic patterns, into north and south divisions roughly by drawing a line from Calcutta to Nagpur. The South India church, in turn, is divided according to the region's linguistic and geopolitical divisions – including Malayalam, Tamil, Marathi and Mysore districts – each district existing as a separate entity with its own annual conference and a vernacular Bible school. These autonomous groups meet biennially in a general conference. As an outgrowth of work begun in the 1920s by Mary Chapman in Travencore State (now Kerala), the Assemblies of God gained from the establishment by John Burgess of a training school for national workers. Soon after the end of World War II, the South India Assemblies of God was organized and registered with the national government. The first superintendent, A.C. Samuel, re-mained at the head of the work until his death in 1970. From 124 churches with 7,350 adherents in 1959, the work continued to grow to 300 churches with 30,000 members by 1980. Presently the movement has grown to include 500 churches and 50,000 adherents. The four Bible institutes have an enrollment of 200 students. The vitality of the move-ment may be seen in the progress of the fifth district. Created in 1981 and numbering 30 congregations, it reported 70 congregations in 1988. The relationship between the DFM and the church in South India was frankly expressed in 1985 by the then superintendent Y. Jeyaraj:

> We feel thankful for all of the missionaries who have felt some call to come to India and work with us. We feel some sadness about a few who did not feel happy to love us and work with us, trying to understand our foreign culture and ways of doing things to strengthen the work of God in India. It makes us feel specially thankful for those missionaries who have lived among us and loved us and worked in cooperation with us even when they may have felt inclined to impose their own will and ideas upon us. These missionaries have contributed much to the growth and maturity of the church, not only by their financial support but by their preaching and teaching and by their example of Christian love, service and sacrifice. We hope and pray that the DFM will work with us in a new spirit of cooperation and partnership so we can see ever increasing growth of the church in India. We do not want to be told what to do and how we must do it, though we will gladly listen to your ideas and suggestions as we sit and work together as equal partners in the mission of the Lord. We no longer feel the need of having missionary 'supervisors,' but we do need friends who will work with us in places where we feel they can use their talents and abilities to strengthen the work of God. We are even willing and happy to use them in positions of leadership as they earn the respect and love of our people by their ministry, dedication, love and respect toward our people. We do not ask that our missionary friends be perfect in every idea, word and action. But we do ask that they be pure in heart and motive. When there are new missionary recruits for India, I expect to be informed at an early stage in the process with full information about their backgrounds, their family, their educational and experiential qualifications and their success in the ministry. We will then prayerfully consider the matter and inform you if we feel that we can use them and where we feel they can be best used. I hope you will understand our desire to work with our American friends as equal partners in the mission of the Church and in the love of Christ our Lord.[28]

'National workers are seeing positive response at a rate far beyond the imagination of earlier missionaries who worked very hard with comparatively few results,' notes an observer of the Assemblies of God work in the area. 'Yet those early pioneers are the ones who laid the solid foundation for this great revival that is taking place all over South India.'[29]

Assemblie di Dio in Italia

The Italian Assemblies of God, the largest evangelical church in that country, resulted from an affiliation with its US counterpart at the

---

[28] Y. Jeyaraj, letter to Jerry Parsley, 1 October 1985.

[29] Stanley Horton, professor at the Assemblies of God Graduate School in Springfield, Missouri, upon serving a guest lectureship in India in 1980.

conclusion of World War II. The Italian government at the time applied a law, enacted under the fascist regime of Benito Mussolini in 1935, that restricted religious activities. Assemblies of God groups were specifically outlawed on the grounds that Pentecostal worship 'was detrimental to the physical and mental state of the race.'[30] The Italian Pentecostal leaders at the time sought the aid of sister organizations in the United States for assistance in their obtaining political recognition, even though Europe was not at the time considered a DFM mission field. In 1949 Alfred Perna, an Italian-born US citizen, felt called to go to his homeland to help Italian Pentecostals, a group who existed as a result of efforts that had begun prior to World War I. Perna's initial years, while he sustained himself largely on his own resources with some help from his home church – Highway Tabernacle, Philadelphia – were difficult but rewarding.

The work Perna found on his arrival had begun early in the century. In 1906 an elderly Methodist woman in Gissi, central Italy, spoke in tongues on her deathbed. Two years later Giacomo Lombardi, recently acquainted with the phenomenon of tongues in the United States, returned to his home town to find this family receptive to his Pentecostal beliefs. About six months later, Luigi Francescon, another expatriate who had received the baptism in the Holy Spirit while in Chicago, arrived in Rome to established a congregation. No revival spread in Italy, but small groups of Pentecostals were established.

At first these believers met no official resistance. Then in 1929, with the signing of a concordat between the Roman Catholic Church and the Mussolini government, the Pentecostals lost their status as a legally recognized religious body. At the time there were about 5,000 believers meeting in 130 small groups. For a decade, from 1935 to the end of World War II, Pentecostals, who were considered agents of a foreign religious movement, experienced severe persecution. At the end of World War II, 200 members of the church in Rome were in jail, and the movement's leader, Pastor Gioretti, was serving a 5-year prison sentence for leading the Pentecostal work. Under the new freedoms that came with liberation the Pentecostals, militant and committed, preached openly. But, when the Allied forces withdrew, once again restrictions were imposed, and the church appealed to the courts on the basis of the constitutional guarantees of religious liberty.

In 1949 the Italian Pentecostals had only minimal organization. Although they wished to receive assistance from their sister organization in the United States, the Christian Church of North America, the reluctance of that group at the time to be incorporated under US law left them without the legal status needed to assist the Italian churches in their constitutional battle. In 1947, when the first World Pentecostal Conference was held in Zurich, Switzerland, representatives of the Italian churches conferred with representatives of the US Assemblies

---

[30] Cited in Thomas Grazioso, *The Italian Pentecostal Movement* (unpublished manuscript), 1.

of God; they returned to Italy and organized their own churches as the Assemblie di Dio in Italia. In 1949 Europe was recognized by the Assemblies of God as a mission field. An organizational meeting convened in Raffadali, Sicily, and the newly elected officers began the process of seeking recognition from the Italian government. In 1953, pressure having been applied in diplomatic circles, the Italian courts finally granted the Assemblies of God recognition. Accordingly, no missionaries were directly involved in the founding of the Italian Assemblies of God.

Since the Italian Assemblies formed an organization only to help their churches obtain official recognition, the Italian churches consider themselves to be autonomous and independent. In the early 1950s the Italian Supreme Court ordered the government to give the Italian Assemblies of God nonprofit status and exemption from taxes, encouraging to the Italians who welcomed assistance from the outside. The DFM Light for the Lost program has made a substantial contribution of literature, providing millions of tracts and other printed materials. About 20,000 Italians are enrolled in International Correspondence Institute study courses. The continuing needs of the Italian church are apparent. About 60 per cent of church members are under 30 years of age and many pastors lack formal ministerial preparation. Located almost entirely in southern Italy and Sicily, only 15 per cent of the church is found north of Rome. The country is divided into 6 zones, each of which is largely free to conduct its own programs. Smaller, dependent congregations, wherever they are found, retain a direct link with the national leadership, however. Most pastors are responsible for two or more congregations. After 42 years of service Superintendent Gioretti was succeeded in office by Francisco Toppi.

Full recognition of the civil status of the Italian Assemblies of God finally came on 29 December 1986. The church received the same privileges and freedoms as the two other recognized religious groups, namely the Roman Catholic Church and the Waldensians. 'There was great rejoicing among the believers in Italy,' the leaders reported, 'especially among the older generation that had lived through the period of persecution and religious intolerance. Now all of this is behind them, they can witness and preach in full liberty as the result of this new agreement.'[31] In 1987 the national church reported 900 congregations, a national ministerial training school, three senior citizen's homes, and an orphanage. Seventy local churches have acquired their own radio stations. One of the advantages of their new status is that the national organization may approve their own ministers, rather than having to request the government to accept given candidates. Deacons of local churches are also now allowed to make hospital visits, and ministers in training are exempt from military service. Radio time

---

[31] Alfred J. Perna, letter to DFM, 9 August 1989.

is available, and the churches are no longer taxed on literature purchased for distribution. 'It hardly seems possible,' exclaimed national leaders upon receiving official notice of their new status. At the time of writing the group has almost 1000 churches with several hundred credentialed ministers and a large number of recognized elders.

Guyana

The Assemblies of God in Guyana dates from 1953 when an independent congregation established a working arrangement with the Assemblies of God in the United States. In 1958 the fellowship was incorporated as the Assemblies of God in Guyana, with one main church, four branch churches in Georgetown, and several outstations. By the eleventh annual conference, held in July 1969, there were 59 churches in various stages of development and 50 national ministers and lay preachers serving a constituency of 3,200 adults.

At the first organizational council in 1958 Melvin Hodges, the Field Director for Latin America and the Caribbean, emphasized the need for the church to be built on 'indigenous principles,' concepts that were written into their constitution. The stage was thus set for the development of the church without reliance on outside assistance. However, since the executive leaders, who were the proprietary pastors of the main congregation, soon withdrew their membership from the new organization, missionary Milton Kersten was elected to serve in their place. In 1970 Kersten refused to continue in office and Errol Bhola was elected to succeed him.

The church in the meantime received a strong impetus from an evangelistic crusade and from English language broadcasts by *Revivaltime*, the Assemblies of God radio ministry conducted by Charles Morse Ward. Attendance at the central church in Georgetown doubled within a few months. Having outgrown their rented facilities, the church continued to meet in downtown theaters until the present building was constructed in 1964. Errol Bhola served as pastor until 1976, when he dedicated himself full-time to serve as the national superintendent. At that time Milton Kersten, the last missionary for several years to serve in the country, left Guyana.

As told by members of the group, the Assemblies of God story is one of growth from a humble beginning under bottom houses (open areas under houses constructed on stilts) and in rented halls to one of the fastest spreading and most dynamic churches in the nation. The young church was aggressive in its evangelism. Outstation churches and branch Sunday schools, radio broadcasts, literature distribution, and personal witnessing are avenues used by Guyanese to communicate the gospel to other Guyanese. Priority is given to the teaching of new converts and training of workers. Since churches often have room to accommodate only

200–300 Sunday school students, they rent bottom houses and halls scattered around the neighborhood to form branch Sunday schools, that sometimes develop into churches. Growth often seems limited only by the number of visionary workers.

Just prior to Guyana's independence in 1961 there were fewer than 500 Assemblies of God church members in six churches around the country. At the church's thirtieth anniversary in 1987, 5,000 believers participated in a parade representing the work in Georgetown. By 1993 the Assemblies of God, without any missionaries, was second only to the Anglican Church in membership, with 194 congregations, 14,600 full members and a participating community of 50,000 people. Reflecting on the transition to complete independence, Errol Bhola commented on the decision of the last Assemblies of God missionaries to withdraw from Guyana.

> There was a mixed feeling in my heart. I was sorry to see the Kerstens leave Guyana, but I was glad and joyful that they had not failed to teach us the Lord's way and plan for His Church. It was not an easy road. Sacrifices had to be made both by our foreign missionaries and our national workers. Many pastors worked at secular jobs while attending Bible school in the evenings to receive training. Many of our men continued to work while pioneering churches, making tremendous sacrifices. Most of the churches were started under houses in those days to avoid the expenses of paying rent until a congregation could be raised up to take care of the expenses of better facilities. Coming from a British background where the churches and missionary societies built all the church buildings and supported all the ministers, there were times when some thought that it would be easier to get brethren in America to help us build the church buildings and support the national workers as others were doing. But our missionaries stuck to the task of teaching our people to be self-reliant and build an indigenous church. Gradually our people began to catch the vision and see the need that if we are going to have a strong church, we will have to make the sacrifices. This meant we will have to build our own buildings, and teach the people to support their ministers. When we looked at the many ancient church buildings built by the British during the time of their occupation of the country, we were the more challenged. Those buildings are falling apart because the funds were no longer coming from abroad and the people who worshipped in them were not trained to take care of the buildings or their ministers.[32]

The Guyana church began a Bible school in 1961 with an enrollment of 45 students. Most of these students were men and women who were already filling positions in local churches. The first graduating class included the later superintendent, the assistant superintendent, the director of the national Sunday school program, and the director of women's ministries. Now 75 per cent of the men and women who are ministers

---

[32] 'End of a missionary era,' *Pentecostal Evangel* (17 February 1976).

are either graduates or students in the Bible school. After 35 years, this training program has become the foundation for the Assemblies of God work in Guyana.

A strategy with a specific focus

J. Philip Hogan, reflecting on the patterns of growth he has observed, likens the growth of the overseas church to crop cultivation.

> Developing a national ministry is very much like farming – like the growing of crops. There are two stages in crop development, and too much rainfall (read 'outside help') at either stage is disastrous. One stage is the seeding time. The other is at maturity. Between the seeding and harvesting – during the developmental period – rainfall is necessary, and when distributed in proper amounts, proves very beneficial. What about this training stage? Many nationals who have been saved out of heathenism without benefit of Christian culture are soon separated from home and family. They are totally without funds. To whom can they turn for training? It is at this point we feel we make the greatest contribution to the national ministry. These Bible schools are the heart of modern missions. It is in these areas of our work that foreign help is most needed and is the least dangerous.[33]

Since the overseas church was largely sustaining its own growth, a question naturally was raised about the continued need for additional missionaries. Would the missionaries' task soon be done? No, not while the great majority of people were still unevangelized. 'Strangely enough,' answered Hogan, 'the indigenous church requires more missionaries, not fewer. Once the believers are in charge of their own national churches they request more and more cooperative help from missionaries in order to face the awesome challenge of the Great Commission.'[34]

---

[33] JPH, *Global Conquest* (November 1959).
[34] DFM Annual Report for 1971, 13.

8

A Pentecostal Statesman

Make no mistake, the missionary venture of the church, no matter how well planned, how finely administered and finely supported, would fail like every other vast human enterprise were it not that where human instrumentality leaves off, a blessed ally takes over. It is the Holy Spirit that calls, it is the Holy Spirit that inspires, it is the Holy Spirit that reveals, and it is the Holy Spirit that administers.

J. Philip Hogan[1]

A world citizen

Throughout the years of his tenure as Executive Director of the DFM, J. Philip Hogan faced enormous administrative challenges. Day-to-day decisions, some of which affected the lives of hundreds of missionaries and the future of the entire overseas operation, hinged on reading correctly the kaleidoscopic changes in world conditions. With an extraordinary grasp of political and social developments, Hogan remained sensitive to new opportunities to advance the missionary cause. He also attempted to formulate appropriate policies and directions for a highly dynamic though underfunded effort. Each decade he traveled one million miles – the equivalent of circling the globe 40 times – visiting virtually every part of the earth and identifying with national leaders, often humble, unrecognized men and women who were the real key to the growth of the Pentecostal movement. 'Thank you for your forward looking leadership,' a colleague on the Assemblies of God executive presbytery wrote on the occasion of his retirement.[2] Having lived through the uncertainty and changes of the post-World War II era, Hogan knew that a leader must keep his eyes on the horizon to discern emerging and often fleeting opportunities.

Hogan was respected and appreciated by his missionary colleagues in the DFM. 'The Division of Foreign Missions of the General Council of the Assemblies of God is the lengthened shadow of J. Philip Hogan,' commented G. Raymond Carlson, the Assemblies of God general super-

---

[1] J. Philip Hogan, 'The Holy Spirit and the Great Commission,' *United Evangelical Action* (October 1970): 4, 5.

[2] Lowenburg, letter to JPH, 2 January 1990.

intendent at the time of Hogan's retirement. In recognition of his colleague's stature and tenacity, Carlson added, 'One characteristic of leaders is that they make things happen. You are admired – never has there been mildew on your convictions.'[3] In many respects, J. Philip Hogan was the best example for his ministerial colleagues – as well as for the laypersons with whom he worked – of a Pentecostal leader. His forceful, well-thought-out, biblical messages left no doubt about his commitment to his Pentecostal heritage. Beyond simply affirming a tradition, however, he demonstrated the relevance, adequacy, and universality of Pentecostal convictions. More than the televangelists who in the 1980s became the focus of media attention, Hogan was the prototypical Pentecostal.

Hogan was involved in the broader evangelical missionary movement that lay beyond his own denomination. He participated in the major missionary conferences and consultations of his era, including the Wheaton Conference (1965), the Berlin Conference on Evangelism (1966), and the Lausanne Conference (1974). He also addressed a plenary session of the Urbana Missions Conference conducted by InterVarsity Christian Fellowship. These events brought him into association with most of the major contemporary missionary figures: George Peters (Dallas Theological Seminary), Eugene Nida (American Bible Society), Donald McGavran (Fuller Theological Seminary), Clyde Taylor (a founder of the Evangelical Foreign Missions Association), Wade Coggins (also of the EFMA), Arthur Glasser (Overseas Missionary Crusade), C. Peter Wagner (Fuller Theological Seminary), and Ralph Winter (Center for World Mission), among others, most of whom he invited to the annual DFM School of Missions at one time or another. Hogan's publications and addresses reflected his awareness of the major issues facing the contemporary missionary movement.

Hogan also came into direct association with his counterparts in the sister organizations of the Assemblies of God in countries where no missionaries were sent. These included the Pentecostal Assemblies of Canada, the Pentecostal churches of Australia and New Zealand, and several movements in European countries, some of which were parallel in their constitution and purposes without bearing the Assemblies of God name. In this respect, Hogan was sometimes as much a diplomatic representative as he was a missions executive. As Brazil and Korea – and eventually scores of Assemblies of God missionary-receiving countries – began sending their own workers overseas, Hogan's emphasis on the reproductive power of the gospel – growing churches that themselves give birth to churches – was vindicated, and missionary endeavour increasingly became a division of labor, providing mutual help, and coordinating efforts.

---

[3] G. Raymond Carlson, letter to JPH, 23 January 1990.

A man for all seasons

Hogan's awareness of major social changes, like mass migration to the cities and growing literacy, as well as of the theological and theoretical tensions that existed within the missionary movement, informed his policies and were apparent in his addresses and writings. On the occasion of the twenty-fifth anniversary of the Evangelical Foreign Missions Association (EFMA) in 1970, Hogan, then the president, made reference to the technological and cultural changes that were rapidly altering the lives of contemporary men and women. Ahead of his time among Pentecostals, few of whom were sensitive to such intellectual subtleties, he warned that secularization, the veneration of science, and indifference toward God – marks of a generation that 'sought to free itself from all standards in search of freedom' – should not blind evangelicals to the fact that 'secularization may be much more shallow than it appears. For all the marvels of life in the twentieth century, multitudes are unconvinced that modern theology, science, or philosophy have really opened the window on the ultimate world. Scientists may try to wall out the supernatural, but the masses are scrambling around and over the walls.'[4] The same sense of strategic timing that Hogan displayed in the Global Conquest program in 1960 motivated his support for expanding the Spanish-language literature program later in the decade and for developing the International Correspondence Institute in the 1970s.

Life Publishers and the International Correspondence Institute (ICI University)

In 1966 the DFM announced that after months of careful study, the decision had been made to move the Spanish Literature Department, founded by pioneering missionary Henry Ball, to Miami, Florida. Loren Triplett, Coordinator for the Spanish Literature Division (later Editorial Vida and Life Publishers), announced the move. Life Publishers eventually produced materials in Italian, French, Portuguese, and Spanish. Its Spanish publications – devotional books, Sunday school literature, and various study guides – made it the largest-in-volume Spanish language press in the United States. These materials were distributed by 67 different denominations or missions in 36 countries.[5]

---

[4] JPH, *Pentecostal Evangel* (21 June 1970). (Notably, Harvard theologian Harvey Cox, whose 1965 best-seller *The Secular City* was at the time being denounced from evangelical pulpits as an indication of the inroads of the 'God is dead' thinking, in 1995 published *Fire from Heaven: The Rise of Pentecostal Spirituality and the Reshaping of Religion in the Twenty-first Century*.)

[5] DFM Annual Report for 1979.

Among his achievements, however, Hogan was especially pleased with the establishment and growth of the International Correspondence Institute, now ICI University, with headquarters in Irving, Texas. In 1967 the opening of ICI was announced with George M. Flattery at its head.[6] Flattery, who was raised in a missionary family in French West Africa, was then completing a doctorate and was in search of a suitable topic for his dissertation.

'I remember getting a call from George Flattery at home in my study one evening,' Hogan recalls. 'I told him I had something that he could help with.'[7] Flattery was dispatched on a trip around the world to survey the educational work – especially the correspondence courses – then offered by DFM missionaries. 'The first memo you dictated here in the office – even before the name ICI was thought of – was the ultimate goal of developing a worldwide, in-depth, correspondence training program where the church, at whatever level it finds itself, can be served, and young people, in any culture anywhere, can have an opportunity to get sound biblical training,' remembers George Flattery. Hogan recalls the program's tentative beginnings.

> Actually, I didn't really know how far it would go, nor did I have a finished concept in mind. I was just reacting to a need. I was very conscious of the fact that we were developing various correspondence institutes around the world. I knew we were probably duplicating some efforts. It had become a burden to me to do the survey work, first of all.[8]

Flattery used a desk provided by the DFM secretarial pool as his first office. Later he placed a small sign reading 'International Correspondence Institute' over a door in the warehouse of the Springfield, Missouri, Mission Village. 'The original building was acquired with $5,000 from the Boys and Girls Missionary Crusade,' Hogan remembers. 'When we started I did not realize it would become this big. That is the miracle of following the Lord's leading step by step. You trust him to lead you.'[9]

'We started with just one course, "The Great Questions of Life," ' Hogan explains. 'This course is the finest thing that has been produced. It was studied, prayed over, and largely developed by Louise Jeter Walker. That course has now gone to 8 million people in 60 languages.'[10]

Early in 1969, Louise Jeter Walker and Carl Malz were assigned to start producing materials. Malz, who had worked in India and the Middle East, understood the strategic importance of mailed materials for reaching some populations. Louise Walker, a missionary in Latin America, had spent years preparing materials for leadership training programs in that

6   *Pentecostal Evangel* (21 June 1970): 18.
7   Ron Barefield, 'ICI's First Fifteen Years,' *Pentecostal Evangel* (11 July 1982): 16.
8   Ibid.
9   Ibid.
10 DFM Archives, ICI file, press release of 12 July 1992, 12

field.[11] Hogan recognized the growing demand for reading materials virtually everywhere, given the then massive programs for adult literacy. 'Millions of people are learning to read, and these new readers yearn to have more to read than has been placed in their hands. The mass media has produced questioning minds and a hunger for knowledge. What people in more developed areas of the world have already discovered, the emerging masses want to learn and learn quickly.'[12]

Flattery later explained that by the early 1970s Hogan saw the need to locate the ICI headquarters outside the United States to ensure that the program from the start would be free from ethnic or cultural barriers. 'We didn't want it to have a "made in America" label.' After considerable searching, Brussels in Belgium was chosen. 'We had several cities in mind,' recounted Hogan, 'including Singapore, Beirut, London, and Brussels.'

> Beirut was then emerging as the queen city of the Levant, and we came close to putting ICI there. At the last moment, we felt constrained not to do so and chose Brussels instead. The sovereign Lord of the universe kept us from being in Beirut during the awful, tragic years to come in that beautiful city. I left Chicago to reach Brussels, but had to overfly the city because of the fog-bound airport. We landed in Frankfurt, Germany. I caught a train for Brussels and got out of the station in a cold, rainy, foggy dawn, in a city I had never been in before, without a telephone number of an address or anyone to meet me, and the extent of my French vocabulary was *oui, oui*. There followed one miracle after another, eventuating in the Waterloo site and the miraculous development of the ICI building.[13]

'The site was ideal,' the two men recall, but they realized that obtaining enough funding would be difficult. 'We started building by faith,' remembers Hogan.

> Bob Combs came as building foreman, but local building codes demanded a local architect. [The architect we obtained] happened to be French-speaking, very expressive, urbane, and sometimes less than Christian in his vocabulary. At the dedication in May, 1975, I mentioned that we had built by faith and had to stop and start several times until our resources caught up with our vision. At the close of my remarks, this volatile French architect exclaimed, 'Monsieur Hogan, it is well to build by faith, but faith is hell on architects.'[14]

In recent years, when the costs of maintaining the Brussels headquarters grew prohibitive and the international character of ICI had long been established, the program was moved to its present headquarters near Dallas, Texas. But its functions continue to expand. 'We're not only a literature program, we're a school. We are teaching by all kinds of media,'

---

[11] Walker's inventory of educational materials in the early years made up as much as 30 per cent of the entire ICI initial curriculum.
[12] 'International Correspondence Institute,' *Key* (October 1967): 4.
[13] Ibid.
[14] Ibid.

insists Flattery.[15] Courses were also made available in audio and video format. ICI Radio Bible School, under the direction of Paul and Violet Pipkin, is on the air in 34 nations weekly, including China, Lebanon, and various countries in Asia and Africa. The *Great Questions of Life* series has been made into a video course available in 15 languages.

When ICI celebrated its fifteenth anniversary in 1982, it reported enrollments in 145 countries. By the late 1980s, more than 6 million students from 164 nations had received ICI Bible study courses. By 1992 the number of ICI students had grown to 7 million, with 25 million courses distributed in 85 languages.[16] Although most materials were published in English, French, and Spanish, additional translations into tribal and Asian languages were provided by the national offices as needed. 'Nothing that the DFM has undertaken in many years gives better promise for immediate success and blessed influence than the formation of ICI,' Hogan asserted in 1967 at ICI's founding.[17] George Flattery and other participants in the program agree that Hogan's support and encouragement through the years have made ICI's progress and widespread outreach possible. Demonstrating imagination, vision, and decisiveness in expanding the operations of the DFM, Hogan went beyond the borders of the Assemblies of God to promote other contributing ministries, especially the work of the Bible Societies.

The DFM and the Bible Societies

Like his predecessors, Hogan avidly supported the United Bible Societies (including the American Bible Society), recognizing the scriptural basis of the Pentecostal message. Because of its growing missionary effort, the Assemblies of God was becoming one of the largest consumers of Bibles overseas. 'We would be remiss in our responsibilities and self-defeating in our missions effort if we did not join "Open the Word to the World,"' Hogan commented in reference to the Bible Societies' motto. Noting that only an estimated one Christian believer in eight has his or her own Bible, the need for accelerated access to the Scriptures remained a basic DFM concern. 'Lasting revival on the mission field depends on new Christians having God's Word,' Hogan asserted.[18]

Not only did the Assemblies of God support publication and distribution of the Scriptures, but also DFM missionaries were engaged throughout Hogan's tenure in various translation and literacy programs. Among these projects were a number involving missionaries in Africa, like Harold

---

15   DFM Archives, ICI files, ICI dateline, 1984.
16   George Flattery, 'ICI – Twenty Five Years of Making Disciples,' *Pentecostal Evangel* (2 July 1992): 22.
17   'International Correspondence Institute,' *Key* (October 1967): 8.
18   JPH, *Advance* (December 1980): 6; idem, 'The American Bible Society: Our Partner in Missions,' *Advance* (May 1973): 7.

and Naomi Lehmann in Ghana and Gail Winters in Zaire. Although at one time the Wycliffe Bible Translators refused missionary appointment to Pentecostals, with growing recognition of the Pentecostal contribution to the evangelical surge and with the wholehearted support of Wycliffe founder William Cameron Townsend, the agency increasingly included Pentecostals among its personnel. In response to this recognition of their contribution the DFM adopted a policy of granting endorsement to Assemblies of God missionaries with Wycliffe, in effect giving these select missionaries dual missionary appointments.

The world missionary conferences

In recognition of Hogan's stature among his peers in leadership positions in other evangelical missions, he and the DFM were invited to participate in the Wheaton (Illinois) missionary conference in 1966. As a joint venture of the Interdenominational Foreign Mission Association (IFMA) and the Evangelical Foreign Missions Association (EFMA), the conference represented a combined total of 15,000 missionaries. Out of the sentiments expressed at the conference emerged the Wheaton Declaration, a statement of social responsibility which the DFM endorsed. Among the presentations was a paper on church growth by Melvin Hodges, the DFM Field Director for Latin America and the Caribbean. 'The presence of an Assemblies of God missions leader on the program, especially handling the subject of church growth,' exulted Hogan, 'is indicative, first, of the acceptance with which the missionary program of the Assemblies of God is received worldwide; and, secondly, it is indicative of the fact that we, by God's grace, have been able, particularly in Latin America, to achieve a degree of success in the vital area of planting indigenous churches.'[19]

The DFM participated in two other major missionary conferences, namely the congresses in Berlin, Germany (1966), and Lausanne, Switzerland (1974). At the former, which coincided with the tenth anniversary of the evangelical fortnightly magazine *Christianity Today*, Carl F.H. Henry and Billy Graham were the chairmen. Delegations came from a hundred nations – approximately 12,000 men and women, from Anglicans to Pentecostals, among whom were participants as diverse in their backgrounds as Oral Roberts, Haile Selassie, and John R.W. Stott. The congress was intended to highlight the advances made by theologically conservative Protestants in offering leadership in world evangelization. In a show of unity the congress planners adopted the theme of 'One Race, One Gospel, One Task' as a prelude to two weeks of reports, position papers, and plenary sessions on the strategy of missions. A 'population

---

[19] JPH, 'The Congress on the Church's Worldwide Mission,' *Missionary Forum* 14 (October 1966): 2.

clock' registered that the human race had increased by more than a million persons during the duration of the congress.

A memorable moment for Hogan occurred at the beginning of the conference when, as part of the ceremonial procession of the flags of the nations, Billy Graham stood on the podium flanked by two Africans, Emperor Haile Selassie of Ethiopia and Lebende Miningou, Superinten- dent of the Assemblies of God in Burkina Faso (then Upper Volta). As Hogan entered the hall and proceeded down the broad aisle toward the front of the auditorium, a widely grinning Miningou defied protocol by raising his hand and waving enthusiastically. Hogan reflects that 'the vastness of the auditorium and the stately march of the nations entering the hall didn't inhibit this humble leader with the tribal marks on his face and his colorful Kenti cloth robe from breaking into a solemn occasion and shouting his greeting to me.'[20]

The International Congress on World Evangelization, known as the Lausanne Conference, brought evangelicals from 150 nations to Switzer- land in 1974. Their major concern was the development of a strategy for evangelism, to be undertaken by AD 2000. The selected theme, 'Let the Earth Hear His Voice,' gave expression to a desire for unity in a common evangelical undertaking and, despite disclaimers, was an obvious effort to provide an alternative missionary voice from that of the ecumenical World Council of Churches. The secular press portrayed it as having a 'strong social consciousness welded to a strategy for preaching the gospel message of salvation throughout the world.'[21]

The closing meeting of the ten-day congress was given to the signing of a document, the Lausanne Covenant, drafted by John R.W. Stott. Carl Henry, who had served as the chairman of the previous Berlin World Congress on Evangelism in 1966, noted that the social aspects of the gospel were made 'more explicit' and were recognized as more 'legitimate' at Lausanne. 'To give only a spiritual content to God's action in man, or to give only a social and physical dimension to God's salvation, are both unbiblical heresies,' Henry advised. Half of the participants were from developing nations. 'If any evangelical stream was under-represented here,' recognized Henry, 'it perhaps was the charismatic or neo-Pente- costal Christians.'[22]

If the world Pentecostal community was considered negligible in 1966, and if in 1974 there was increased recognition that the Pentecostals were more important for the task of world evangelization than had been previously recognized, the publication in 1982 of David Barrett's *World Christian Encyclopedia* cast entirely new light on the growth of this sector. Barrett's comprehensive profile of world Christianity clearly placed the

---

[20]   JPH, letter to author, 10 January 1996.
[21]   Los Angeles Times News Service, *San José Mercury* (California), 26 July 1974.
[22]   Carl F.H. Henry, 'Lausanne '74: Let the Earth Hear His Voice,' *World Vision* 18 (September 1974): 11.

Pentecostals in a leading role as the most rapidly growing, global, and inclusive form of evangelical Christianity.[23]

Perhaps the larger role that Pentecostal missions now played in the missionary enterprise resulted in Hogan's tending to be especially circumspect in adopting DFM policies. In respect to the legal status of overseas personnel, for example, he avoided taking measures that would threaten the DFM with reprisals or legal action. 'We are not a tourist visa organization,' he insisted.

> We want to go where we can operate on an official basis, so that our people will know *how* and *why* they're there, so they can live, learn the language, and plant the church of Jesus Christ. We believe that ideally this is the way to do missionary work. Where you cannot operate this way, you do the next best thing. In some of these countries, this is through ICI. [National directors, however,] operate the ICI programs in lands where we cannot place missionaries. In a sense, the mailman becomes our missionary.[24]

Hogan rejected talk about closed doors in missions. 'Doors are never totally closed because you cannot close them to the Holy Spirit.'[25] Whether in currency exchange, legal entry into a country, or the securing of permits and licenses, Hogan wanted the DFM operation to remain transparent. When some evangelicals promoted Bible smuggling, Hogan followed the lead of Billy Graham and other evangelical notables in urging for the use of available legal methods to provide materials whenever possible. Hogan's policies derived from what he believed to be better sources of information about the availability of legal channels, and from regular communication with the State Department and diplomatic offices around the world. Hogan also believed that some sensational programs based on illegal methods compromised missionaries ethically and could in some cases jeopardize Pentecostal believers.

J. Philip Hogan's missiological statement

J. Philip Hogan's later statements reflected his maturing Pentecostal philosophy. His address to the EFMA in 1970, as president of that association, represented one of his clearest statements of what he believed the Pentecostal strategy to be.

> Some years ago Hendrik Kraemer, the noted missions professor, spoke to a group of missions administrators in the city of Chicago. At the conclusion of his address, the subject of Japan and its recent history came into discussion. It

---

23 Barrett, *World Christian Encyclopedia*. Hogan was so enthusiastic about the positive light it cast on Pentecostal efforts that he permitted missionaries to purchase the expensive volume as part of their normal work expenses.
24 Cited in Barefield, 'ICI's First Fifteen Years.'
25 Ibid.

was observed by different participants in the discussion that immediately following World War II, when the Emperor had renounced his deity, the inevitable spiritual vacuum created by this act afforded one of the greatest opportunities any nation has ever known for evangelism. Further observations were made concerning how propitious it would have been if the churches in the rest of the world had focused their attention on the Emperor himself. If he had accepted the claims of Jesus Christ, perhaps a whole nation could have been won in a day! Mr. Kraemer listened to this for some time, then remarked, 'I never did agree with you Americans. You seem to have the idea that by getting together and using the proper methods you can do anything. You leave out of consideration the operation of the Holy Spirit.' This blunt Dutch professor indeed said it all and said it well. In Acts 5:32 we read, 'And we are witnesses of these things; and so is also the Holy Ghost, whom God hath given to them that obey him.' This indicates that the task of worldwide witnessing is a joint task. It is a cooperative endeavor between the Lord of the harvest and His Church made up of human vessels.

For more than twenty years I have been privileged to be intimately related to church planting and evangelism in more than eighty countries of the world and to be somewhat related and acquainted with the work of God in the whole world. A great deal of my time has been taken up with the human side of the missions enterprise. I have dealt with people, their successes, their personalities, and their problems. I am overwhelmed and humbled before the moving of the Spirit's own sovereign presence in the world. Make no mistake, the missionary venture of the church, no matter how well planned, how finely administered and finely supported, would fail like every other vast human enterprise, were it not that where human instrumentality leaves off, a blessed ally takes over. It is the Holy Spirit that calls, it is the Holy Spirit that inspires, it is the Holy Spirit that reveals, and it is the Holy Spirit that administers.

From the long viewpoint of history, there have been times when men have doubted the ceaseless, sovereign presence of the Spirit of God in the world. Elijah's scathing words about Baal have at times seemed almost applicable to the Lord of Heaven. 'God sits in Heaven and does nothing,' grumbled Thomas Carlisle. H.G. Wells in his last statement declared man to be played out, the whole world system jaded and devoid of recuperating power, the only possible philosophy left one is stoical cynicism.

I have long since ceased to be interested in meetings where mission leaders are called together to a room filled with charts, maps, graphs and statistics. All one needs to do to find plenteous harvest is simply to follow the leading of the Spirit. When one engages in this truth and begins to live by this principle, there will be communities, whole cities, whole nations, whole cultures and whole segments of pagan religions that will suddenly be thrust open to the gospel witness. Witness the sovereign freedom of the Holy Spirit today. We are witnessing an outpouring of the Pentecostal experience on groups and individuals that our prejudices and our provincialism are sometimes slow to accept. I have just returned from the heart of Latin South America where my brethren confronted me directly to say, 'What should our attitude be toward hundreds of Catholic priests who are testifying to the reality of the baptism of the Holy Spirit?' They said, 'These men, five years ago, were throwing rocks at us and doing everything possible to contain the Protestant message. Now they have covered up the stations of the cross in their cathedrals and have in turn emblazoned the message of Pentecost.' What can I say when priests and bishops and powerful leaders of liturgical groups around the world tug at my sleeves in airports or in other crowded areas of the world to confidently whisper, 'Brother Hogan, you will be surprised to know that I pray in tongues every day.' If I had been designing the persons or groups upon whom I felt the sovereign Spirit would fall, some of these are the last ones that my provincialism would have dictated should receive this blessing. However, thank God, the essential optimism of Christianity is that the Holy Spirit is a force capable of bursting into the hardest paganism, discomfiting the most rigid dogmatism, electrifying the most suffocating organization and bringing the glory of Pentecost. Stand in awe, my friend, and witness in these days the wonder of the ages, the Spirit of God is being outpoured upon persons and in places for which there is no human design and in which there is not one shred of human planning. The inscrutable ways and origins of the Spirit indeed place a stranger than fiction-like quality to serving God in these days. There are times when I feel like a spectator with a box seat, watching the greatest drama of all time unfold before me.[26]

---

[26] JPH, 'The Holy Spirit and the Great Commission:' 4, 5.

9

The Pentecostals' 'Social Strike'

The Pentecostals do not *have* a social policy; they *are* a social policy.

Jeff Gros[1]

The Pentecostals' 'social strike'

According to many assessments, both religious and secular, the Pentecostals have long been on a social strike.[2] Given to preaching exclusively to save souls, according to this widely held thesis, Pentecostals are indifferent to saving the temporal lives of their adherents. Their message, reads the indictment, is an 'opiate' for people in desperate conditions; it provides distraction from wracking poverty and hopelessness, but fails to address the underlying economic and political causes of misery. Perhaps so, but little effort had been made by secular observers to understand the social involvement of Pentecostals prior to 1990, when David Martin and David Stoll in their studies of Latin American Pentecostalism addressed the issue and put Pentecostal groups in a different light.[3]

---

[1] Jeffrey Gros, 'Confessing the Apostolic Faith from the Perspective of the Pentecostal Churches in the Ecumenical Movement,' *Pneuma: The Journal of the Society of Pentecostal Studies* 9 (spring 1987): 12.

[2] Wagner, *Look Out!* provided an early sympathetic discussion of the issue. The allegation of a Pentecostal social strike was advanced by the Swiss sociologist Christian Lalive d'Epinay, *Haven of the Masses* (1969), followed in succeeding years by criticism of alleged Pentecostal support for dictatorships and reluctance to support liberation theology and national revolutionary movements. Articles, such as those by Deborah Huntington, 'The Prophet Motive,' *NACLA* 18 (1984): 4–11, and Penny Lernoux, 'The Fundamentalist Surge in Latin America,' *Christian Century* (20 January 1988): 51–54, maintained that Protestant fundamentalists, including Pentecostals, were negligent if not antagonistic to social advance.

[3] Stoll, *Is Latin America Turning Protestant?* and Martin, *Tongues of Fire*. Criticism of the Pentecostals' lack of social action appears often to have been directed at their reluctance to use political means – especially violence – to achieve their goals. They have, in fact, only rarely identified with militant political groups, making them appear indifferent to social action and passive toward injustice and exploitation. Given resistance to theological liberalism and implied or overt hostility to the social gospel, Pentecostals seemed indifferent to human suffering. Such statements, however, do not address the real issue for Pentecostals, namely, the manifestation of compassion and concern that derive directly from the Pentecostals' basic beliefs and practices.

Pentecostals have seldom responded to their critics in this, as in other areas, but had there been an interest to go beyond the stereotypes to the realities, it would have been possible long ago for observers to see the inaccuracy of such libels. All along, though increasingly in his later years, J. Philip Hogan made clear his belief that the gospel, intended to effect profound changes in human character, was bound to have temporal as well as eternal results. As early as 1965 Hogan stated that the DFM priority was to love people as Jesus did. 'It sometimes surprises people to know that, while we have never been primarily a relief and rehabilitation organization, we do put out some effort along this line. What we have done is only a drop in the bucket. But it has been done by people who not only have given food but also have brought the message of eternal life.'[4] In 1986 Hogan reiterated the commitment of the DFM to social concern. 'The Communists may out-think us, out-talk us, out-argue us, out-work us, and out-live us, but they cannot, they must not, they will not, by God's grace, out-love us. We will continue to show compassion in a manner representing the love of Jesus.' In reference to a particular operation, the Latin America ChildCare program, he reported that on a given day '60,000 children in the world will have a nourishing meal and clean clothes and will read or hear the gospel, and they had none of these things before we gave them to them.'[5] To critics who argued that such programs were only palliative, obscuring the need for thorough structural change, Hogan responded that the gospel 'must strike at the depths of the structures of human culture and life.'[6]

The two mandates, to evangelize the world and to show compassion for the people who are evangelized, cannot easily be separated as underlying motives of the Assemblies of God missionary enterprise. Faced with the overwhelming material needs in their fields, some missionaries early on undertook social action by founding leprosariums, orphanages, and schools. Such activities, unwittingly illustrate the Pentecostals' concern for the manifestation of the kingdom of God in this age.[7]

While the *laissez-faire* posture of most Pentecostals has resulted in little coordination of effort, the movement may well have achieved more with inspired volunteerism than it would have accomplished by means of duress

---

[4] JPH, 'Feeding the Hungry,' *Pentecostal Evangel* (16 May 1965): 19.
[5] JPH, DFM Annual Report for 1986, 5.
[6] JPH, DFM Annual Report for 1980, 12.
[7] McGee, *This Gospel*, 2:171. McGee points out that among Pentecostals there has long been theological ambiguity on the issue of social concern. In some quarters McGee detects support for active intervention in human social problems, while in others he sees denial. Frank M. Boyd, a widely read student of eschatological matters, asserted that the kingdom of God, while presently in the world, could not be 'unveiled' (170). His contemporary, the one-time Assemblies of God superintendent Ernest S. Williams, however, provided a basis for social action by denying that the kingdom of God is entirely hidden from the church. 'We must conclude that the [visible] church and the spiritual kingdom are one and the same with slightly different connotations.'

or a prodding sense of duty. David Martin sees Pentecostals, whom he portrays as marginal groups huddled together for survival in a hostile world, as believers who are nevertheless aware of their own growing strength and who have on occasion employed their collective resources to address social needs.[8]

What is clear is that Pentecostals march to the beat of their own drummer, feeling little compulsion to combine efforts with non-Christians whose motives or methods they may question. Leftist political groups that have appealed to the Pentecostals' sense of solidarity with the impoverished masses have been met with little or no response, despite the benefits Pentecostals supposedly would derive from efforts to change exploitative social structures. Pentecostals are not likely to respond to appeals that tend to draw them into conflicts and causes that appear to have little practical or moral justification. Not only does this tendency keep them from collaborating with progressive Christian movements (like those fuelled by liberation theology), but it also inhibits cooperation among Pentecostals themselves in social action programs. To be a Pentecostal usually has meant being free to decide when and how one goes about about fulfilling one's calling, governed only by a sense of divine leading.

The doctrine of abundant life

On the face of it, as people who for many years characteristically came from needy or marginalized sectors of society and whose existence was defined largely by deprivation, the Pentecostals' rejection of tangible or social blessings seems illogical. In fact, Pentecostals, who have never foresworn temporal blessings, have often testified to divine provision in receiving health and healing, employment, safety, improved social circumstances, and restored relationships – the rewards of temporal life. Pentecostals are hardly mystical recluses, however much they may be motivated by self-sacrifice in respect to the evangelistic task.

Moreover, Pentecostals collectively have had enormous social impact, whether observers recognize it or Pentecostals themselves deny it. Virtually every Assemblies of God community in the world maintains some kind of self-help program for member families. In small churches individuals and pastors attend to families in desperate need, while in larger churches a committee is instituted to collect and disburse goods in kind, provide enough money to pay electricity bills, and help the unemployed find jobs. All of this may be overlooked because it is not the congregation's main concern. 'Pentecostal churches do not opt for the poor,' explains Brazilian sociologist Cecilia Mariz, 'because they are already a poor

---

[8]   Martin reports that the converts he interviewed did not expect material aid as a motive of conversion, but he notes that at the same time 'they said they could be sure of assistance in time of need;' Martin, *Tongues of Fire*, 222.

people's church, and that is why poor people are choosing them.'[9] The recently published study by Douglas Petersen on Latin American Pentecostal social concern has greatly expanded the discussion of Pentecostals and their temporal needs and aspirations. His investigations demonstrate what a great deal of literature has overlooked, namely the socially redemptive effects of these groups, made more notable by their being the efforts of grass-roots congregations.[10]

Changing assessments

By far the most important studies of Pentecostal social concern are not those published by evangelicals and their religious sympathizers, but rather the findings of secular social scientists, who generally seem to be more aware of Pentecostal efforts than many missiologists or advocates of militant social action. One example is the small but growing body of literature that deals with the social involvement of Pentecostals in Latin America, a region where the charges of social neglect have been especially frequent. For example, Cecilia Loreto Mariz, a Brazilian professor of sociology teaching in Rio de Janeiro, rather than viewing evangelical religion (in this case specifically Pentecostalism) as an obstacle to social advancement because of alleged encouragement of passivity, has argued that religious fervor has given Brazilians the initiative and confidence to improve their positions in temporal life. She observes that Pentecostals 'are more motivated than [non-Pentecostals] to survive by avoiding self-destructive behavior, such as drinking and gambling.'[11] Similarly John Burdick's study of Brazilian evangelicals led him to conclude that 'Pentecostals can be heard as often as anyone else decrying bad drinking water, dangerous buses and roads, unstable tenure of house plots, and the lack of electricity.' He adds regarding the Pentecostals' independence in political action, 'We have yet to hear the believers' [*crentes'*] last word.'[12]

A publication that did much to turn secular scholars toward a reappraisal of the Pentecostals' social impact was the doctoral dissertation written by Elizabeth Brusco. She demonstrated that Pentecostals were effective in changing destructive traditions of male dominance by empowering women in their own homes. David Martin, a British sociologist who has spent his life studying the role of religion in effecting social

---

[9]   Mariz, *Coping With Poverty*, 80.

[10]   Petersen, *Not By Might Nor By Power*.

[11]   Mariz, *Coping With Poverty*, 24.

[12]   John Burdick, 'Struggling Against the Devil: Pentecostalism and Social Movements in Urban Brazil' in *Rethinking Protestantism*, eds. Garrard-Burnett and Stoll, 223. In another example, Annis, *God and Production*, reported some Guatemalan's use of the expression *del suelo al cielo* ('from earth to heaven') in recognition of the impact of the gospel on economic behavior. See the Introduction to Miller, ed., *Coming of Age*, xiv–xvii.

change, summarizes the mechanisms Brusco identified in these Pentecostal churches.

> [They do] this partly by promoting a form of personality inimical to the stereotype of the Colombian male and partly by a strategic alteration in the priorities of consumption. Evangelical religion literally restores the breadwinner *to* the home and restores the primacy of bread *in* the home. The woman finds her refuge in the church and tries to bring her husband along too, if he is still around, or else she finds a supportive husband from within the fellowship. [When conversion occurs] the atmosphere of the home changes. [Sometimes] the man relapses because of the ostracism of his peers, but quite often he attends often enough to be integrated into the standards of the community. His wife, meanwhile, has joined a whole series of women's organizations, and attends women's services, where the dominant images are those of cleanliness and good food. Moreover, the person who usually presides at these meetings is the pastor's wife.[13]

Thus, while Pentecostals, unlike more theologically liberal groups, have not pretended that their message is primarily for the social well-being of their converts, they nevertheless have been extraordinarily effective in addressing such needs. Roman Catholic ecumenical leader Jeffrey Gros, explaining Pentecostal influence, has observed that 'Pentecostals do not *have* social policy; they *are* a social policy.'[14]

A cup of cold water

While little institutional attention was given to social concern during the formative years of the DFM, a review of the policies and statements during the Hogan years indicates that, while Hogan concurred with the prevailing view that social concerns were subordinate to the task of evangelism, he asserted that they were nevertheless legitimate and biblical. In 1964 Hogan summarized the social policies of the DFM.

> The Assemblies of God has not engaged in extensive institutional programs, in keeping with our concept that our contribution to world evangelism is primarily spiritual and that, according to Acts 15, we are called to 'take out a people for His name.' God has given us an energizing spiritual message and we must use our talents and resources to propagate that message. Therefore, we exercise a certain priority in our work. We are not critical of missions that emphasize medical and educational programs, nor are we unmindful of the physical and material needs of people in countries where we serve. We never have appointed a medical doctor and it is unlikely that we will do so in the foreseeable future. Our medical work overseas is on a clinic and dispensary

---

[13] Martin, *Tongues of Fire*, 182.

[14] Jeffrey Gros, 'Confessing the Apostolic Faith:' 12.

basis only, conducted by missionary nurses. Our clinics, dispensaries and orphanages require only an insignificant percentage of our missionary dollar.[15]

In an article published in the *Pentecostal Evangel* in 1965, quoted earlier in this chapter, J. Philip Hogan noted that he was often asked what the DFM did to alleviate the physical hunger of the world. Last year we distributed abroad approximately 296,680 pounds [148 tons] of food supplies. They were secured largely from the surplus commodities agencies of the United States Government, and consisted of wheat, flour, beans, dried milk, animal fats, and other such staple commodities. We also distributed 40,000 pounds of used clothing and hospital supplies, almost all of which came by free-will contribution from our churches. Miscellaneous relief goods made up an additional 18,000 pounds.'[16]

Almost a quarter of a century later Phil Hogan reiterated the legitimacy of encouraging compassion as a part of evangelism.

> We have invested millions of dollars and devoted countless lives to feed starving people, clothe poor people, shelter homeless peoples, educate children, train disadvantaged adults and provide medical care for the physically ill of all ages. We have always generously responded to the pleas of foreign nations after natural disasters – hurricanes, floods and earthquakes. As the director of this fellowship's overseas efforts, I want the world to know that the reason we do these things is because Jesus Christ did them. The reason we love people is because Jesus Christ loved them. We have no other motive than that. Our relief efforts are inseparable from our gospel witness. Unlike some agencies who help the suffering in their temporal needs only, we minister to their need for Christ as well. For us, that's the bottom line of everything we do. And it's working! Israel understood God's law for the reapers of the harvest: 'When you reap the harvest of your land, thou shalt not wholly reap the corners of thy field, neither shalt thou gather the gleanings of thy harvest . . . Thou shalt leave them for the poor and the stranger: I am the Lord your God' (Lev. 19:9, 10). Suffering people are under the care of the reapers. The Division of Foreign Missions understands this divine principle. While evangelism, church planting and training of national believers remain paramount in our activities, disaster relief, refugee work and physical nurture are also necessary parts of our harvest-time strategy. Matt. 25:40: 'Inasmuch as ye have done it unto one of the least of these my brethren, ye have done it unto me.'[17]

Regardless of discussions about the legitimacy of social programs, the DFM policies tended to develop gradually, as a result of concrete situations and of increasing recognition that social concern had long been implicit in the Assemblies of God understanding of the missionary task. 'The historic aim of Pentecostal missions has been the evangelization of the lost before the return of Christ,' writes Assemblies of God historian

---

[15] JPH, 'How Do We Compare?' *Missionary Forum* (3rd quarter 1964): 7.
[16] JPH, 'Feeding the Hungry:' 19.
[17] *Mountain Movers* (June 1989).

Gary McGee. 'Yet, at the same time, sizable funds and energies have been directed to those with physical needs.'[18] The orphanage established by Lillian Trasher, the work of Florence Steidel among lepers in Liberia, and European relief efforts in connection with the Church World Service during and after World War II all were indications that, in practice as well as in theory, social concern was an integral part of Assemblies of God overseas efforts.

Developing a policy of social concern

In 1961, only months after J. Philip Hogan took office, he encouraged Jere Melilli, an Assemblies of God medical doctor from Louisiana, to survey DFM work in Africa with a view to instituting a medical program. Dr Melilli's findings seemed to justify the emphases the Assemblies of God had previously placed on more direct approaches to evangelism. Medical programs, Melilli reported, 'are very much secondary and many times unnecessary. They have their place, but should never become the prime motive or the first avenue of endeavor in establishing a missionary program. It was my observation that medical missions do not increase the spiritual harvest to a great extent.'[19] After addressing the candidates and veteran missionaries assembled at the School of Missions on the CBI campus in July 1961, Melilli added: 'If I were going to be a full-time missionary today, I would not go to Africa as a medical missionary, but rather as an evangelist.' A decade later concerns about the evangelistic impulse of the enterprise being compromised by the health care services and the funding of medical facilities prompted Hogan to write that 'We have kept our emphasis at the cutting edge of evangelism and church planting and we have sought for, supported, and appointed the kind of people who can best carry out these tasks.'[20]

Dr Melilli's sentiments, apparently reflecting the view of most Assemblies of God members, nevertheless could not stand unanswered for long. Other spokespersons recognized that the priority of evangelism did not exclude or even imply exemption from social programs, especially since many precedents for such efforts had been carried over from earlier Assemblies of God missionary work. At the time of the 1967 Biafran War in Nigeria, a mission field where the Assemblies of God had enjoyed particular success, General Superintendent Thomas F. Zimmerman pronounced a view that stemmed directly from evan-

---

[18]   McGee, *This Gospel*, 2:60. Although the denomination had an amicable association with the Church World Service of the National Council of Churches previously, upon its affiliation with the National Association of Evangelicals there were strong pressures to withdraw from that relationship thereafter. Cecil M. Robeck, Jr., 'A Pentecostal Looks at the World Council of Churches,' *Ecumenical Review* 4, no. 1 (1995): 60–69.

[19]   Cited in McGee, *This Gospel*, 2:249.

[20]   Ibid.

gelistic, not just relief, concerns. 'As God-fearing men and women we cannot stand idly by while thousands of Assemblies of God believers die of starvation in a land that for nearly thirty years we have tried to evangelize. We must show them that we love them enough to care about their present suffering.'[21] Within a short time, tens of thousands of dollars had been designated for Biafran relief. In later years relief help was also forthcoming for Thailand, Vietnam, Bangladesh, and several countries in Africa.

Hogan frequently urged for help for victims of other natural disasters. He pointed out that whenever a natural disaster occurs in any country where the Assemblies of God performs missionary work, emergency funds are available for immediate release to those missionaries and national church leaders who are at the scene of the disasters and request the funds. The DFM also responds to natural catastrophes by sending financial appeal letters on behalf of the stricken country. The writing, printing, and delivery of those letters takes time, however, so Hogan suggested that concerned people should respond to natural disasters even before they receive appeals for help. 'If a Christian hears of a natural tragedy anywhere in the world and wants to do something to help the people there,' he said, 'he can send his offering to us. As long as he designates his contribution for the relief efforts in that country, we will get those funds to the locations where they can do the most good.' According to Hogan very few places exist where the Assemblies of God cannot provide direct disaster relief through their own contacts. 'We have more than 1,500 missionaries ministering in 120 countries, and we maintain a working relationship with national church bodies and legitimate international relief organizations in other nations. People who send their gifts to us can rest assured that we will get them to the people who need it most.'[22]

The impossibility of addressing their spiritual needs without compassion for the people among whom Assemblies of God missionaries worked was articulated by Dale Preiser, a missionary in Haiti. 'I want to preach. I know I've been called to declare the Word. But I've been out in the country and preached to an audience of people who couldn't stay awake because they lacked proper nutrition.' Occasional relief projects were insufficient for the ongoing needs of the people, Preiser observed, raising questions about combining evangelism and direct material help to desperately needy peoples.[23]

---

[21] Cited in ibid., 250.
[22] JPH, 'Assemblies plays key role in aiding disaster victims in Bangladesh and the Caribbean,' *Pentecostal Evangel* (6 November 1988): 12.
[23] Cited in McGee, *This Gospel*, 2:250.

Health care ministries

With the physically needy receiving increased attention, Assemblies of
God church members and missionaries began to voice greater concerns
for policies of caring for temporal needs. A proposal for increased medical
aid was presented by Paul R. Williams, a pediatrician and Assemblies of
God church member, to the DFM in November 1982. As a result a study
committee was appointed to consider social programs. In a historic move,
the board approved the development of Health Care Ministries, to be
directed by Dr Williams. Despite the long record of humanitarian
endeavors initiated by DFM missionaries, this decision by the board
marked a level of endorsement and encouragement not known before.
On a continuing basis, Health Care Ministries takes the initiative in
country after country, organizing medical programs in conjunction with
evangelistic efforts, although without discrimination or pressure to convert.[24]

Presently three institutional programs reflect the thinking that has
gone into the social concerns of the DFM: the Lillian Trasher Orphanage
in Assiut, Egypt; Latin America ChildCare in 19 republics of the
southern hemisphere; and the Mission of Mercy program in Calcutta,
India, begun by DFM missionary Mark Buntain. These programs are
too large and strategic to be considered representative of other DFM
undertakings, but they clearly reflect the denominational thinking that
sustains them.

Lillian Trasher and the Assiut orphanage

Although Lillian Trasher first went to Egypt under the auspices of another
Pentecostal organization – the Church of God (Cleveland, Tennessee) –
she had been associated through most of her career with the Assemblies
of God. Little had been heard of her for years, but the relief needs of her
Christian community in Egypt in the post-World War II years gave her
fascinating ministry a large popular following in the United States. At the
very end of her career Trasher appeared in Springfield, just after J. Philip
Hogan became the foreign missions director. A picture of a portly, slightly
shabby matron of indomitable determination emerges from Phil Hogan's
recollections.[25]

'She arrived at the Assemblies of God headquarters in Springfield,
Missouri, in 1961, after twenty-five years without a furlough,' Hogan
wrote. 'She was wearing an old, black dress. She carried one battered
cardboard suitcase and was wearing a straw hat.' Hogan secured a room
for her in a local hotel and arranged to pick her up the next morning.

24 Ibid., 252–254.
25 JPH, letter to author, 13 February 1995.

About eleven o'clock at night, she called him, confessing that she couldn't enjoy the comforts of the elegant room and wanting to know if some other arrangements could be made for her. Hogan placed her in a private home and went on to learn more about her in the coming weeks. At the time she was caring for about 850 children in her orphanage, all of whom she considered as her own children, and whom she could not forget in their clean but spare situation while she was relaxing in unaccustomed comfort.

It was soon clear that Lillian Trasher expected her orders to be carried out promptly and completely – without excuse or protest. It was this kind of heavy-handed administration and unflinching determination that had made the operation of the Assiut orphanage a success despite overwhelming obstacles. At the end of her service in Egypt, however, and unable to continue her work but unwilling to relinquish control, she was encouraged by Hogan to think about how to leave the institution in the best possible condition to guarantee its continuance after she was gone. Although she seemed determined to remain to the very end, a sick and exhausted Lillian Trasher called Hogan late one night and agreed that she must make a decision about the future of the orphanage. He helped her make the necessary arrangements and guaranteed that her wishes would be respected as much as possible during the transition.

When Lillian Trasher was honored posthumously by the Egyptian government on the occasion of the seventy-fifth anniversary of the orphanage in February 1986, Hogan was invited to participate in the official ceremonies. Present were the governor of Assiut and his staff, along with several cabinet members. 'There was nothing compromising in the atmosphere that day,' recalled Phil Hogan, reporting on the young people who sang Christian songs, prayed, and listened to public reading of the Bible. 'After seventy-five years – and twenty-five years after Lillian Trasher's death – the original purposes of the founding of the institution are still strongly in evidence. The director, George Assad, had grown up in the orphanage. Under his administration two new buildings were under construction though, as in the past, there were not sufficient funds for the project. The institution was still operating by faith.'[26]

Hogan noted that 80 per cent of the orphanage budget – $500,000 a year – comes from Egyptians.

> The orphanage clearly has a powerful influence in Egypt and is well respected. The fact that most of the funds come from people in a predominantly Muslim country is a striking, ongoing testimony to the fact that this woman followed the call of God, worked hard, and was more of a servant than anything else. It is also a testimony of God's love for the people of Egypt (where the average monthly income is about $60) still being demonstrated through the Lillian Trasher Orphanage.[27]

---

[26] JPH, 'The "Mamma Lillian" Meeting,' *Pentecostal Evangel* (13 April 1986): 22.
[27] Ibid.

Latin America ChildCare (LACC)

The Liceo Cristiano, a school founded by missionary John Bueno in San Salvador, El Salvador, presents another institutional development that demonstrates the holistic concern of Pentecostals for the populations among whom they work. From a three-classroom primary school with 81 students in 1963, the Liceo had grown during decades of political turbulence to become a national educational institute with 34 campuses and 24,000 students, the vast majority from some of San Salvador's poorest slums. The school eventually provided education from kindergarten to university level. For students excluded by poverty and disruptive conditions from acquiring even basic skills, the school offered an opportunity for a meaningful life and a significant career. Further the Liceo provided at least rudimentary medical and dental services and supplementary nutritional and welfare assistance for the students and their families.

The Salvadoran churches had formed almost spontaneously among the landless, wage-earning coffee workers of the country's western region just before World War I. A Pentecostal missionary in 1949 described the condition of these laborers.

> About a block from our church we saw row after row of persons, some wrapped in thin blankets and some without covering, asleep on the bare ground. There they live, hundreds and sometimes thousands of them. During the four months of coffee harvest they have no shelter. The world does all it can do to get the few pennies they earn with liquor, lotteries, gambling and entertainment. We try to reach some of these people with the message of salvation.[28]

Though at first it served the educational needs of the largely poor and marginalized Pentecostal community, the central school, the Liceo Cristiano Reverendo Juan Bueno, was later extended to various poor *barrios* that grew as refugees, from the political violence in outlying areas, fled to the city. When their own meager funds prevented further expansion, grants were obtained from other overseas agencies, including the Christian Children's Fund and World Vision. The schools were built and operated as a service to the neglected populations, including some Pentecostal families, for whom the government did not have either the resources or the interest to provide education.

In 1978 concerns about dependency and the wisdom of relying on a single source of funds led the directors to develop their own program within the Assemblies of God both for funding Latin America ChildCare and for developing a comprehensive philosophy of education. As a result a system of patrons to support schools in various Latin American countries provided a fiscal foundation for LACC, and a philosophy of moral development was defined.[29] LACC has emerged as part of an effort to

28 Arthur Lindvall, 'Priest Finds Genuine Peace,' *Pentecostal Evangel* (23 April 1949).
29 Petersen, *Not By Might*, 162.

break the poverty cycle that traps poor families by providing an alternative education. The program at once offers relief for children by providing them with schooling, structure in their often chaotic lives, improved nutrition, and most importantly by being concerned with their complete social, physical, intellectual, and moral development.

Joaquín García, the administrator of the El Salvador Assemblies of God schools, explains their purpose in these same broad terms.

> God has given us the enormous and delicate mission of transforming – or at least improving – our society by putting under our care children and young people that study in our schools. They represent the future of our nation, and if we win them for Christ, also winning their families, we will have a better society in the future. In El Salvador one finds the infamous 'zonas marginales.' These are extremely poor communities, made up for the most part of people who migrated from the country in search of better opportunity, but who do not have adequate preparation for life and work in the city and, thus, became part of the enormous army of the underemployed. Homes in these areas have been constructed of discarded materials. They lack even basic services like running water and sewers. Persons grow accustomed to the lack of hygienic services and to lives of promiscuity. Often the children of these areas are full of intestinal parasites, suffer from the growth of fungus on their skin and, due to poor nutrition, become sick or are physically retarded.
>
> Eleven years ago, when we placed our first school in one of these zones here in San Salvador, we immediately realized that these children needed more than education. We could educate them to take them out of poverty in the long run, but how could we help children intellectually who attended school without an adequate diet, suffering from malnutrition and disease? How could we expect children to practice hygiene and dress neatly when they had a hard time finding even rags to wear?
>
> We then heard the words 'I was hungry and you gave me something to eat, I was thirsty and you gave me something to drink, I was a stranger and you invited me in, I needed clothes and you clothed me, I was sick and you looked after me. Whatever you did for one of the least of these brothers of mine, you did for me.'[30]

In effect, the Liceo became a mechanism for social transformation. 'We began to build schools and churches in the marginal sections of San Salvador, increasing the number of children who would be given an opportunity to escape a life of poverty and desperation,' John Bueno later explained.[31] During the 1970s and '80s, while El Salvador's brutal civil war claimed 80,000 lives, new schools were opened on sites selected according to the unavailability of public education and the severity of the

---

[30] Joaquín García, 'Nuestra responsibilidad como servidores de una institución educativa cristiana,' unpublished SIEELA proceedings, San José, Costa Rica, 1984, 11.

[31] Cited in Everett A. Wilson, 'Latin American Pentecostalism: Challenging the Stereotypes of Pentecostal Passivity,' *Transformation* 11 (January–March 1994): 19–24.

needs of families with poor incomes and housing. The Liceo's first satellite campuses targeted slum settlements, especially areas on the periphery of the city where the Ministry of Education had not opened schools because of the residents' precariousness. In 1977, 86 per cent of the Liceo's total enrollment of 2,671 children received instruction at the main campus, while in 1982 only 47 per cent of the total 6,333 students still met at the original campus.[32]

With completion of projects in the marginal areas, there was concern that many students at the satellite campuses were not performing well academically because of the high incidence of malnutrition and disease. As a result, the Liceo began to offer services which evolved into the Clínica Médica Cristiana and the feeding program of the Sección de Beneficios Estudiantiles. In 1992 the LACC schools in El Salvador provided a million meals, representing a lunch each school day for 7,000 children. The Liceo reported that 18,000 of its 23,000 students received some form of assistance, including tuition scholarships, meals, uniforms, and medical and dental care.

The task of educating children from impoverished families was often discouraging. Despite usual parental support, the problems of economic instability and inadequate health and nutritional conditions had to be confronted without adequate resources. Nevertheless, many examples had already been noted of children who were well on their way to fruitful lives and often to promising careers upon completion of their studies. The Liceo formed parent associations and recruited the donated services of sympathetic professionals in nutrition, counseling, and health care. Remarkably, the operation of these institutions is funded largely by Latin American Pentecostals themselves, with an estimated less than 30 per cent of funds provided from outside sources.

Concerned with supporting children emotionally and spiritually, the language of the reading primers used in LACC is rich in descriptions of the concepts of love, hope, and most importantly, empowerment. In recognition of these basic needs, the slogan adopted by the Liceo Cristiano is 'Forging New Spirits.' Building on the basic premise that all people are created in God's image, LACC has developed a Christian education curriculum for each grade level, from grades one to six that focuses on six major topics – spiritual life, Bible, theology, the role of the church, Christian service, and Christian ethics. In LACC this message of being created in God's image is referred to as the 'pedagogy of hope.'[33] It is recognized that a child's needs are material as well as educational and that teaching must be preceded by instilling in the child a sense of human dignity and self-worth. Children usually enter the program with low self-esteem and a feeling of social inferiority; LACC believes that the best hope for a child to comprehend and demonstrate self-dignity and self-

---

[32] Petersen, *Not By Might*, 158.
[33] Ibid., 169–176. See also Johns, *Pentecostal Formation*, 238.

worth will be through a personal relationship with God. 'Ultimately, LACC sees the rescue of children from dismal, hopeless poverty as only the first phase of their transformation. Eventually, they must acquire a sense of responsibility for changing the conditions that perpetuate poverty and powerlessness.'[34]

Assessing the achievement of Pentecostal schools

While El Salvador's Liceo Cristiano has always been an outstanding effort, it has not been unique. The simultaneous development of similar schools in the Dominican Republic, spontaneous and unrelated to the program evolving in El Salvador, as well as those founded later in Guatemala, Colombia, Panama, Argentina – in a total of 19 Latin American republics – provides a gauge of the social concern found among Latin America's burgeoning Pentecostals. The development of Latin America ChildCare in Honduras is representative of the way in which the program developed in several countries in the 1980s. In Honduras, Mario Canaca, a professor of education at the Universidad Autónoma Nacional de Honduras, began schools in 1983 as Centros Educativos Cristianos under the auspices of the national Assemblies of God. In Colombia, where the first LACC school was not begun until 1993, six schools, with a total of 1,500 boys and girls, have operated for 20 years without any outside help. Similarly, countries of the southern cone, Uruguay, Argentina, and Chile, have 21 Pentecostal schools, few of which receive foreign assistance. Increasingly, however, schools of these national organizations have developed educational programs in cooperation with LACC, an umbrella agency created to raise funds for the operation and capital development of schools.

LACC schools are typically found in deeply distressed areas where public schools are either not available or inadequate. Rural and marginal schools often have high rates of student and staff absenteeism, partial curriculums, and a high percentage of students who are required to repeat the previous year of study. These schools are always developed in relationship with a local congregation, often by a pastor with a vision for assisting the families of his congregation and for serving the surrounding community. Administrators comply with the requirements of the Ministry of Education in curriculum and policies. Since each school in these national programs requires a professional administrator as well as qualified teaching staff, the pastor must be in agreement with the educational objectives of the school and to some extent must share leadership in the evangelical community with a layperson, often a woman, whose formal education almost invariably exceeds his own. The merits of such an arrangement, which requires professional educators to direct their efforts

---

[34] Petersen, *Not By Might*, 179.

holistically to the spiritual and social as well as the narrowly educational needs of children, and which, in turn, helps pastors address immediate social concerns, offers perhaps one of the best indications of the conceptual balance of the system.

With about 300 schools, an estimated two-thirds of the total number operated by Latin American Assemblies of God congregations, the LACC schools are training a combined enrollment of 75,000 students from kindergarten through to their professional studies in the region's largest such private, non-Catholic network.[35] Each national educational system operates under the auspices of an autonomous national church responsible for its own administration, funding and programs.

Clearly, some Latin American Pentecostal churches, in the area of their children's education, have adopted self-help solutions effectively and on a significant scale. While efforts in a given country may be negligible, or easily diluted by deteriorating social and economic conditions, the emergence of these programs indicates the Pentecostals' commitment to temporal improvement for themselves, their children, and their neighbors. Considering the multiplication factors that can be assumed in the personal and social salvation of each child rescued from demoralizing circumstances, the Pentecostals have yet to see the fruit of their educational efforts to fight paralyzing indifference, frustration, and cynicism.

Mission of Mercy, Calcutta, India

If the Latin American schools program was the largest major social program undertaken by the DFM, it was not the last, or even the most highly publicized. In 1977 missionary Mark Buntain dedicated the Assemblies of God hospital in Calcutta, India. The culmination of a lengthy process of evangelism, church planting, and vision for developing leadership, the work was an extraordinary effort that defied tradition and opened new vistas to Assemblies of God social concern. Mark Buntain's emergence as a remarkable figure in Assemblies of God missions is told by his biographer, Ron Hembree, who traces the experience of the Methodist pastor's son from the time his family was influenced by Dr Charles Price (who came to Winnipeg, Manitoba, in 1925). Later Mark Buntain followed in his father's footsteps and entered the ministry. After his marriage in 1944, Buntain felt called to work in India, where he took his wife Hulda and their four-month-old daughter in 1953. A turning point in Mark Buntain's ministry came when he was told, 'Don't try to give us food for our souls until you give us food for our stomachs.'[36]

---

[35]   Information supplied by the Association of Christian Schools, International, Whittier, California, 9 July 1993.

[36]   Scott Shemeth, 'Buntain, Mark' in *DPCM*, 102.

In the 1980s the program he instituted fed 20,000 persons daily. His ministry of health care developed into a hospital and a nursing school, six village clinics, a drug prevention program, and a hostel for youth. Since its opening, the hospital has treated more than 100,000 patients.

The development of these programs was a result of the specific needs Buntain encountered when he inaugurated his evangelistic center in Calcutta in 1959, the first Protestant church to be built in that city in a century. The church on Royd Street, the site of a cemetery, was dedicated on Christmas 1959, just a few days before J. Philip Hogan assumed the directorship of DFM. Then, as the ministry grew, some other Christian institutions in the city reacted by expelling employees who were associated with Buntain's work. When he sent buses through the city of Calcutta to pick up children for the Sunday school, the names of these children were noted and they were given notice of their expulsion from school. The following Monday Buntain arrived at the church to find 250 recently dismissed children and their parents demanding to know what he was going to do about it.

'Traditionally,' writes Ron Hembree, 'the Assemblies of God has stayed away from social concern, to concentrate instead on spiritual problems. As soon as he was able, Mark Buntain took his concern for a school to the Foreign Missions Board in Springfield, Missouri. They listened. They understood, but still they had to think of the implications for the rest of the world, not just Calcutta. After all, the denomination was worldwide – and if they set a precedent, would they lose their distinguishing and effective missionary emphasis? It was a difficult time for both Mark Buntain and the men who served on the board.' As Hembree relates the account, DFM Director Hogan presided at the meeting.

> 'Mark, I'm sorry. We believe everything you say. We understand your need, but we cannot help you. If you insist on starting a school, you will do it totally on your own.'
>
> 'But I'm not asking for money,' Mark replied, 'I'm asking for permission.'
>
> Another board member jumped up and said, 'I object to giving Mark permission. Why should he be allowed to raise money from our churches for a school, when we have such a desperate need for a Bengali church in Calcutta.'
>
> In a flash of inspiration Mark jumped in. 'Sirs, if you will give me permission to build my school,' he told the board, 'I will raise the money for the Bengali church.'
>
> The tide turned and the board granted Buntain permission. They allocated no funds for Mark's school. He was indeed on his own. However, he could tell churches about the need – and if they wanted to help, that was their business.[37]

---

[37]   Hembree, *Mark*, 167.

The school that Mark Buntain went on to establish soon grew in reputation. Parents who had once had their children in the Anglican and Catholic schools wanted to transfer them to the Assemblies of God institution. The institution reached hundreds of Hindu and Muslim children and eventually began to make an impact on Calcutta.

Soon after he had arrived in Calcutta, Buntain started a small clinic in the church compound, which, because of the demand, provided around-the-clock care. Buntain realized that a much larger facility was needed. As unlikely as the acquisition of property was at the time, Buntain found himself with the title to a suitable piece of land and the funds to begin the construction of a hospital. Called the Mission of Mercy, the hospital was inaugurated in 1977, receiving recognition from World Vision and the Government of Alberta, among other agencies, for the service it was providing. *Christian Life* magazine made Buntain the subject of a cover story. While the work in India may not be repeated in the same manner elsewhere, each day tens of thousands of men and women are reminded of the compassion of Christ through the ministries of missionaries associated with Assemblies of God churches.

By 1989 Assemblies of God overseas relief funds were distributed in more than 20 countries. Sensitive to human need, the Pentecostals, whose roots were in the poorer social sectors, directed overseas efforts in substantial amounts to such people. As Pentecostal historian Gary McGee points out, DFM personnel are increasingly engaged in work in cities, where their efforts are invested, for the most part, in the most destitute and hopeless of the world's populations.

In 1989 the DFM magazine *Mountain Movers* printed a statement by J. Phil Hogan affirming his commitment to the needs of people around the world.

> We have invested millions of dollars and devoted countless lives to feed starving people, clothe poor people, shelter homeless people, educate children, train disadvantaged adults and provide medical care for the physically ill of all ages. We have always generously responded to the pleas of foreign nations after natural disasters – hurricanes, floods and earthquakes.

Hogan emphasized the biblical rationale behind this concerted effort.

> If our providing social assistance opens doors that would otherwise be closed to our missionary endeavors . . . good! But if not, we will still continue to provide relief. Because opening doors is not our reason for sharing in other people's sufferings. Demonstrating the truth of Christ's words and sharing the love of God are our intent.[38]

---

[38] JPH, *Mountain Movers* (February 1989): 5.

10

Perils of Power: Schisms and Scandals

The foreign missions effort of the Assemblies of God is by far the largest and most powerful missions work in the world. That may sound chauvinistic, but I say it with reason. If anything would be allowed to weaken or hinder the foreign missions efforts of this Fellowship, it would deal a horrendous blow to God's plan in general, and a tremendous victory for the powers of darkness in particular.

Jimmy Swaggart[1]

Pentecostal power

During J. Philip Hogan's DFM tenure, the representative stereotype of Pentecostal evangelism tended to change from the storefront mission to the televangelist. The change, however, was not entirely positive. For much of the viewing public, some Pentecostals seemed arrogant, crass, attention-seeking, and unrestrained in their eagerness for recognition and power.

But power, supernatural power, after all, is what Pentecostalism is about. Demonstrations of power have been the stuff of sometimes dramatic reports about faith healing, celebrity conversions, gospel music sales, comparative growth statistics, lavish spending, and effective use of the electronic media. Given an opportunity to exercise influence, to demonstrate collective strength and to command respect, Pentecostals have few inhibitions about making use of the tools that they feel God has placed in their hands.[2]

Pentecostal power, however, goes beyond the kinds of power sought by other religious and secular associations. Believing in the immanence (as opposed to the transcendence) of the supernatural, the distinguishing

---

[1] Jimmy Swaggart, *The Evangelist* (August 1983): 12.

[2] This concern with power is inherent in Pentecostalism. Pentecostals, from the most humble believer to the movement's most prominent figures, frequently quote Acts 1:8 (in the Authorized Version): 'And ye shall receive power after that the Holy Ghost is come upon you' (sometimes, however, neglecting the remainder of the verse that revealed the purpose ('Ye shall be witnesses') for which the power had been conferred). Bible students with even a smattering of Koine Greek know that the New Testament text reads *dunamis*, from which is derived the word *dynamite*.

characteristic of Pentecostalism, adherents understood power as referring to the divine grace which is evidenced, usually, by a climactic emotional experience and is followed by an ongoing sense of God's presence and at least some occasional objective confirmation. The vindication of a person's faith – healing, transformed personal character, putative miracles, the changes in apparently impossible circumstances – is a cardinal tenet of Pentecostalism and makes its appeal broadly applicable and vital. Inner resources, reduced by behavioral psychology to personal mechanisms for coping, for Pentecostals are divine empowerment to help them survive, achieve, or change, whatever the need may be.

Notions of what evidence, sentiments, and conduct are demonstrably 'Pentecostal' – especially healings, miracles, signs and wonders, fervor, avoidance of worldliness, extraordinary faith – tend to vary according to individual beliefs and sometimes constitute the distinguishing boundaries between various Pentecostal groups. Although glossolalia, for example, is for most Pentecostals a litmus test, popular Baptist speaker and writer Anthony Campolo, in a curious affirmation of Pentecostal beliefs and practices by denying its signature experience, has argued that tongues is not essential to being Pentecostal after all.[3] But, tongues or no, power is ultimately defined by Pentecostals as it is for everyone else: 'Power is the unimpeded ability to do work,' even if for Pentecostals this 'unimpeded ability' is often primarily affirmation of the believer's worth and inherent dignity and a vindication of one's faith in the context of day-to-day life.[4]

Pentecostal leaders like J. Philip Hogan have had to deal with power, spiritual and otherwise. Questions about charismatic authority, not simply ecclesiastical chains of command, have had immeasurable bearing among

---

[3]   Campolo, *How to Be Pentecostal*.

[4]   Pentecostal power, in the sense of the aggregate strength of its constituents, however, is extremely diffused. It shows up frequently in prosaic expressions, as, for example, in the exponential statistical summaries and projections issued by missionary researcher David Barrett. Pentecostal power also has appeared in articles in business magazines like *Forbes* and *Business Week* on the implications of Pentecostal growth in developing nations for consumerism and enlarged overseas markets. Pentecostalism has even become the topic of a considerable number of doctoral dissertations at leading universities, especially those that deal with creating wholesome personal and family values and, as well, has been on the agenda of ecumenical consultations and those dealing with the implications of Pentecostal growth for the political processes of nations where no genuinely popular movements have ever entered the political arena. Pentecostalism by the 1970s, at least, had become an irrepressible religious phenomenon. As a result of its increasing resources and recognition, however, the character and mission of the movement itself has been threatened. What the sociology of religion revealed about the apparently inevitable winding down of revival movements generally, scholarly assessments like Dan Morgan, *Rising in the West* (1992) and Poloma, *Assemblies of God at the Crossroads*, actually documented about the institutional if not the spiritual development of the Assemblies of God. Apparently, what external opposition could not accomplish through ridicule and resistance, the subtle erosion of Pentecostals' faith through affluence, social acceptance and complacency could accomplish in a surprisingly brief time.

Pentecostals on recognition and acceptance of a person's leadership, on denominational policies, on the raising of funds, and on priorities and strategies. The acceptance of leaders has often depended on their having established legitimacy and having built a consensus. Hogan, both ethically transparent and administratively astute, was portrayed by an admiring colleague at the former's retirement as being a 'mixture of both the pragmatic and the idealistic.'[5] Obviously, to a notable degree he succeeded in gathering strong support, but his achievements were not without decisive contests of legitimacy and spiritual authority.

J. Philip Hogan, like any Pentecostal leader, had to convince his denominational peers that he, rather than someone else, spoke for God – no easy task when numbers of other highly regarded contenders were asserting that they were more in tune with the Lord than he was. When some other voice asserted its greater legitimacy or the superiority of an alternative strategy, Hogan either had to redirect his efforts in order to co-opt the competition or he had to stand his ground and defend his, and the DFM's, course of action. Sometimes Hogan's notion of how to grow an overseas Pentecostal church was too slow for some of his colleagues, too indirect for others, and too exclusive for still others.

Accordingly, the question for the DFM became: Where does the mission direct its resources and efforts? At best, a lot of potential Pentecostal human and material resources have been allowed to lie idle without their being effectively applied to the evangelistic task. At worst, much potential Pentecostal power has been selfishly squandered in prodigal self-aggrandizement, especially noticeable in (but certainly not confined to) the PTL debacle with Jim Bakker in 1978. But apart from these extremes of neglect and abuse, when Pentecostals have resources to contribute, where should they – and where did they – direct their energies, resources, and empowerings?

Characteristically divided, independent, and egalitarian, even when they concur in their support of certain strategic goals and basic beliefs – for example, the importance of evangelism – Pentecostals have often disagreed on priorities and approaches. Pentecostals may all be led by the Spirit, but in their exclusiveness, competitiveness, impatience for results, and pragmatism, unity is sometimes hard to discern. Clearly the Pentecostals have not shown marked achievement simply because they all subscribed to the same church growth theories or worked in choreographed harmony. 'The difference between Roman Catholics and Pentecostals,' goes the joke, 'is that the Catholics only have one Pope; the Pentecostals have thousands!'

Given these splintering, centrifugal tendencies, J. Philip Hogan's substantial achievements were attributable in large part to his keeping the DFM in focus, thereby preventing the mission's self-destruction. His conviction that the nurturing of an overseas church was the primary task

---

5   G. Raymond Carlson, letter to JPH, 23 January 1990.

was often contested by prominent figures who wished to take the mission in other directions. With no end of persuasive proponents of a 'better way,' the avowed DFM 'indigenous church' strategy was repeatedly contested.

The T.L. Osborn Association for Native Evangelism

Among the competing proposals advanced in the 1960s was the Thomas L. Osborn program of 'native evangelism.' One of several independent or loosely affiliated Pentecostal evangelists to acquire a large following in the 1950s, Osborn was considered by Edwin Harrell, Jr, historian of the 1950s 'healing' movement, as one of the more capable and reliable of the men and women then on the evangelistic circuit.[6]

As a young Oklahoman Pentecostal Church of God evangelist, Tommy Osborn had spent a discouraging year as a missionary in India in 1946 before settling in Oregon. There he encountered Hattie Hammond (whom Hogan had heard speak at CBI during his college days), through whose ministry Osborn was deeply touched. He attended a William Branham healing meeting, where he reported to have received a spiritual gift similar to that of Branham, then considered the 'dean' of the healing evangelists.[7] Setting out to conduct evangelistic campaigns with a healing emphasis, Osborn soon acquired a large following and began to register notable success in foreign campaigns, reportedly preaching to hundreds of thousands of listeners in 11 countries within five years of the launching of his ministry. An 'island-shaking' revival in Cuba reportedly resulted in 50,000 professions of faith. In Chile a reported 100,000 persons packed a stadium to attend a single Osborn service. The evangelist then announced that he was moved by the 'alarming challenge of the heathen masses everywhere dying without Christ and felt compelled by the Spirit to bear a miraculous gospel to all the world.'[8]

Osborn's missiology soon crystallized into a scheme for mass crusades that would be conserved by local evangelists recruited and paid for by his Association for Native Evangelism. Reportedly Osborn's organization was formed after consultation with various Pentecostal missions, including the Assemblies of God. By 1957 the Tulsa-based ministry was printing 250,000 copies monthly of his *Faith Digest*. Osborn was not under the auspices of any denomination, and Harrell reports that 'the growing treasury at his disposal made him a man to be courted' by the various denominational mission boards.[9]

Then in May 1958, with the healing ministries generally in decline, Osborn announced abruptly that he was making missions his primary concern.

---

[6] Harrell, *All Things Are Possible*, 106.
[7] Ibid., 64.
[8] Ibid.
[9] Ibid., 65.

I feel that God has given us the greatest calling on earth – that of evangelism among the unreached. When the truths of faith and healing were revealed to me, God impressed me to take the message to the heathen as Paul did . . . That is why God has so abundantly blessed our lives.[10]

When Osborn first embarked on his 'native evangelist' mission in 1953, he had approached various denominations with the offer to raise money for the support of paid overseas workers. At that time the Assemblies of God Missionary Secretary, Noel Perkin, responded to the offer with a policy statement.

We have recently been approached by T.L. Osborn (the evangelist who has had outstanding meetings in Latin America) with an offer to secure support in his [US] meetings for native evangelists in foreign lands. This offer is not being extended to the Assemblies of God alone, but to a number of Pentecostal groups such as the Church of God, the Foursquare Movement and others. The thought of our Brother Osborn is that the mission field is so vast that the missionary will never be able to complete the task of world evangelism but each country must ultimately be evangelized by its own nationals. Inasmuch as we are seeking to promote self-supporting churches, we do not normally encourage the giving of support from foreign funds to native pastors. However, some natives who are engaged in pioneer or missionary work may be supported to advantage.

Although Perkin had some reservations, the Foreign Missions Committee considered the offer thoughtfully. 'M.L. Hodges [Field Director for Latin America] speaks well of the work done by Brother Osborn in Central America,' the minutes of the Foreign Missions Committee read. It was noted, however, that 'Our missionaries are endeavoring to get the work in Latin America established on a self-supporting basis, and for this reason it would be preferred if Brother Osborn were to send in funds designated for Native Evangelism [to be disbursed by the national church] rather than for national workers [paid directly from the US].'[11]

At the time the matter of private corporations within the Assemblies of God gave rise to discussions about the healing evangelists. Beyond issues of financial accountability and tolerance of an autonomous agency within the organization, the issue of conflicting philosophies and approaches led to growing concerns.[12] Nevertheless, the *Pentecostal Evangel* continued to

---

[10] Ibid., 66.

[11] Minutes of the Foreign Missions Executive Committee [hereafter FMC], 28 May 1953, 292A.

[12] According to the published 'Criteria for Independent Corporations,' *Assemblies of God Minister* (executive quarterly newsletter), 28 May 1962, in addition to restrictions on accounting, promotional statements and administrative procedures, General Council ministers were to refrain from 'agreements with independent organizations entailing the use of solicitation of funds, or the ministry of persons representing these organizations when such cooperation involves the identifying of our work with, or the giving of

print reports of Osborn's meetings, even after it discontinued making reference to other such evangelists because of their alleged 'unacceptable extremes.'

In February 1955, however, Osborn sent copies of his book, *Frontier Evangelism*, to about 40 Assemblies of God missionaries, requesting a complete list of missionaries so that he could send copies to the entire roster. Some members of the committee thought that he also intended to send complimentary copies of the book to all Assemblies of God national pastors who read English. As a result, the committee requested copies of the book before considering its authorization.

The outlook of the DFM toward the Osborn program changed abruptly at this point. In June 1955 Melvin Hodges reported to the committee that the Osborn plan was 'wreaking havoc with workers on some of our fields.' He pointed out that some of the new workers were receiving more support than some of the pastors who had been in the service for years. 'In a number of cases, men who were endeavoring to get a work established on a self-supporting basis have left our employ in favor of receiving a salary from Brother T.L. Osborn.'[13]

In November 1955 the Foreign Missions Committee received a letter from T.L. Osborn stating that he had decided to send support for foreign workers directly to the missionaries supervising their activities. The Committee agreed that a letter should be written to Osborn pointing out some of the undesirable aspects of such a procedure. It was further felt advisable to put a note in the *Missionary Forum*, the internal publication issued to DFM personnel, advising Assemblies of God missionaries to operate according to policy by turning such donations over to the national leadership from whom national evangelists should receive their allowances, rather than disbursing funds directly to national pastors and evangelists.[14]

A publication in January 1956 included a statement explaining the relationship between the DFM and the T.L. Osborn Association for Native Evangelism.

> In the beginning it should be stated that all members of the Missions Committee have the highest regard for Brother Osborn personally, and wish to express full confidence in his sincerity and integrity. We appreciate the fact that he has chosen to distribute the funds which he handles through existing full gospel missionary agencies, rather than attempting to establish independent missionary work on the various fields. The Foreign Missions Department is also in accord with the general objective toward which Brother Osborn is working, that of assisting national workers reach their own people.

publicity to, organizations over which the General Council has no proper working relationship.' As a result of the adoption of these guidelines, several highly regarded overseas ministries thereafter were reorganized on an independent basis.

[13]   FMC, 7 June 1955, 694; and FMC, 25 February 1955, 655.

[14]   FMC, 15 November 1955, 800.

However, while all of this is true, we can see no advantages but rather some definite disadvantages in our Assemblies of God churches and people channeling their missionary giving through an independent missionary agency rather than directly through the Foreign Missions Department set up by the General Council to serve our fellowship. Our Assemblies of God missionaries are engaged in every phase of missionary activity, literature, radio, schools, relief. That our missionaries have for years been particularly active in training and encouraging national workers is evidenced by the fact that there are approximately five thousand national workers [in 1956] holding credentials on the various fields where we have Assemblies of God missionary representatives. This is further evidenced by the fact that we operate fifty-two Bible schools – more than any other missionary agency. The Foreign Missions Department still follows its historic policy of using all missionary offerings only for the specific purpose designated by the donor.

Brother Osborn feels that two conditions were absolutely essential to the successful conduct of his program. He requests that funds distributed under his auspices be sent to individual missionaries who serve as 'missionary supervisors' and are responsible to submit to him regular monthly reports concerning the activities of the national under their supervision. To follow this arrangement is to revert to a system which the Foreign Missions Department has been endeavoring to correct. It is better to avoid having any national working for and paid by an individual missionary. Inevitably this develops a sense of personal obligation to the one from whom the money is received, and in spite of the best intentions, tends to prejudice the nationals toward the missionary who is in a position to distribute funds most freely. Experience has proven that it is much better to weld both missionary and national together as fellow workers in a general field council, and to disburse all funds through a field treasurer under the directions of a committee or presbyter board on which nationals serve as well as missionaries.[15]

J. Philip Hogan was concerned with the far-reaching implications of a policy that seemed reasonable to many people.

For us to engage in such a venture would be turning the clock backwards forty years or more and would be a denial of the efforts of scores of wonderful missionaries who have planted the seeds of an indigenous church. Yes, we do have national workers, but only a few of these are supported by American money, and this number grows less year by year. At the present time we list 4,883 national workers. Would anyone dare to suggest that we trade this noble band of pioneers who are sacrificially living and ministering for ever so large a band of men supported by foreign money?[16]

---

[15] J. Philip Hogan stated the matter succinctly: 'No church either at home or abroad can progress very far down the road toward being a stable, witnessing church until it assumes, sometimes at great sacrifice, the support of its own ministry and leadership.' JPH, *Key* 4 (January–February 1956).

[16] JPH, 'Harvest Hints,' *World Challenge* (December 1956).

By March 1958, the Foreign Missions Committee concluded that the Osborn program was drawing funds away from the Assemblies of God missionary program.[17] However, even then the committee agreed to allow missionaries on each field to determine whether or not they wished to accept assistance from the Osborn fund. The matter was only resolved in the mid-1960s after further statements were issued about the reasons for not endorsing the Osborn plan.[18] At this point an open letter, explaining the DFM objections to paying overseas workers, was circulated among the denomination's pastors and district leaders. The policies of the DFM thereafter received such strong support that despite criticism about 'bureaucratic controls' and 'quenching the Spirit,' the controversy soon disappeared.[19]

The DFM and Youth With A Mission (YWAM)

Even before the Osborn matter was settled, another alternative method of doing missionary work appeared. This program used large numbers of short-term volunteers as auxiliaries to long-term resident missionaries. Although the matter was resolved in an amicable manner, with Youth With A Mission becoming an independent ministry, it was nevertheless difficult at the time and led to a painful parting of the ways for some Assemblies of God personnel. If the settlement was decisive for the future of YWAM, the concerns were ongoing for the DFM, since the now independent YWAM continued to draw substantial numbers of Assemblies of God young people, including promising leaders, into its program. The possibility that the DFM and YWAM were both ultimately better off not working within the same administrative framework has sometimes been considered. In any event, the withdrawal of YWAM left the Division of Foreign Missions free to pursue the policies that it had long supported.

About 1960, Loren Cunningham, son of the assistant superintendent of the Assemblies of God Southern California District, formed an association of young people to work overseas, adopting as its main stated purpose: 'to employ individuals in secular work on mission fields to relieve missionaries of many of the mundane tasks associated with their ministries.'[20] The next year Cunningham received DFM approval to travel in Europe as a missionary evangelist and, working under the supervision of

---

[17]   FMC, 11 March 1958, 1403.

[18]   FMC, 24 February 1961, 2184.

[19]   FMC, 28 February 1961, 2184B. Although thereafter Osborn's ministry had less visibility, his interdenominational efforts in 1964 had extended to over 40 countries, with notable successes in Kenya, Indonesia, Formosa, Japan, Java, Holland, Chile, Switzerland. Reportedly, he still remains active as an overseas evangelist with notable success. See R.M. Riss, 'Osborn, Tommy Lee' in *DPCM*, 655–56.

[20]   FMC, 26 September 1962, 2468G.

the Southern California District, began to extend the program among young people in the United States.[21] In 1962 a committee of the General Presbytery discussed the possibility of the program being adopted by the DFM but failed to take conclusive action. During the discussions, however, it was pointed out that the new organization did not conform to the recently established criteria for 'separate corporations' adopted by the General Presbytery, and, even if it did, the philosophy of YWAM appeared incompatible with that of the DFM. Making reference to undesirable situations that had already developed overseas, the committee decided to withhold approval. The resolution read:

> Continued problems arise where independent corporations like Youth With A Mission base their support in Assemblies of God churches and seek to relate their activities overseas to the Foreign Missions program. There is inevitable confusion and a fragmentation of the missionary thrust. The Foreign Missions Board therefore requests that Youth With A Mission be dissolved, and the sincere efforts of both leadership and lay young people be directed into the mainstream of constitutionally authorized Foreign Missions advance.[22]

When Loren Cunningham and the superintendent of the Southern California District met with the Missions Committee, they were informed that to some members there seemed to be more concern with interesting and occupying youth than with meeting the needs of the missionaries overseas. J. Philip Hogan pointed out that there are many difficulties involved in sending young people to foreign fields – problems arising from lack of maturity, as well as from language and cultural barriers. Hogan also emphasized the danger of separating the 'secular' from the 'sacred' functions of missionaries. The committee suggested that YWAM should consider greater emphasis on home ministry, becoming a domestic youth service corps rather than an overseas missionary program.

Loren Cunningham then appealed personally to Thomas F. Zimmerman, the General Superintendent, believing that he could convince Zimmerman of the merit of his approach. Reports from the group's recent project in the Bahamas, Cunningham believed, would persuade denominational leaders that the program should be adopted just as he had envisioned it. 'Our plan was actually working!' exulted Cunningham, who argued that he had opened his program to all denominations but still wanted to stay within the framework of the Assemblies of God. But the meeting with the General Superintendent, as Loren Cunningham reported it, was disappointing.

> Brother Zimmerman shook my hand cordially and then sat down and looked at me across his desk. Indeed he had heard about the Bahamian experiment. But if I were expecting a quick endorsement and a blank check to work interdenominationally and still maintain my standing as a minister with my

---

21 FMC, 24 February 1961, 2484.
22 FMC, December 1962, 2524L; and FMC, 26 March 1963, 2547E.

church, I was mistaken. The problem, I gathered as we sat talking quietly, was that new works like ours needed to be brought under the organizational umbrella – not remain outside and autonomous. There was a place for me in the Assemblies, but of course I would have to be a full team player. In the end I was offered a job. A good one, too, there at headquarters, complete with a fine salary, a staff, a budget.

'You can continue with your vision, Loren, but you'd be taking out more manageable numbers – say ten or twenty young people a year.'

My heart dropped to my knees as the very gracious offer came out – it sounded so reasonable, so secure. Only it was far from what I believed God had told me to do: send out waves of young people from all denominations into evangelism. I tried to explain what I had thought God was saying to me about what was about to happen. It was much, much bigger than twenty a year and larger than any one denomination. 'Sir,' I said, 'there's another generation coming. It's different from anything we've ever seen –' I floun-dered, for I could hear how foolish it sounded. Brother Zimmerman assured me he had worked with young people for decades and knew them well. As he tried to explain his reservations about my plans, I could truly see his dilemma. If I had his responsibility of leading a large movement, I would need submitted people – ready to play by the rules for the good of the whole. But here I was, hearing a different drummer, out of step. That's more or less what Brother Zimmerman said, too. He was sorry, but I'd have to leave the team – resign – if I couldn't play by the rules. 'God, is this really you?' I said quickly to myself. And I thought I heard the answer that it was indeed His leading. I knew what I had to do. If I was really sure what God was telling me, then I had to obey and accept the consequences. Brother Zimmerman agreed, but he had no choice either.[23]

Separated from the Assemblies of God in 1964, the mission grew steadily thereafter to 15,000 YWAMers in 1983. Youth With A Mission activities at the 1972 Munich Olympic Games and the establishment of the Pacific and Asia Christian University (PACU) in Hawaii, gave the program a more institutional, less spontaneous image. In time YWAM was often reported to be the US-based mission with the largest overseas staff.[24] In the meantime, various short-term overseas programs developed satisfactorily within the DFM guidelines, involving, if not 'waves,' sub-stantial numbers of young people each year, some of whom later became appointed Assemblies of God missionaries.

Television and the DFM

Although television offered a great deal of promise for accomplishing the missionary task, for J. Philip Hogan it produced the greatest ordeal of his

---

23   Cunningham, *Is That Really You, God?* (1984), 65.
24   J.R. Zeigler, 'Cunningham, Loren' in *DPCM*, 232, 233.

administration. While the issues compromising the indigenous policies and adopting an alternative short-term missionary philosophy may have simply sharpened the focus of the DFM, the use of the electronic media, first by Jim Bakker and then by Jimmy Swaggart, greatly raised expectations, influenced the denomination's entire missionary program, and left a gaping hole when the television ministries collapsed.

The long-held belief that television could be a major tool in evangelism, virtually limitless in its global extension, appeared to be realizable through Jim and Tammy Bakker's PTL Club Christian talk show and Jimmy Swaggart's televised evangelistic rallies, the latter featuring a winning formula of music, affirmation of cherished beliefs and prejudices, and an attractive, popular style that had broad appeal. Given the close association of the Swaggart ministries with the DFM, and the evangelist's representativeness as a Pentecostal spokesman, the marriage between the DFM and Jimmy Swaggart appeared to be especially satisfactory. With the advent of national – even international – television ministries, the Pentecostal movement seemed to have outgrown its parochial styles and limited access to the centers of media power.

Jim Bakker and the DFM

In 1977 Jim Bakker, whose PTL Club had already acquired a considerable following, began to emphasize missions. 'Overseas evangelism was a cornerstone of the Assemblies of God,' explained *Charlotte Observer* reporter Charles G. Shepard, who followed PTL closely. In Shepard's opinion, for television ministries like those of Jim Bakker, 'missions were also a proven stimulus to charitable donations.'[25] After beginning this expanded emphasis with the Spanish-language version of PTL that met with at least qualified success, Bakker soon launched into an ambitious missionary program.

On 13 June 1977, before a live audience, Bakker invited his talk-show guest, Assemblies of God minister Paul Yonggi Cho of Seoul, Korea, to become PTL's surrogate in Asia.[26] Cho, according to Shepard, was stunned. He answered Bakker's suggestion with a polite, 'Praise God, Amen.' But Bakker continued, 'We can do the same thing [in Asia that] we are doing in Latin America. If Dr. Cho can help us to get the time, we will produce it and we will raise the dollars to buy the time.'

Yonggi Cho agreed to make arrangements when he returned home to Korea, and the following month a PTL vice-president left for Korea to begin drawing up plans. For weeks thereafter the Asian mission took center stage on the telecast. Soon PTL announced that it had raised $277,000 for Korean television, and Bakker portrayed the project as all

---

[25]   Shepard, *Forgiven*, 77

[26]   Yonggi Cho adopted the 'Christian' name Paul as an adult convert. In recent years, as an indication of a changed personal perspective, he has begun using the name David.

but complete. 'We are getting ready to ship the cameras. We are going to have a special packet of cameras for Korea,' he said in October 1977.[27]

Even as he poured millions of PTL dollars into the Heritage US theme park, Bakker proclaimed his commitment to missionary work. 'I love missions so much,' he told his studio audience, 'it brings me to tears sometimes to see [missionaries'] dedication. I've lived so comfortably here in the United States. We all have. It's only right that we support those who go among disease and need in other places to share the gospel.'

But other projects diverted attention from Bakker's plans for an Asian PTL. In fact, no cameras had been purchased. In May 1978 a telecast guest asked point blank: 'You are on in Seoul, aren't you?' As the anniversary of Bakker's offer to Yonggi Cho approached, according to Shepard, Yonggi Cho and his staff grew frustrated and embarrassed. On 8 June 1978 a member of Yonggi Cho's staff wrote to Bob Manzano, head of the PTL missions department, complaining that overseas visitors kept asking to see the studio that PTL had built. 'They all think it is up and going.' Eight days later the assistant wrote to Bakker that Yonggi Cho was disturbed by the slow progress. During Yonggi Cho's worldwide travels people everywhere were always telling him how wonderful it was that he now had TV studios in operation, all paid for and provided by PTL.[28] When, however, funds were eventually disbursed for two overseas projects – PTL in Seoul, Korea, and a Brazilian PTL – both Pastor Yonggi Cho and Robert McAlister turned down the funds. 'If I had been in his shoes,' responded Jim Bakker regarding the Brazilian project, 'I would have taken the money.' To which Manzano retorted, 'Jim, that's the difference between you and McAlister.'

Eventually Yonggi Cho received $350,000 and McAlister accepted substantial amounts, and Bakker emerged from his world trip with a professedly renewed passion for missions.[29] Once again, he declared overseas evangelism to be the PTL ministry's priority. He promised to send more money to a program for the hungry in India, and his staff drafted a plan to put ten per cent of each day's receipts into a separate missions account.[30] Later, when Bakker was called to testify before the Federal Communications Commission, he still insisted that missions was a matter of high priority: 'I've always said: Pay missionary commitments right up top. They're important. It's part of my ministry. I've had to change staff members, and we have rectified this situation.'[31] Missions thereafter, however, were of little concern for Bakker, and overseas evangelism largely disappeared from the PTL scene long before his empire came crashing down.

27   Shepard, *Forgiven*, 97.
28   Ibid., 101.
29   Ibid., 114.
30   Ibid., 127.
31   Ibid., 76.

The DFM and Jimmy Swaggart Ministries

Meantime, in the early 1980s, as Jimmy Swaggart's television ratings rose impressively, the evangelist made overseas missionary work a motif of his ministry.

> A short time ago the Holy Spirit quickened my heart, instructing me to place the full weight of this ministry toward a massive, worldwide missions effort to reach many of the heretofore unreachable multitudes with the glorious Gospel of Jesus Christ. This may well be the most energetic, important, and timely missions thrust ever undertaken by a single ministry, but one that should and must be undertaken to reach millions who have never heard.[32]

Since Jimmy Swaggart chose to direct his missionary efforts largely through DFM channels, there could be no mistaking the denomination's satisfaction with his efforts. A letter from J. Philip Hogan to Swaggart in September 1978 assured the evangelist that the DFM was pleased with the way their programs had dovetailed.

> Dear Brother Swaggart:
> This is just a note to indicate how grateful we are for the relationship we in the Division of Foreign Missions of the Assemblies of God enjoy with the Jimmy Swaggart Evangelistic Association. You have worked closely with us from our initial contacts, and have faithfully portrayed exactly the right emphasis on the projects we have been able to interest you and your board in. Some of us on given occasions are able to monitor the broadcast, so that we can know what you are saying, and on every occasion we have reported to each other that your portrayal is in no sense exaggerated and, as I have indicated, exactly the emphasis we have asked you to place. Furthermore, you have accepted most sacrificially and generously the promotion and fundraising for some of the vital overseas projects. On every occasion you have done exactly what you said you would do, sometimes considerably in advance of when you thought you might have the money raised. Going down the list of projects one by one, we note that the funds are already here and have been sent on to the projects. This is just to say again, by way of clarification, that our working relationship is most agreeable. There is, as far as we are concerned, not a shadow across it, and we are anxious to maintain this relationship.[33]

In the years that followed it became clear that Swaggart indeed had made an extraordinary contribution to the DFM. The enthusiastic support for Swaggart's involvement was attested to in Swaggart's magazine, *The Evangelist*, which regularly ran statements of DFM approval.

Then in July 1986 *The Evangelist* asserted that a year previously God had given Swaggart a vision of reaching the world with the gospel through

---

[32] Jimmy Swaggart, *The Evangelist* (March 1983).
[33] Cited in *The Evangelist* (November 1978).

the vehicle of his weekly broadcast; that vision was becoming a reality with releases in 135 countries and an actual audience of 260 million viewers. Swaggart reported the potential viewers in the combined television markets as 2 billion people.[34]

> God has told us to take the Gospel to the world via television (along with building churches, Bible schools, and schools for the children, plus distributing literature). This is a monumental task. Five years ago, it was almost impossible to get on television in foreign countries, and now we're getting so many calls for the program that it's impossible for us to meet the need. And the sad thing is that in many of these countries, it is the only avenue of the Gospel that the people have.[35]

In October 1987 *The Evangelist* revealed Swaggart's growing missionary pretensions. Swaggart reported the precise words of his prayer: 'Lord, I could never hope to have even a portion of the great touch or mandate that You gave the Apostle Paul or the great prophets of the Old Testament, but I do thank You that You allow me to labor in this great vineyard.' According to Swaggart, the presence of the Lord came over him, and responded in these words: 'I have given you the responsibility for touching the world with My gospel as I have given that opportunity to no one else.'[36]

Swaggart reported sensing a terrible awe and responsibility at the time and went on to explain that his television ministry was possible only because of the cooperation of a team, 'a vast army,' that helped him with the task. 'Firstly, there is no way we could see accomplished what the Lord is helping us to see were it not for Godly missionaries who are able to garner the harvest. If we did not have good Holy Spirit-filled churches to put the converts in, then the harvest would be squandered. But in country after country, some of the finest men and women of God in the world are making it possible for us to do what we do – and most are accomplishing this in addition to their myriad other duties.'[37] Swaggart at the time was especially appreciative of the DFM, regarding it as 'possibly the most powerful missions effort on the face of the earth today, under the leadership of Foreign Missions Director J. Philip Hogan. All that we have been able to do and see for the cause of Jesus Christ would have been so severely limited and hindered were it not for Phil Hogan's help, guidance, and administration, and naturally, that goes for the hundreds of missionaries under his direct supervision.'[38]

On other occasions as well, Swaggart related his appreciation for the denomination and its missionary outreach.

---

[34]   Jimmy Swaggart, *The Evangelist* (July 1986).
[35]   Idem, *The Evangelist* (December 1986).
[36]   Idem, *The Evangelist* (October 1987), 47.
[37]   Ibid.
[38]   Ibid.

Recently missionary Mark Buntain and I were discussing the manner in which the Lord has blessed this Fellowship – the Assemblies of God. Brother Buntain made this statement: 'Jimmy, I believe God has placed His seal of approval upon the Assemblies of God for two specific reasons. The first is holiness, and the second is evangelization of the world.' As I sat there considering this much-respected missionary's remark, I found myself in total agreement. Missions was a major factor in the establishment of the Assemblies of God. And over the years missions has brought untold blessing from God to the movement because it observed and accepted the Great Commission of Jesus Christ as outlined in Mark 16:15. I have traveled all over the world in my effort to support the work of God. In my travels I've seen firsthand the work accomplished by the missionaries of this great Fellowship, and it does not take a back seat to any effort of its kind anywhere. It is a work of which every single contributor can be proud. It is, in my estimation, the brightest star in the proud record for the Assemblies of God. The foreign missions effort of the Assemblies of God is by far the largest and most powerful missions work in the world. That may sound chauvinistic, but I say it with reason. If anything would be allowed to weaken or hinder the foreign missions efforts of this Fellowship, it would deal a horrendous blow to God's plan in general, and a tremendous victory for the powers of darkness in particular.[39]

Typical of Swaggart's approaches were his ventures into children's programs based on the work originated in the Central American republic of El Salvador by missionary John Bueno, who at the time had accepted Swaggart's support for his educational program.

John Bueno, who administers the efforts of the Jimmy Swaggart Children's Fund in all of Latin America, has spent twenty-two years of service in El Salvador. John lives and ministers among the Salvadoran poor. Though

---

[39] *The Evangelist* (August 1983). Swaggart's frequently expressed enthusiastic support of Assemblies of God missions was reflected in correspondence to Phil Hogan from James Woolsey, a former Assemblies of God missionary who had worked with Jimmy Swaggart in Central America before emerging as his principal missionary coordinator. The implications of both a growing interrelationship and the strains between the two agencies were, however, apparent almost from the beginning of their association.

> Dear Brother Hogan:
>
> As you know, Jimmy Swaggart Ministries has become heavily involved in foreign missions projects and missionary support around the world. We believe *missions* [his emphasis] is the very heartbeat of God. Presently, Jimmy Swaggart Ministries supports over 350 missionaries and gave over 8 million dollars to missions last year. Most of this was channeled through the DFM. Brother Swaggart has the utmost confidence in you and the Division of Foreign Missions' ability to oversee the world's finest missionary effort which we believe is light-years ahead of any other missionary board's endeavors. Jimmy Swaggart Ministries is a missions work and wants to do everything possible to help take the Gospel to the four corners of the earth. (James Woolsey, letter to JPH, 24 February 1984).

Brother Swaggart had been helping hungry and needy kids in poor Third World nations since 1979, he received the inspiration for the Jimmy Swaggart Children's Fund from the Holy Spirit in a hotel room in El Salvador on September 15, 1981. About 2 a.m., the Holy Spirit awakened Brother Swaggart, instructing him to take the 'total care for children' concept being pioneered by John Bueno, into every needy Third World nation that would accept it.[40]

Not content with merely working to support the DFM program, however, Swaggart increasingly put his own ministry at the center of his operations. In March 1986, two years before his personal shortcomings were revealed, he proposed raising funds not for the DFM but for his own enterprises. However easily the medicine went down for his own followers, Jimmy Swaggart was unabashedly naming himself the apostle of high-tech, global evangelism. 'Help me reach millions around the world with the gospel,' he pled in his monthly publication.

This is one of the most important articles I've ever written for *The Evangelist*, and I think after you read it you will understand why. We are making the largest effort we have ever made in the history of the Jimmy Swaggart Ministries to recruit new World Outreach Partners. This is a World Outreach Ministry. We are covering the entire globe with the Gospel of Jesus Christ. And we desperately need believers like you to support this worldwide effort. Before you decide whether you will become a World Outreach Partner or send a gift, there are four points I would like you to consider.

1.   God has called me to do what I am doing. As the Apostle Paul was the apostle to the Gentiles and Peter was the apostle to the Jews, due to the modern times in which we live and the advancement of technology, God has called me to preach the Gospel of Jesus Christ to a lost and dying world.

2.   We are attempting to reach the entire world. Many people talk about World Outreach, but this Ministry is *doing* it. We have an opportunity unparalleled in the history of the human race to touch this world for the Lord Jesus Christ.

3.   Our telecast is reaching more people with the gospel than any other single effort in history. At the time of this writing, the Telecast is seen in nearly 120 countries around the world by 150 million people each week. In the last two years we have received over a million letters from people telling us in one way or another that they've come to the Lord as a result of the telecast. There has never been anything in history like this, and of course the Lord is the author of it all.

4.   We operate the largest para-church missions organization in the world. Our total missions effort goes into 181 countries around the world. We have helped build some 59 Bible Schools to train national pastors by the thousands to reach their countrymen with the Gospel. We have built 92 schools and provide support for more than 204,000 children daily. We have helped build

---

[40]   *Pentecostal Evangel* (November 1985).

90 churches, distributed over 20 million pieces of Bible-based literature and support 490 missionaries on the field.[41]

The tendency for Jimmy Swaggart to take credit for ministries that were not entirely – or even primarily – his was increasingly clear in his publications. While he was partially correct in his statements, his error was assuming, as did many of his viewers and readers, that television (or any other impersonal mechanism) was necessary for conveying the gospel. While God's work may make use of virtually any medium of communication, television, despite its gripping influence, is nevertheless nothing more than a means to an end. God's work is simply not subject to human limitations.[42]

At his peak, for many observers, as well as for many DFM personnel, Jimmy Swaggart was a Pentecostal champion who represented well the benchmarks of traditional Pentecostal belief and practice. A forceful, uninhibited, down-to-earth, honest-to-goodness, bigger-than-life, charismatic, country-western hero, Swaggart could be counted on, often enough, to express many of the prevailing, pent-up frustrations and grievances of Pentecostals, as well as the essential Pentecostal message, in a technically appealing fashion before a national television audience. If Swaggart later could be accused of calculated ingenuousness, of high-pressured marketing techniques, of subtle, self-serving use of criticism (virtually everyone at some time or another was on his hit list), of a well-nourished martyr complex, of gross exaggeration and clever misinformation, these and other weaknesses were either overlooked entirely or glossed over in the euphoric glow of success and exercise of power – Swaggart's and that of the Assemblies of God – that pervaded his ministry.

The rise of Jimmy Swaggart and the other televangelism ministries grew to a climactic crescendo in January 1987 with the attention focused on the forty-fourth annual convention of the National Religious Broadcasters. 'Amid the glitter and glamour of show business style some 4,500 people gathered in Washington, D.C., January 31 to February 4, for the 44th annual convention of the National Religious Broadcasters,' reported the *Pentecostal Evangel.*

Glamour and glitter are inevitable when the leading figures of religious television and radio get together. After all, the names of several religious TV evangelists have become household words. And sessions like NRB's attract an entourage of promoters pushing all sorts of programs, supplies, and equipment. With this kind of clout in the media, it isn't surprising that the NRB convention attracts a great deal of attention in religious, secular and

---

[41] Jimmy Swaggart, *The Evangelist* (March 1986): 35.

[42] Similarly, Swaggart called his magazine, *The Evangelist*, 'The most read publication in the world today by preachers.' The publication went on immodestly and dubiously to say that readers 'have learned more about the Bible and about God [by] reading *The Evangelist* than any other religious periodical.' Jimmy Swaggart, *The Evangelist* (February 1987): 25.

political fields. Where but at NRB, for example, is a person likely to see Jimmy Swaggart, Jerry Falwell, and Richard Roberts all on the same platform at the same time – along with 50 or so other significant media people? Campus Crusade for Christ President Bill Bright said NRB represents 'the most influential body of men and women in the Christian world.' One delegate said the whole atmosphere was somewhat like a circus. But that is only one side of the story of NRB. Jimmy Swaggart, America's most-watched TV evangelist, concluded the NRB gathering with a strong challenge to get out the gospel. 'This generation has been given technology no other generation has had, and it is for the express purpose of taking the gospel of Jesus Christ to the world. We have the solution, Jesus Christ,' he said in speaking of the world's problems. 'We must not waste time on foolishness or fables. Ministries must emphasize Jesus as Savior, Healer, Deliverer, and Baptizer with an awareness of the preciousness of airtime. We must not waste it,' he declared.[43]

Two years earlier, Swaggart told his 1987 NRB audience, his telecasts could be seen in 65 countries. 'Today it is on 3,000 TV stations in 143 countries, with a good possibility of it being seen in China soon.' Swaggart went on to claim that since the spiritual harvest would be primarily outside the United States, he had canceled most of his US crusades and was now spending more time in overseas evangelism.

While most evangelicals would contend for the proclamation of the gospel, insisting that the gospel by itself is timely, appropriate, and effective, the evangelist's arrogance in placing himself in apostolic succession and taking credit for what was only partially a result of his efforts was unpardonable. Within weeks of the NRB meeting the first of the two major scandals to burst on the evangelical world within a year erupted. On Thursday, 19 March 1987, news broadcasts reported that, 'Jim Bakker, popular religious TV talk show host, resigned and turned the reins of his $129-million-a-year PTL ministries over to Jerry Falwell.' For his part, Falwell recognized the severity of the crisis for televangelism. 'I am not naive enough to think that a ministry of the magnitude of PTL could go through a dilemma such as this without creating a backwash that would hurt every gospel ministry in America, if not the world,' Falwell said.[44] Formal investigation of the charges against Jim Bakker had begun the previous week. But for the Assemblies of God and J. Philip Hogan, the worst was yet to come.

One year later, several days prior to Jimmy Swaggart's 21 February 1988 public confession, J. Philip Hogan received the devastating news at home in his study: 'The national wire services will soon release the story

---

[43]   Swaggart recounted for his NRB audience a vision the Lord had given him of a cotton field, noting that the harvest is ready as never before in history and the worst storm ever is building on the horizon. 'God will delay the storm to give the church time to gather the harvest,' he said. God promised to unlock doors but told him, 'You must open them.' Quoted in the *Pentecostal Evangel* (1 July 1985).

[44]   Quoted in the *Los Angeles Times* (Saturday, 21 March 1987).

that Jimmy Swaggart had been implicated in immoral acts with a prostitute.' Stunned – and unwilling to accept the report on hearsay – Hogan, despite previous indications that not all was well in the Swaggart operation, found it difficult to face up to the overwhelming implications of Swaggart's sudden, precipitous fall. As an executive officer of the Assemblies of God, Hogan was soon informed of the details – sordid, painful, and involving other prominent figures in the Pentecostal movement – which exposed the Swaggart organization's moral and financial profligacy to the whole world. Although it was a matter for disciplinary action that came under well-established policies and rehabilitation procedures, supervised by Superintendent G. Raymond Carlson and Assistant Superintendent Everett Stenhouse, Hogan was present for the discussions that determined the evangelist's future with the denomination. Given the sensationalization of the scandal, however, his information – even the anonymous tips and informants who came forward with allegations – scarcely kept ahead of developments appearing daily in the media.

The necessary damage control of the disheartening situation was handled as best as possible, but clearly no one at the denominational headquarters could prevent the embarrassing fallout. Across the street, where a tent had been erected on a parking lot to accommodate the press, reporters and camera crews turned the usually serene, headquarters building into the backdrop for a distressingly profane information-feeding frenzy. Telephones rang incessantly in the third-floor executive offices. The reliable functioning of their organization had often made headquarters staff proud that they could run God's work with competence, but under the onslaught of the outside world they suddenly seemed woefully parochial. They struggled to handle the flood of callers, many of them ministers, whose relentlessly repetitive comments ranged from urging the Assemblies of God to 'Take every measure to separate us as quickly as possible from this mess,' to the question, 'Why have we abandoned one of our most effective evangelists to face this libel without our movement's wholehearted support?'

J. Philip Hogan faced his own public relations challenges, responding personally to the calls of scores of missionaries and national leaders of the worldwide Assemblies of God network. The DFM offices in the headquarters building, connected by satellite telephone services and facsimile machines to virtually all the world's capitals, was immediately inundated with questions, reports, and requests for authorizations. Many communications were merely 'say-it-isn't-so' pleas denying the reports carried by the broadcasting services and CNN. Some missionaries desperately hoped to avoid the bitter disappointment of nationals loyal to Swaggart, as well as the gleeful taunts of local critics happy to celebrate the evangelist's compromising conduct. Some calls came from missionaries whose identification with the Swaggart ministry had been so complete that they could foresee – beyond a suspension of funding – canceled crusades, ongoing television contracts, possible lawsuits, and unfinished

construction projects remaining for many years to mock future undertakings. Eventually the problem of titles and deeds would emerge with the
Swaggart managers' efforts to recover properties that had been deeded to
national churches.

As the implications for the DFM were discussed in the press, the
international reading public learned that Jimmy Swaggart's receipts in
1987 had risen to an annual level of $150 million, of which a reported
$12 million had been directed to DFM projects and appointed mission-
aries. Although Swaggart funds represented about 15 per cent of the total
DFM receipts for the year, the nature of the underwriting, much of it
one-time funding for capital programs like schools and churches, did not
make the Swaggart support indispensable.

The relationship between Jimmy Swaggart and the DFM required
explanation. As Hogan reported, the flow of funds had in fact been
disrupted a full month before the revelations of misconduct, causing a
near panic even before the humiliating account came to light. Jimmy
Swaggart, whose recognition as a successful evangelist had been established in the late 1970s, gradually had brought his virtually independent
ministry almost entirely within the operating framework of the DFM. J.
Philip Hogan explained to the press the specifics of what had generally
been considered a mutually beneficial relationship.

> In the late 1970s, Brother Swaggart began to make overtures [to the Division
> of Foreign Missions] about his desire to support some of our missionaries, as
> well as missions projects that had been established by DFM. We told him at
> that time we would be pleased to receive gifts for our missionaries and their
> missions projects, *as long as this did not in any way usurp our own goals, philosophies,*
> *or global strategies* [Hogan's emphasis]. Swaggart agreed, and that arrangement
> has been the basis for our continued relationship.

Swaggart had been especially generous with funds, handing out from
tens to hundreds of thousands of dollars for specific DFM projects and
individual missionary support. The DFM had in turn endorsed his
programs and allowed him to identify closely with ongoing ministries to
which his contribution was not always strategic and on occasion could
not be considered more than a token participation. As Hogan explained,
'Virtually all of the overseas projects that Jimmy Swaggart Ministries
[have] promoted are projects that are directed by the DFM.'

> The overseas crusades that were held by Jimmy Swaggart were conducted at
> our invitation, in cooperation with our fraternal national churches. Only
> Swaggart's overseas television broadcasts could be said to be totally his
> property. Yet even those programs were often arranged with the assistance of
> our missionaries and national leadership.[45]

---

[45]   The DFM insisted early on that the overseas ministry projects promoted by Jimmy
Swaggart Ministries were 'virtually all' operations of the DFM. *Mountain Movers* (August
1983): 12.

Hogan detailed areas of ministry that were affected by the loss of Swaggart's funds. These ministries included overseas relief efforts, such as feeding programs and disaster aid; building of churches and Bible schools; medical clinics and vans; literature outreach and training programs; the ministries of the Lillian Trasher Orphanage in Egypt and missionary Mark Buntain's work with children in India. Hogan said that the school programs – 'in place many years before the Jimmy Swaggart Ministries stepped in to help' – were in urgent need of assistance. Another area in need of immediate funding was transportation of supplies destined for famine-stricken areas of Africa.

Six months after the crisis, J. Philip Hogan announced that the DFM had survived the ordeal without having to abandon any of its programs, although several ministries to children lost contributions of $200,000 per month. Although Assemblies of God church members increased their giving measurably, total missions giving for 1988 was down by $1.4 million.[46] 'Despite a loss of revenue linked to Swaggart's dismissal as an Assemblies of God minister,' Hogan affirmed, 'the DFM expects to continue and to increase its ministry in the affected outreaches.'

What initially had been a fairly uncomplicated collaboration, one with overwhelming benefits for missionaries who needed funds to promote high-cost projects, had grown into overlapping jurisdictions and an increasingly tangled set of problems which demanded resolution long before Swaggart's hurried exit. While Assemblies of God missionaries clearly benefited from Jimmy Swaggart's funding, issues of policy, personnel controversies, priorities, and general philosophies caused strains. The Swaggart 'organization within an organization,' predictably, became unworkable, especially as Swaggart delegated critical areas of responsibility to staff members whose approaches and priorities were not acceptable to DFM leadership. Increasingly, Jimmy Swaggart had become less available to DFM leadership, contacts being left largely to staff members who screened his calls.

For Hogan and the DFM, growing dependency and dictates to the DFM over the priority of projects was only the first cause for concern. There was also the underlying fear that the eventual collapse of the Swaggart empire would gravely endanger various commitments made by the DFM around the world. Thus, prior to the cessation of Swaggart support, measures had been taken to find alternative funding for several of Swaggart's major programs. When, in fact, the ministry crashed and funds abruptly dried up, some arrangements, like that for Latin America ChildCare, were already in place to pick up the slack. Because pastors and members of the Assemblies of God rallied to support the endangered overseas operations, the transition was made with limited disruption to ongoing programs.

---

[46] JPH, monthly letter to DFM missionary personnel, May 1988.

For J. Philip Hogan the self-destruction of Jimmy Swaggart was a bitter, personal ordeal, even apart from the loss of a major source of funding and the loss of a missionary champion for the DFM. Hogan had strongly supported Swaggart's overseas ministry, which he considered by and large as a legitimate and effective evangelistic effort. The two men, if significantly different in many respects, were brought together by their mutual concern for the success of DFM projects. Each man was capable of enormous vision, and each had a great deal to gain from the growth and positive representation of the DFM. Principally Jimmy Swaggart saw the task of communicating the message – especially through the powerful, penetrating medium of television, with himself in the limelight – as having priority; J. Philip Hogan was concerned with national churches' taking root throughout the world on a broad, durable base. Hogan was not simply accepting Swaggart's financial, television, and crusade efforts pragmatically; he believed wholeheartedly in such enterprises – as long as they promoted the overseas church. Even if no concessions are made to the possibility that Swaggart and his associates were driven primarily by unrestrained ambition, Swaggart's interests in overseas evangelism apparently lay more in the unique opportunity that missionary work gave him to extend his ministry.

Hogan supported Swaggart so strongly that he was embarrassed not only by the evangelist's crisis, but for not having seen the impending fall. While the two men were not personally close friends, Hogan had visited Swaggart's offices on two occasions to help define working arrangements. In retrospect, Hogan admitted to having begun to sense that ambition and arrogance were appearing too frequently among Swaggart's associates, an indication other observers attributed to Swaggart's own example. Both knew, however, that the relationship in missionary work between them was made tenuous by their differing philosophies. Only the success of the cooperative ventures and the ability to reduce tensions at intervals had kept the Jimmy Swaggart Ministries and the DFM efforts coordinated. The intimation of total agreement between the DFM and Swaggart's overseas ministries, made frequently in Swaggart's publications, was misleading, as it only referred to the specific individuals who had benefited from Swaggart's support. Some other missionaries and national leaders had severely criticized the Swaggart team's policies. The Italian Assemblie di Dio, refused to work with his program.

Eventually, Swaggart's hubris had to be confronted. While Jimmy Swaggart may have assumed that he was assisting the DFM program, essentially he did not understand the limits of his own efforts nor what nurturing the overseas church was about. A joke that circulated even before Swaggart's downfall illustrates the differences in perspective and the self-centeredness that prevented the evangelist from seeing God's hand at work. One version of the story, repeated endlessly in countries where Swaggart used interpreters, was about a Latin American pastor of a rural church who was asked what he thought about the Swaggart crusade taking place in a large sports stadium in the capital. The humble servant of God was obviously impressed. The huge crowds and the bright lights and the great response of the people to the gospel were exciting, almost beyond belief. 'The only thing that bothers me,' the pastor added, 'was that every time the speaker gets started, that *gringo* interrupts him to say something unintelligible in English!'

Viewing the task only from his own perspective – and forgetting, apparently, that his work relied on an already existing infrastructure of national churches, on dedicated national workers, on the goodwill already generated in the community, and an effective follow-up – Jimmy Swaggart, and many of his supporters, did not understand that ultimately overseas evangelism relied little, if at all, on a given evangelist's charisma. Without the Spirit's preparation of hearts for the sowing of the seed, all evangelistic efforts are in vain. God may use a Jimmy Swaggart and many others to achieve his purposes, but he really does not need any one in particular.[47]

Whether Jimmy Swaggart was using missions to enlarge his own empire, as some critics have contended, is beside the point. Jimmy Swaggart, however much he contributed to the proclamation of the gospel at a given time and place, came and went while the work of the Lord continued without him. The power of Pentecost is hardly in the possession of a given ministry or in any association of churches, including the Assemblies of God; it lies in the empowering of millions of humble believers, who recognize their own need to share their hope and strength with their world – a truth that the DFM's recognition of autonomous national churches took into account.

Shortly after the Swaggart debacle, Edith Blumhofer took the evangelist to task for asserting that the Pentecostal evangelistic effort would falter if he did not continue his ministry:

> Equally disturbing is the Swaggart organization's explicit statement that a variety of missionary projects would be jeopardized unless the JSM continues. In fact, ChildCare International, through which Swaggart channeled substantial funds to help feed hundreds of thousands of children around the world, is not a Swaggart program at all. It was established by the Assemblies of God long before Jimmy Swaggart rose to prominence. Those who want to continue to support that and other special projects (like building Bible institutes, schools and hospitals) can do so by contributing directly to the Assemblies of God. Designated funds will support precisely the same projects. Jimmy Swaggart served as a skilled publicist who enhanced the visibility, and

---

[47] Poloma, *Assemblies of God at the Crossroads*, 181. For sociologist Poloma, the real issue was that Swaggart was simply too powerful for the Assemblies of God executives to control. At a time when his telecast reportedly was reaching some two million households, leaders in the Assemblies lacked a forum of their own to challenge his power. Assemblies of God leaders were apparently unwilling or unable to silence him until he was brought down by his own failures.

thus the resources, of such programs, but they will go forward without him. The denomination plans to continue its recent practice of devoting more than 70 per cent of its total expenditures to world ministries. Some 1,500 Assemblies of God missionaries supervise these programs around the world; none of these is likely to be recalled if Swaggart no longer raises funds. The magnitude of Swaggart's giving has obscured the steady growth of grassroots-sponsored Assemblies of God missions.[48]

For J. Philip Hogan, the respect that he felt for Jimmy Swaggart as an effective evangelist and the common interest the two men had in missionary work made the ministry's collapse traumatic. Frankly identifying it as the 'worst disappointment of my ministerial career,' Hogan afterward was unable to recall any clue to the evangelist's personal problems that might have interrupted their collaboration. Nevertheless, on reflection, the strong statements Swaggart made about the exclusive importance of his ministry troubled Hogan. 'When I heard Jimmy Swaggart say, in effect, that if he did not reach the world, the world would not be reached, I knew something was terribly wrong.' Nevertheless he admits, 'I did not see the problem coming and, despite administrative friction at times, I tried to maintain a continuing, fruitful relationship with Jimmy Swaggart.' 'Ultimately,' Hogan reiterated, 'world evangelism belongs to the Lord of the harvest who oversees, directs and empowers the workers who are engaged in bringing about His purposes.'[49]

---

[48] Edith Blumhofer, 'Swaggart and the Pentecostal Ethos,' *Christian Century* (6 April 1988): 333–335.

[49] In addition, Phil Hogan was forced by the time of the elimination of Swaggart's funds to distinguish between what he himself believed to be true about missions and what had been forced upon him for the sake of cooperation. This latter included taking a hard look at what procedures would be used in qualifying missionary candidates, specifically whether psychological tests or professional psychologists whose approaches did not fit with Swaggart's criteria would be part of the DFM screening of candidates. While other conservative voices were also strident on this issue, considering secular psychology to be 'humanistic' and unspiritual, the fact remained that the practices previously adopted were for a time suspended during Swaggart's ascendancy. After Swaggart's fall, Phil Hogan and other former associates tried to communicate with the evangelist with little success. After February 1988, Phil Hogan never spoke with Jimmy Swaggart.

[11]

The Formation of a Fellowship

During the Congress I saw men whom I have known, loved, and worked with for more than thirty years and who now lead great movements, some rivaling or superseding the US Assemblies of God in numerical strength.

J. Philip Hogan[1]

The Seoul meeting of the World Assemblies of God Fellowship (WAGF)

Monday, 29 October 1994, dawned on a miracle. A well-publicized prayer rally, with an anticipated attendance of one million Koreans and guests, was scheduled to be held out of doors on the expansive military parade grounds on the banks of the Han River, central Seoul, Korea.

The threatening clouds and forecasts for dismal weather only slightly dampened the mood of the guests – delegates, who days before had gathered for the first congress of the World Assemblies of God Fellowship. Rain or sunshine, the occasion was a monumental, unique, representative display of the diversity and extension of the Pentecostal movement. Having the attention of Assemblies of God adherents all over the world focused on this single location made the occasion also undeniably 'Pentecostal' – 'They were all together in one place' waiting for the 'sound like the blowing of a violent wind' from heaven. The 'house where they were sitting' on this occasion would have as its roof the open, beclouded firmament, and it was 10,000 miles and culturally half a world away from the Midwestern town of Springfield, Missouri, where the building at 1445 Boonville Avenue bore an inconspicuous sign that presumptuously identified it as the 'International Headquarters of the Assemblies of God.'

The crowd in Seoul gathered well before the appointed hour. Each delegation was shuttled with smooth precision to the areas previously designated for them. A half-hour before the announced starting time, with all of the delegations in place and the approaching rain clouds visibly drenching adjacent sectors of the city, Pastor Yonggi Cho indicated that the service would begin.

---

[1] JPH, 'It's A Dream Come True,' *World Link* (January 1995): 12, 13.

A 2,000-voice Korean choir and orchestra led the several hundred thousand worshippers to unite in words of praise in the languages of many nations – including Swahili, Urdu, Arabic, Portuguese, Ukrainian, Bengali, Mandarin, Fijian, Japanese, Thai, Zulu, German – the families of humankind rendering homage in, for the most part, the mutually unintelligible but perfectly understood language of devotion. The moment was transcendent; the worshipers' feeble efforts to express their sentiments were amplified as their resonating voices carried on the storm currents swirling above them.

For an instant time stopped as a surge of emotion overwhelmed the many men and women in attendance who could appreciate what had been required for such a gathering to take place. The libation of praise swelling about them could not be expressed in a liturgy, no matter how beautiful. Their feelings were too profound, too intense, too exalted to be contained in human language. An unexpressed sense of elation from deep in their soul gave way to the dawning realization that the decades of vision, sacrifice, tenacious faith, and unrelenting commitment of national pastors, missionaries, and faithful laypeople had not been in vain. God had responded to their pleas for an outpouring of spiritual fervor, a penitent melting of hearts, and a yielding to their presentation of the good news.

The Pentecostal pioneers who had sown the seed, the men and women who had labored for this gathering, had long since passed from the scene. But their efforts had not been in vain. Their confidence that God was leading them was vindicated in the extensive vision and effectiveness of the groups that they had brought into being. Each delegate present was a flesh-and-blood human being with complicated personal fears, aspirations, needs and desires to be needed. Each delegate represented a personal history, each one had a story, a 'testimony,' to tell. Each of the celebrants felt the same gratitude for the light of the gospel that they had received. Each one acknowledged a sense of divine acceptance as a gift of grace which, in turn, demanded a response of praise and an act of renewed dedication. The worshipers felt the freedom of the Spirit that enabled them to soar above the restrictions of human limitation in which they had once been imprisoned. Each one felt with renewed conviction that the task of conveying the glorious gospel of Christ, the promise of redemptive, transformed life, was the most important commission they or anyone could receive.

On the dais, J. Philip Hogan stood enraptured by sights and sounds he had long hoped to witness, seeing not only his work, but also the vision of generations of missionaries focused on the purpose for which these delegations had gathered. 'I am a fairly well-contained person, having seen enough victories and experienced enough defeats in forty years of missionary ministry to be calm in most circumstances. However on this occasion, I almost lost my composure,' Hogan admitted in what seemed to be a gross understatement. 'During the Congress I saw men whom I have known, loved, and worked with for more than thirty years and who now lead great movements, some rivaling or superseding the US Assemblies of God in numerical strength.'

> Men were there whom I [had] ordained, married, whose children I baptized, preached to, spent long days traveling with, sometimes in danger and often in less-than-comfortable circumstances. Men attended the Congress who had spent years in prison for their testimony. Men were there whose families and congregations have suffered starvation. Nations were represented where mighty, sovereign, Holy Ghost revival has broken out, undesigned by human planning. Attending were pastors of great churches in the world's cities – churches built as a result of Assemblies of God labor and resources. The Assemblies of God is now a worldwide entity. It is growing faster, penetrating deeper, and maturing more than ever in our eighty-year history. With God's continued blessing, we have become a major force in church planting and evangelism in Christendom.[2]

The prayers that followed were offered for the suffering and oppressed peoples of all nations – the men and women, the congregations, the national churches that met for worship in a climate of deprivation, hostility, and fear. Stepping to the microphone, Loren Triplett, the Executive Director of the US Division of Foreign Missions, called attention to the several millions of Pentecostals, on every continent, across the world's time zones, that would participate in the event through advanced telecommunications.

> We are in the throne room of God with peoples from many lands. This is perhaps the greatest prayer meeting in the history of the Christian Church, and the greatest prayer is 'Thy Kingdom come, Thy will be done on earth.' We pray for the coming of our Lord, and we pray for the saving grace of God for countries where the story of Jesus has never been told. Today we pray, tomorrow we must give feet to our prayers. A million voices must be His witnesses into all the world. We make our vows today to work faithfully in God's kingdom until Christ returns, so help us God![3]

While the rainstorm passed over Seoul, the Plaza received only a few sprinkles. 'The clouds looked like a giant doughnut encircling the plaza, with the hole right overhead,' a guest observed.[4] Although the participants expected showers at any minute, the rain came only after the meeting was over.

A global Fellowship

The miracle of that Monday was not the behavior of the weather, but the emergence of the grass-roots, worldwide Pentecostal movement, of

2   Ibid.
3   Loren Triplett, quoted in 'A Historic Gathering,' *World Link* (January 1995): 15.
4   George O. Wood, General Secretary of the Assemblies of God, quoted in ibid.

which the gathering was merely a token group. The initial convocation, held in the Yoido Central Church on the previous Thursday evening, for many participants who had come from long distances was hardly less moving. That first plenary session of the recently formed World Assemblies of God Fellowship began with a parade of flags, many of them carried by national Assemblies of God superintendents. The names of each country, announced as they entered, demonstrated the denomination's global coverage. Beginning with Albania, where a thriving Pentecostal church has emerged despite, until recently, the ban on religious proselytism, the standards of the nations entered the church until the appearance of the final representative from the flourishing, thirty-year-old church in Zimbabwe.

Attendance was a triumph for many of the delegates; some had never before left their homelands. One of the most recent churches to open, the Hope Assembly in Ulan Bator, Mongolia, was represented by two deacons. Proudly carrying the flag of Vietnam was Paul Ai, the national superintendent, who had spent almost ten years in prison for the sake of his ministry in that country. The flag of Iran was carried by Edward Hovsepian Mehr, brother of Haik Hovsepian, the former superintendent who had also spent time in prison and been murdered a few months previously, his body dumped in a park just days after his release. Among the other national Assemblies of God church leaders were representatives from Buddhist Nepal, where the Pentecostal work continues despite persistent and deep distress, and from Communist Cuba, the flag carried by Humberto Rodríguez Sabó, the national superintendent whose church is experiencing an intense spiritual movement.[5]

Once assembled, the representatives were formally welcomed by Pastor Yonggi Cho, who told them, 'You are not [here as strangers] in a foreign land; [because] you are my brothers and sisters. You have come to your brother's home. I'd like to hold your hands [as we] march together until we reach our heavenly home, having victoriously done all that God has entrusted to us.'[6]

The main speaker of that initial meeting was J. Philip Hogan, founding chairman of WAGF, whose vision was in large measure responsible for the gathering. He spoke about the conception and planning that had given rise to the event. 'In the spring of 1987, the leadership of the Division of Foreign Missions was in a prayer retreat,' he began.

> On the second day, a spirit of intercession moved among us. We found ourselves burdened in seasons of prayer, interspersed with times when the gifts of the Spirit were manifest. At the close of the period, we began to say to ourselves, 'We are part of a worldwide fraternal fellowship. We are in no position to command anybody to do anything, but at least we are hopefully a respected member of a great world fellowship called the Assemblies of God.'

---

5 Ibid., 4.
6 Ibid., 14.

We decided that we would step out in faith and invite leaders from more than 100 countries in the world to join us in the coming spring, that of 1988, in Springfield, Missouri, to talk about stepped-up activities and programs for world evangelism. For promotional purposes we discussed the name we should give this new venture, and we settled on the term Decade of Harvest. We wanted to have a time aspect in it, and we wanted it to have the thought of evangelism. One of the great benedictions of my administrative career was the fact that there was almost unanimous response immediately from more than one hundred leaders around the world, and among them an amazing amount of them said, 'Brother Hogan, this is what God has been talking to us about.' In 1988 about one hundred delegates came, and that meeting resulted in the formation of the World Assemblies of God Fellowship. In that initial meeting we discussed the idea of a mid-decade meeting, should our Lord tarry, to ascertain whether the Decade of Harvest was a vine of God's own planting, and to see what God had done with and through us. Today we are here, the largest single gathering in the history of the Assemblies of God, and quite likely the largest gathering of Pentecostal believers the world has ever known.[7]

Hogan effusively recounted how just a few months after the initial planning meetings the reports of revivals in national countries had begun to stream in.

I wish all of the plenary members could have been present with us [in the early meetings], chiefly to hear the reports. We had to keep reminding ourselves that only a few months previously, we had met for the first time and signed a covenant committing ourselves to a mighty effort to complete the task of evangelism and to make possible the return of our blessed Lord by the end of the decade, this century, and the millennium. The reports were staggering when you consider that less than two years previously we had met together with nothing more than a burden and a dream.[8]

Pentecostal solidarity

Reports of the extension of the Pentecostal movement were given in the sessions that followed. None of the other reported revivals, however, compared with that of China, where there are now estimated to be as many as 65 million Christian believers, though at the time of the expulsion of missionaries in 1949 Chinese believers numbered at best several millions.[9] The fraternal worldwide fellowship of the Assemblies of God is by far the largest Protestant constituency with an estimated 30 million adherents.[10]

---

[7] Ibid.
[8] Ibid.
[9] An estimate of one million believers is given by Hudson Taylor III in the foreword to Adeney, *The Church's Long March*, 9.
[10] While this figure has been cited often, J. Philip Hogan used the estimate of from 22 to 24 millions in 1988; JPH, Editorial, *Mountain Movers* (December 1988): 3.

At a later indoor gathering, Peter Kuzmic, Director of the Evangelical Theological Seminary in Osijek, Croatia, whose people had long known political and ideological turmoil, referred to the precariousness of all human existence and the reassurance that comes from experiencing God's provision. 'The church never panics,' Kuzmic told his listeners, 'even under adverse circumstances, even when there is persecution. The church that knows the presence and the power of the Lord understands that He will have the final word. He is the Alpha and Omega, the first and the last One.' Referring to the collapse of Soviet Communism, Kuzmic saw in that event a matter of God's timing. 'The final word in history will not come from Moscow, Beijing, New York, the United Nations or Washington, D.C. The final word belongs to our Lord, the risen Lord, the returning King of Kings. So He says, "It's already November 1989? And the Assemblies of God has announced the Decade of Harvest?" So He starts moving a little faster with the left hand, changes history, and brings down the enemy so that we can have a great harvest.'[11]

The following day the Congress met at Prayer Mountain, the prayer retreat of the Yoido Central Church, interceding for worldwide revival. An inspired 50-voice choir from the Marshall Islands sang, their worship flowing to an island rhythm. A Friday night prayer meeting and Saturday's two plenary sessions preceded the climax of Monday's outdoor prayer rally.

Although the Seoul gathering was not deliberative, the capacity of such a broadly representative group to make a forceful statement led to the formation of a World Assemblies of God Relief Agency (WAGRA). The goal was stated by Dr Prince Guneratnam, General Superintendent of the Assemblies of God in Malaysia and WAGRA International Co-Chairman. 'The World Assemblies of God is a caring, loving and supportive fellowship,' he explained. 'Whether the need is for finance or time, the worldwide Assemblies of God will rally together, not only to preach the gospel but to meet human needs. Jesus preached the gospel, but He also fed the multitudes. He is our example.'[12] A total of $2 million was pledged to endow the fledgling enterprise. 'When tragedy strikes, as it often does these days,' the WAGRA news letter pointed out, 'we can rush to the aid of our suffering brethren. When a movement is 30 million strong, to do otherwise is to neglect a basic biblical premise.'[13]

In another display of solidarity, a group of 5,000 Pentecostals carried petitions to a number of embassies, consulates, and legations in Seoul to protest against the recent assassination of several Iranian Assemblies of God leaders. 'There is power in unity,' said a spokesperson. 'When an Assemblies of God superintendent from a Muslim country was cruelly martyred recently along with some of his coworkers, Assemblies of God believers mounted an outcry against the offending government.'[14]

---

[11] Peter Kuzmic, 'God Has Changed History,' *Mountain Movers* (September 1994): 20.
[12] *World Link* (January 1995): 15.
[13] Ibid.
[14] JPH, 'It's A Dream Come True:' 13.

'An outgrowth of the Congress was a heightened sense of unity of purpose among the ninety-four general superintendents attending,' the leadership of the gathering noted. 'Some [national leaders] had never had the opportunity to fellowship with leaders from other countries. The prayer times were very powerful, creating a bond of love between nations.' The Superintendent of the Assemblies of God of Samoa, Max Haleck, Jr., captured the sentiments of many of the delegates when he said that these meetings were a 'beautiful confirmation of the unity with other believers that his church was already feeling.'[15]

Prior to the first plenary meeting of the WAGF in Seoul, the affairs of the new organization had been attended to by a committee of representative national leaders. At a meeting in Oslo, Norway, in 1991 David Yonggi Cho was elected to succeed J. Phil Hogan as chairman, while Hogan remained on the 14-member executive committee as elected honorary chairman. At the time of writing 60 national churches are participating in the loosely structured organization, which claims no authority over member national churches. Cooperation and coordination in missions and evangelism are the exclusive concerns of the WAGF. 'Neither the world nor the church needs another high level religious organization,' insisted Hogan. 'Let our gathering be moments for renewal, which, in another way, is simply saying, "God, send us revival." '[16]

Emergent national leadership

The Seoul meeting brought together for the first time a number of national Pentecostal leaders. The WAGF executive committee included the leader of the world's largest Pentecostal group, José Wellington of Brazil, as well as Sri Lanka pioneer Colton Wickramaratne, Jeremiah Motsatse of South Africa and Andrew Evans of Australia. But less-well-known leaders predominated. Charles Osueke, for example, General Superintendent of the Nigerian Assemblies of God, served for a number of years as a national evangelist before election to his executive position. Trained initially at a Nigerian Assemblies of God Bible school, he received additional academic training in the United States at Central Bible Institute and the Assemblies of God Theological Seminary – both in Springfield, Missouri. These experiences whetted his appetite and vision for evangelism, church-planting, and missions. In his national leadership position he insisted that all aspiring pastors attend one of the nine regional schools operating in his country. Beyond formal preparation, this prerequisite provides pastors-to-be with the character-building influence of mature leaders and the support of colleagues with similar vision. The one-million-strong national movement Osueke represents has undertaken an

---

[15] Max Haleck, Jr., *Pentecostal Evangel* (26 June 1988).

[16] JPH, 'Though Thy Beginning Was Small,' *Decade of Harvest World Report* (June 1992): 1.

aggressive effort to reach into new fields, focusing on the establishment of new churches among the Kogi people. Between 1960 and 1993 the group initiated 1,537 new churches, an added 400,000 new members, almost doubling the size of the Nigerian Assemblies of God.

African leader Lazarus Chakwera, Superintendent of the Assemblies of God in Malawi, is in his early forties, like many of the representatives at Seoul. Raised as a Presbyterian, he became identified with the Assemblies of God after being filled with the Holy Spirit during his university days. Before his election to executive office in 1989 he served as a pastor, then as a teacher in Malawi's only Assemblies of God Bible institute. 'Lazarus Chakwera is an insightful and congenial leader who moves forward with a clarity of vision towards the goals the church has set,' a friend has observed. 'He is recognized as an influential, transorganizational leader among the other executive Assemblies of God leaders in East Africa.' Chakwera received his formal training at the University of Malawi and then continued studies at the Assemblies of God Bible school. In 1995, with 900 congregations, the Malawi Assemblies of God has set for itself the goal of placing a church in every one of the country's 1,800 towns and villages.[17]

Jean Pawntaore Ouedragaogo represented the church of Burkina Faso at Seoul. As the son of a pioneer pastor, Pawntaore Ouedragaogo learned church planting from the example of his father, who is still actively starting new congregations. The French-speaking leader attended the Assemblies of God Bible school in Ouagadougou and pursued studies in Bible at the International Bible Training Institute in England. Later he went to the United States for study at the Assemblies of God Theological Seminary.

The growth of the Assemblies of God in Burkina Faso, long a vigorous, healthy movement, is impressive. In a country of 8 million people, Assemblies of God membership has grown from 75,000 to 200,000 during a period of six years. The movement's churches and Bible schools are full to capacity. Seventeen Burkinan missionaries were reported to be ministering in eight countries. 'We now have 200 students enrolled in four Bible schools,' reported Pawntaore. 'Some of our most promising students are studying in Europe and America. These are our future leaders, teachers, and missionaries.'

Manuel Lazaro, Superintendent of the Assemblies of God of Tanzania, East Africa, reported in 1990 that a ten-day Bible conference and training seminar in the capital city of Mbeya drew some of the largest crowds ever for any religious event in Tanzania, more than 30,000 people. Church leaders thereafter started a survey of the 120 tribal groups living in the country, most of whom are unevangelized. According to Lazaro, often the best way to reach a given tribal group is to assist a young person to return to evangelize among his or her own people.[18]

---

[17] Don Corbin, letter to author, 16 February 1995.

[18] Immanuel Lazaro, 'Executive Reports: Tanzania,' *Decade of Harvest World Report* (May 1990): 3.

African leaders such as Jeremiah Motsatse from South Africa and Fernando Panzo from Angola, in reporting on the continuing growth of their respective national churches, emphasized the importance of training programs to equip emerging pastors and other leaders. According to Panzo the Assemblies of God of Angola, with 75 churches, operated the Instituto Biblico de Angola, a three-year residential program focusing on preparing leaders for the growing church in Luanda and other cities.[19] The East Africa School of Theology, where several missionaries assist the national staff in training national leaders, regularly receives requests from Ethiopia to train men and women among the 300,000 'indigenous' (nonaffiliated) Pentecostals. 'Remarkably open doors like this abound throughout Africa,' spokespersons reported.[20]

Reports from Asia

Patrick Lau, the Superintendent of the Singapore Assemblies of God, looked on the Seoul meeting with appreciation for the opportunity it gave his delegation to meet other Pentecostals.

> I thought it was significant because this would be the first time that we would gather as Assemblies of God world leaders. This would afford the Assemblies of God leadership a time when we could sit down together and plan ways to reach the world for Jesus Christ. I was very encouraged after the meeting. It was wonderful to hear news firsthand about what God is doing all over the world. I was especially encouraged by the news from areas such as the Eastern Bloc nations and Africa – areas about which I seldom hear anything. As I left the Decade of Harvest meeting I thought it is wonderful to know that God is not only moving in our own nation, but around the world. I am also happy to know there are many people who are concerned about reaching the people of this world for Jesus Christ. If we work together, we will create a great impact. This meeting truly helped us to see the world vision.

About the church in his own country, he pointed out that Singapore had 32 churches with 18,000 members. 'In Singapore God seems to be touching professional people,' he observed.[21]

Prince Guneratnam, General Superintendent of the Malaysian Assemblies of God and pastor of the country's largest Assemblies of God church, with 3,500 members, pointed out the restraints imposed on work in that Muslim country.

> We have always been very restricted by the government here in regards to conducting any kind of open evangelistic meetings. However, recently we

---

[19]   Fernando Panzo, 'Executive Reports: Angola,' *Decade of Harvest World Report* (November 1991): 4.

[20]   'Kenya, East Africa,' *Decade of Harvest World Report* (December 1992): 9.

[21]   Patrick Lau, 'Singapore Sets Goals,' *Decade of Harvest Update* (January 1989): 1.

invited a European evangelist to conduct meetings. When we applied for his visa and permission to use the government stadium, to the surprise of all of us, we had very little opposition. Seemingly, there has been a change of attitude [on the part of the authorities]. We conducted the evangelistic meetings for six nights. The newspapers carried the story. The last few nights the crowd numbered nearly 140,000 – the largest crowds we have ever known in such a meeting. The meetings emphasized salvation, healing and miracles. Each night a strong appeal was given for salvation. We prayed for the sick in every service in a mass type of prayer. People were healed and came up afterwards and told what God had done for them. One night the baptism of the Holy Spirit was stressed and many nominal Christians, including leading Anglicans, were seen praying for the Pentecostal experience. We are really thanking the Lord for the change of attitude and the possibility before us of being able to conduct more public meetings in Malaysia.[22]

Eli Javier, the General Superintendent of the Assemblies of God in the Philippines, on the other hand, commented on the religious freedom his church enjoyed. With 1,432 congregations the Filipino church has encountered no pressures from political leaders. 'God is raising up strong lay people as shepherds who work closely with the pastors. There is also a strong partnership with the missionaries – especially those from the United States, Australia, and Singapore. Last year 210 churches were planted, more than we had expected.' In a multicultural society, with nine major languages and 85 dialects, a variety of approaches to church planting have been taken, he pointed out. The church has achieved a great deal through radio. 'Some segments of our society cannot be reached by the Filipinos, but respond readily to foreign missionaries.'[23]

The leaders from the Chinese congregation in Manila pointed out that a feature of the Pentecostal movement there is its vision for reaching overseas Chinese throughout southern Asia. Begun in the 1950s, the church has had a succession of pastors, some of them missionaries, who encouraged the congregation to direct its resources not to its own needs, but to the expatriate Chinese community. The church of 300 members (80 per cent Chinese) in the late 1980s had 14 home cells and had purchased property to enlarge its own facilities. In addition to supporting workers among the Chinese elsewhere in the Philippines, the church also supported 16 full-time missionaries in China, and another 40 Chinese workers had been supported for shorter periods of time in various parts of Asia. More than 80 per cent of the congregation's budget of $5,000 per month is invested in missionary work. Two Chinese workers have been studying Tibetan; others have maintained contact with Christians in Tibet.

---

[22] Prince Guneratnam, 'Executive Committee Reports: Malaysia,' *Decade of Harvest World Report* (May 1990): 2, 3.

[23] Eli Javier, 'Interviews with Church Leaders,' *Pentecostal Evangel* (1 October 1989): 1; see also 'Asia Project 2000,' *Decade of Harvest World Report* (June 1992): 4 ,5.

Kawa Waga, Superintendent of the church of Fiji, reported that the intensive effort of the Decade of Harvest since 1989 has already produced 25 new churches, a growth in membership from 16,348 in 1986 to 33,000 in 1992. 'Never before have we heard so many national leaders, parliamentarians, church leaders, government institutions, community leaders, chiefs, and people crying out to God to bless and lead our nation. The Assemblies of God, with local churches all over the nation, has played a role in this spiritual impact on government, business and our communities, and institutions. In addition, we are presenting the gospel in Fiji through the media. We now have four weekly, half-hour programs on a station that broadcasts all over the country to reach our nation of 770,000 Fijians.'[24]

Other national leaders of notable effectiveness have emerged in Asia, including Roslim Suwandoko, General Superintendent for Indonesia and the pastor of the largest Assemblies of God church in the world's largest Muslim nation. In Japan Dr Akiei Ito, Pastor of the Shinohara Assemblies of God church in Yokohama, has been the General Superintendent of the Assemblies of God for 12 years. In Vietnam the Assemblies of God under the leadership of Tran Ai grew from 22 to 125 churches since the end of the Vietnam conflict.[25]

A *Time* magazine article that reported on the Pentecostals in Korea noted that 'Asian Pentecostalism has prospered most spectacularly in the aftermath of turmoil.' But looking beyond 'crisis evangelism,' the journalists found other reasons for this growth, including charisms of healing and glossolalia, the converts' feeling of immediate spiritual equality, and the 'tendency of missionaries in the classical Pentecostal denominations to turn over leadership to local followers sooner than other missionaries have done.'[26]

Reports from Latin America

In Guyana, the national Decade of Harvest committee held a conference on evangelism for all ministers and church leaders in the capital city of Georgetown. After a week set apart for concerted prayer in January 1990, a three-month, nationwide evangelistic campaign featuring a number of evangelists was conducted from April through to June. A 15-minute radio program was broadcast daily. 'In response to the broadcast,' reported Superintendent Errol Bhola, 'the government of Guyana (which previously had stated that they wanted no religious broadcasts in this country) called my home and asked if I would be interested in doing one and one-half hours of radio broadcasts locally each week.'[27]

---

[24] Pita Cioli, 'Executive Reports: Fiji,' *Decade of Harvest World Report* (December 1992): 2.
[25] Robert Houlihan, letter to author, 16 February 1995.
[26] 'The Spirit in Asia,' *Time* (8 October 1973): 102.
[27] Errol Bhola, 'Executive Reports: Guyana,' *Decade of Harvest World Report* (May 1991): 2.

Other notable Latin American leaders include Rodolfo Sáenz, the President of the Council of Assemblies of God national executives (CELAD); leaders of the Assembleias de Deus of Brazil, the world's largest Pentecostal movement; and, in a strategic situation, Humberto Martínez Sabó, the Superintendent of the Assemblies of God work in Cuba. With 600 students preparing for ministry in Cuba, Superintendent Sabó was enthusiastic about the future of his work. 'I believe that Cuba is at the point of a great revival. Thousands are flocking to Assemblies of God churches, drawn by miracles of healing and salvation. Even many communists are coming to Christ.' According to Sabó, Cuban authorities closed about a third of the churches after the revolution. Christians are not permitted to build new church buildings, but the Assemblies of God is buying houses and using them for churches. He added that the Assemblies of God has 320 churches in Cuba, more than 15,000 believers, and many young people are being trained for ministry through correspondence courses.[28]

In Argentina mass meetings conducted by Argentine Pentecostal pastors themselves have made that country a leader in the current global revival. Pastor Claudio Freidzon, who ministers frequently outside his own country, has led a crowd of 65,000 in Pentecostal worship in the same Vélez Sarsfield stadium where, as a boy, he dreamed of someday playing professional soccer. In his recent book Freidzon tells how after his calling and preparation for ministry he remained for 7 years as a pastor without a flock – no one would attend his meetings, not even when they were conducted in the open air in parks. But in the wake of the Falklands War and along with the stirring ministry of Carlos Anacondia, Ed Silvoso, and other evangelists, a spontaneous spiritual awakening has affected large sectors of the Argentine society. Not only was the revival found in the urban churches, with multiple services and testimonies of extraordinary ministry, but also in the impulse to evangelize, pastors and evangelists have gone to the outlying provinces, and nearly a hundred missionaries have gone overseas to Africa, Europe, and Muslim nations.[29]

Reports from Eastern Europe

Jozef Brenkus, President of the Apostolic Church in Kosice, Slovakia, reported at the Seoul meeting that it was reassuring to be part of such a large group of worshipers. Expressing confidence in the future of the ministry in his country, Brenkus thanked his fellow ministers throughout the fellowship for their concern and assistance to the countries of Eastern Europe. The prospects had not always been so encouraging. But by the end of 1994 the church in Slovakia had increased to 17 congregations,

28   Humberto Martínez Sabó, 'Executive Reports: Cuba,' *World Report* (May 1991): 8.
29   'Pastor Finds the Path to Success Is Full of Failures,' *Joy* (Great Britain) (July 1996): 17–20.

from 6 in 1990. Five churches had local Bible schools, and a Pentecostal Bible Academy and Theological Mission Seminary had been developed. The church also had a department of missions, which sent short-term teams to Albania, Macedonia, and Ukraine.

In 1990 Peter Kuzmic reported on the general state of the Pentecostal churches of Eastern Europe, indicating that the Pentecostals in the Central Independent States (CIS) were forming their own union, separate from the other evangelicals with whom they had formerly been associated. Reportedly there are from 140,000 to 160,000 Pentecostals in the recognized churches of the United Evangelical Church, about 70 per cent of the total evangelical Christian community. This association at the time operated two Bible schools.[30]

Pentecostal regional associations

The formation of an ongoing association of sovereign national Assemblies of God churches is not a recent notion. A resolution was approved at the US General Council in 1957 to determine the advisability of developing an international Fellowship of the Assemblies of God. Similarly, in each of the Assemblies of God fields, roughly corresponding to the continents, the national organizations of the Fellowship have formed regional associations to coordinate their efforts. While only loosely linked, the growing significance of these fellowships appears to reflect the similarity in purposes and concerns of their member organizations.[31] Beginning with an initial meeting in Nicaragua in 1959, the Central American churches called together national delegations from each of the national churches to outline a pattern for future meetings. This resulted in a national leaders institute where common problems could be discussed. The notion of an international organization was dismissed in favor of an association intended for fellowship and consultation. The upshot in Latin America of these efforts was the formation of two regional associations: the Assemblies of God Council for South America (Consejo de las Asambleas de Dios de Sur America – CADSA) to serve the southern countries of the continent (Argentina, Chile, Uruguay, Paraguay, Bolivia, and Peru); and the Executive Council of the Assemblies of God for Latin America (Consejo Ejecutivo Latinoamericano de las Asambleas de Dios – CELAD) to serve the 14 northern republics and Puerto Rico (from Ecuador north).

A similar plan for the Far East was launched at a meeting convened in Hong Kong, 1–6 July 1978. The result was the formation of the Assemblies of God Asian Mission Association (AGAMA), a confederation of ten national churches with a concern for developing leadership, uniting in educational efforts that are beyond the resources of individual countries,

---

[30]   Peter Kuzmic, 'Pray, Plan, Strategize, and Move Ahead Boldly,' *Decade of Harvest World Report* (May 1991): 5.

[31]   Bob Houlihan to author, February 1997.

and encouraging churches to send and support missionaries around the world.[32]

Similar associations are found regionally among the African Assemblies of God and, most recently, in Eastern Europe. The representatives of various national Pentecostal movements at a meeting in Bratislava, Czechoslovakia, in October 1990, issued a 'Declaration of East European Pentecostal Leaders' regarding their relationship, their situation, and their aspirations. Among the representatives were Michal Hyudzik (Poland), Committee Chairman, Roman Bilas (Russia [CIS]), Jozef Brenkus (Slovakia), Rudolf Bubik (Bohemia), Attila Fabian (Hungary), Peter Kuzmic (Yugoslavia), and Viktor Vircev (Bulgaria).[33]

Given the limits of missionary influence, the importance of the Seoul meeting for the national executives was that many of these leaders for the first time participated in an association larger than their own regional meetings. No longer dealing with each other through the mediation of the US-based DFM, pastors and elected executive officers could and did develop multilateral relationships with their counterparts from other countries. For many national leaders, for the first time, the Assemblies of God became not merely the name of the mission from which they had received foreign personnel and assistance, but the name of an international association of like-minded national Pentecostal leaders, whose constituents collectively far exceed that of the US Assemblies of God. In virtually all instances, moreover, these national churches are entirely independent financially and are not beholden to any foreign agency for their operations and growth. Such regional fellowship does not restrict the national autonomy of the member organizations, and the fact that American missionaries serve with the approval of a host national church provides evidence of that autonomy.

The strength of each association, consequently, has been the vitality of each national church. Given their vastly different environments, limitations, and opportunities, each national church has developed along its own lines. In several countries, for a variety of reasons, the Assemblies of God national body does not use as a title the local equivalent of 'Assemblies of God' (the church in Slovakia, for example, is called the Apostolic Church) and in several countries, given the divisions existing between ethnic and cultural groups, more than one Assemblies of God organization has emerged. When the Assemblies of God overseas shows aggregate growth and development, this global effect is actually a reflection of the vitality of a large number of individual units.

In recognition of this diffusion of spiritual life, social scientist David Stoll has observed that 'If [Pentecostal] churches were really built on handouts, they would be spiritless patronage structures, not vital, expand-

---

[32] 'Beyond Indigenization,' DFM Annual Report for 1986, 17–18.
[33] *Decade of Harvest World Report* (November 1991): 8.

ing grass-roots organizations.'[34] Individual national organizations, each facing its own challenges and showing varying degrees of effectiveness, demonstrate initiative, proprietary control, and comprehension of their own problems. Thus the overseas Assemblies of God resembles a mosaic that produces in the observer impressions ranging from concern to wonder, depending on the course the local movements have taken.

National leaders recognize that the collective leadership of the Pentecostal movement is distributed around the world, exercised not only at a national but also at an international level by men and women whose organizations, independent and uncompromised, enjoy the respect of their counterparts in numerous other countries. The leaders who have emerged in these national movements, while responsible solely to their own constituents, nevertheless often acquire international influence, a cross-fertilization that militates against parochialism and provides a loose system of checks and balances.

Long before the end of his executive leadership of the DFM, J. Philip Hogan recognized that the churches that had received assistance from the US Assemblies of God would by their nature become missionary-sending churches themselves. The growing number of missionaries sent out by churches in countries still considered to be a mission field themselves, according to Hogan, reflects the vision these churches have received for continuing evangelization.

While US missionaries continue to serve the national movements as foreign personnel, they have adapted to the changing needs of the churches. For all of Africa, for example, there were a reported 2,320,000 Assemblies of God members and adherents in 32 countries (1990), with a missionary couple or a single missionary for each 14,500 people in the community. Clearly, the work of expatriate (overseas) North American Assemblies of God missionaries is not essentially to serve in pastoral roles. Missionaries' work includes a wide array of functions, from oversight of institutions to specialized forms of evangelism, all of which, in the view of the national church leadership, with the concurrence of DFM leadership, are strategic for a given field. If the ratios of overseas adherents to DFM missionaries is not in all cases as high, the point is clear: missionaries are more closely related to the formation of national leadership than directly to the membership in most countries where they work. Most foreign missionaries, as in the past, are involved with pastoral training, including teaching in Bible institutes (totaling 377 in the 1990 DFM annual report), as well as other strategic ministries like communications, correspondence courses, and specialized work with children and youth.

Even when missionaries are involved in pastoral and evangelistic efforts, they are generally not ministering just – or even primarily – to a

---

[34]   David Stoll, 'Is There a Protestant Reformation in Latin America?' *Christian Century* (17 January 1990): 447.

given congregation. They are more likely to be assisted by national pastors who play an integral part in the campaigns and who will assume responsibility for the work as it develops, leaving the missionary free to proceed to some other city or ministry. In the process, generally, the training of national leaders and the modeling of leadership roles is more important than the concrete results achieved by the campaign effort. According to J. Philip Hogan:

> We never set out to establish a worldwide, American structure in lands afar, but to foster and encourage the indigenous church with fraternal ties rather than constitutional, organic ties. Several of these overseas fellowships rival us in size and are growing far faster than we are here at home. The largest churches I preach in are overseas.[35]

He goes on to say,

> I am often asked what I attribute this growth to, and I am happy to respond. The sovereign wind of the Holy Spirit blows around the world. The Division of Foreign Missions in concepts and its leaders, from its inception until now, have believed in, depended upon, welcomed, and sought the wind of the Spirit.[36]

---

[35] JPH, 'From Azusa Street to the World,' *Pentecostal Evangel* (10 April 1994): 11.
[36] Ibid.

The Paradox of Pentecostalism

Pentecostals used to say that their doctrine was 'true' because it was small and pure, now it is 'true' because so many are drawn to it.

Martin Marty[1]

An enigma

If Pentecostalism was understood poorly when J. Philip Hogan first came to the leadership of his denomination's missionary program, for many observers it still remains incomprehensible. Apart from the more obvious concerns about the movement that trouble non-Pentecostals – ecstasy, glossolalia, faith healing, prophetic statements, behavior attributed to private divine mandates – none of which is regularly and universally agreed upon by practitioners themselves, vexing questions arise about fanaticism, inconsistencies of doctrine and conduct, apparent appeals to extra-Biblical authority, and the spread of Pentecostalism among people who are too volatile, too uncritical, or too lowbrow to inspire confidence.

How then does one explain a movement that fits so poorly into some conventional categories of historical Christianity (e.g. the movement's almost total neglect of the sacraments and the tendency to deny its debt to preceding theological traditions) while so effectively promoting biblical belief and time-honored Christian piety? The Pentecostals, observes a Roman Catholic charismatic writer, 'are better at new evangelization – ultimate challenge, decision and conversion – than we are.'[2] From the outset of any discussion about Pentecostal effectiveness, it must be recognized that the movement is better suited for promoting faith than for any other function. In the long run, the perpetuation of Pentecostal emphases is justified only by their application to a single task: Christian conversion and spiritual development. Either Pentecostalism is an aberration (as some critics continue to insist) or it must be recognized as the product of the same vision, motivation, and dynamics – the initiative of

---

1 Marty, *Nation of Behavers*, 106.
2 Kilian McDonnell, cited in Edward Clearly, ' "John Paul Cries Wolf": Misreading the Pentecostals,' *Commonweal* (20 November 1992): 8.

the Holy Spirit – that appear to have given rise to other revivals of the Christian faith.

While particular branches of the movement have withered or have appeared by some criteria to distort the Christian message, the Pentecostal mainstream has veered little if at all from the cardinal tenets of the faith. Despite considerable opportunity for error because of its internal diversity, spontaneity, and popular character, Pentecostalism, for the same reasons, is inclined to be self-correcting. As sociologist Luther P. Gerlach explains, Pentecostalism 'prevents effective suppression or cooptation of the total movement through its redundancy, multiplicity of leadership, and self-sufficiency of local groups.'[3] Nor can the movement easily become the self-serving mechanism of one, dominant leader, no matter how charismatic they are. On the basis of his investigation Gerlach concludes that Pentecostalism 'generates an escalation of effort and forward motion through the rivalry and competition among its various segments and leaders.'[4]

After almost a century of expansion, this still not easily categorized religious phenomenon has produced tens of millions of apparently sincere, committed Christian believers, whose personal lives and church communities have inspired renewal and imitation throughout the historic churches. Despite rejection, criticism at various levels, and predictions of disaster, the movement has become a modal form of the Christian faith.

Stated positively, Pentecostalism is increasingly viewed as a dynamic movement with an extraordinary capacity for advancing contemporary Christianity. Gerlach believes that Pentecostalism is a movement which is likely to 'disturb those who wish religion to maintain established ways and values;' he early on identified it as a movement of 'personal transformation and revolutionary change.'[5]

> The very characteristics of ecstatic religious behavior – ceremonial dissociation, decentralized structure, unconventional ideology, opposition to established structures – which might appear to be marks of a sect of misfits and dropouts, are indeed the features which combine to make Pentecostalism a growing, expanding, evangelistic religious movement of change.[6]

The Pentecostal missionary movement, the result of the remarkable motivation, vision, and initiative of mainly unknown believers in the developing nations, ultimately must be attributed to that which is inherent to Pentecostalism – a personally satisfying, transforming religious experience and its accompanying values and world-view, which in turn have produced cell-like congregations that readily identify with aspiring

---

[3]　Luther P. Gerlach, 'Pentecostalism: Revolution or Counter-Revolution,' in *Religious Movements*, ed. Zaretsky and Leone, 381.
[4]　Ibid., 681.
[5]　Ibid., 680.
[6]　Ibid., 685.

peoples and extend the message of the gospel with considerable energy and enthusiasm. In country after country the era overseen by J. Philip Hogan witnessed the rise of national leaders capable, without foreign dependency, of extending their own movements. This fundamental fact of Assemblies of God missionary effectiveness, often overlooked by missiologists – and even many Assemblies of God constituents – has been the operational secret of the mission's rapid growth and remains its most distinguishing feature, one that sets it apart from virtually every other US missions agency.

In response to questions about their collective impact, Pentecostals are inclined to explain their growth simply as 'a sovereign move of God' to extend the gospel in the last days of the church era. Thus their Pentecostal beliefs and emphases become the cause and champion of their numerical growth and continuing dynamism. This response, however, places a heavy responsibility on subtle theological explanations of the kind that Pentecostals themselves have been slow to examine in any great depth.

For, while some Pentecostals adhere resolutely to their particular doctrinal emphases – premillenialism, signs and wonders, prosperity, spiritual warfare, and kingdom teaching – these cannot be demonstrated to have been the exclusive or even the primary reason for the movement's rapid expansion. Pentecostal groups have often developed quite well without special reference to any of these emphases. The most widely read and persuasive explanations of Pentecostal effectiveness, rather, have been functional studies published by non-Pentecostals, mainly secular social scientists, often with considerable methodological sophistication, though sometimes with corresponding disdain for the Pentecostals' theological distinctives.

Ultimately these analyses indicate that Pentecostals have not needed substantial resources, brilliant leadership, or theological consistency to make an impact. Their successes, though often marred by serious failures, can only be explained by the subjective experience of now tens of millions of grass-roots believers from virtually every nation, ethnic group, culture, and social standing. These are people who, unless considered victims of a religious contagion, have found both intense personal spiritual satisfaction and a remarkably appropriate basis of association in a local unit of the body of Christ.

The verdict of secular scholars about the impact of Pentecostalism has been, in brief, that the movement's effectiveness has resulted from remarkable cultural appropriateness and unerring timing – over which even the most committed missionaries and national ministers have had little control – both of which lend support to the Pentecostals' claim that they are guided and empowered by the Holy Spirit.

Meanwhile, there is no end of observers who predict the collapse of Pentecostalism. While many of these writers refer primarily to laws of growth and decline, there are relatively few intellectuals, statesmen, educators, or social critics of note who appear to be comfortable discussing the phenomenon. At best, for most scholars, Pentecostalism tends to be a religious efflorescence that is symptomatic of a disintegrating, postmodern culture. Ironically, the writers most likely to recognize the vitality and strength of the Pentecostal movement – attributing to it remarkable achievement in mobilizing socially marginal masses – are least likely to attribute its effectiveness to transcendent causes. Pentecostals, as always, are left dangling, dependent only on their belief in God's desire and ability to sustain them. Whether projections about the demise of Pentecostalism will prove true, accordingly, depend on the Pentecostals themselves, especially on their continued exercise of the beliefs and practices that have made their movement so extraordinarily vital.

It would seem that if the Pentecostals are to continue making a positive contribution to global evangelization, extending human hope for the future, or providing some practical solutions to the larger evils of our time (as opposed to finding limited, subjective satisfactions), they must find the answers within themselves and in the demanding – and not always realized – values that underlie their expression of the Christian faith.

But what is this Pentecostal essence to which adherents must recur? Even if not in *theory* Pentecostals in *practice* are more likely than other Christians to declare that *their strength lies in their weakness*. They often take seriously the biblical appeal to become living sacrifices, and to that extent they acquire real if intangible spiritual resources.

While Pentecostal beliefs and practices, as often alleged, may provide adherents with a certain degree of diversion and anesthetic, their sustained personal confidence and collective power is apparently based more on the subjective reality of God's presence than on a comprehensive theology, or confidence in denominations, movements, or religious celebrities.

Do Pentecostals offer their adherents real solutions to the uncertainty and frustrations of contemporary life? That this 'supernatural assistance' – J. Philip Hogan's 'blessed ally' – is not simply a case of mind over matter is demonstrated by the believers' having to put their faith into action. Whether or not God really does answer prayer, no matter how many individual testimonies can be adduced to support the assertion, is in fact writ large in the history of the Pentecostal movement itself for everyone to examine critically. Nor is the adherents' faith merely a mystical escape from the temporal world – they pray fervently for their daily bread, physical healing, the resolution of troubling circumstances, and power either to overcome or put up with apparently unendurable situations. Yet they often deny the world and sometimes turn their backs on means and goals that are generally considered legitimate, when they consider these temporal avenues less worthy than the radical but attainable ideal of a life lived in harmony with New Testament precepts.

Whether or not this movement will continue to grow without the loss of spontaneity and transparency remains to be seen. Left to human efforts alone, no matter how pious and well-intentioned, a kind of religious Second Law of Thermodynamics would seem to govern the destinies of

Christian renewal movements like Pentecostalism, leading to their inevitable decline.[7] If the Pentecostal movement after almost a century still displays vitality, there must be some sustaining energy other than its adherents' own inner resources that gives it life. The withering of Christianity has often been predicted; most recently, ironically, during the very years that the Pentecostal movement was gaining an extraordinary following.

True, the Pentecostal solution taken at 'full strength' requires renunciation and abject faith. But for tens of millions of Pentecostal Christians the challenges of the New Testament, to experience divine guidance and empowering for discipleship, are as contemporary as their most recent reading of Peter's sermon in Acts 2: 'This promise is for your and for your children and to them that are afar off, and to as many as the Lord our God shall call.'

The paradox of Pentecostalism

The great Pentecostal paradox, which looms above the many other paradoxes that complicate analysis of the movement is this: Pentecostals, who have no 'visible means of support,' no adequate human resources to explain their achievements beyond the resources available to energize any believer, may not take credit, any credit at all, for their achievements. They may not attribute their successes to extensive material resources, profound theological insight, exemplary piety, superior administrative skills, or outstandingly wise or charismatic leaders.

As Martin Marty has correctly analyzed the dilemma, either Pentecostals have to deny what they have always contended, namely that God has used them rather than other equally inadequate 'earthen vessels' primarily because Pentecostal adherents have been more willing to let him direct the action; or, affirming as in the past their abject dependence on God, they will have to refrain from taking too much credit for their personal and collective achievements. Having long claimed that God has used them precisely because they were admittedly helpless, Pentecostals cannot then claim to possess spiritual – or any other kind of – superiority.

Ultimately, Pentecostals must simply acknowledge that their usually very ordinary efforts have been blessed – far beyond reasonable human expectation – to become something that they cannot adequately explain. At best they can point to their willingness to respond to inner promptings and their faithfulness to specific enterprises that, left to their own inadequate resources, were destined to failure. Moreover, many of the movement's apparent successes were achieved by men and women who, on

---

7   The Second Law of Thermodynamics, referring to the theoretical tendency in physics for the universe to 'wind down,' has been applied to social situations to describe declining energy, effort, and enthusiasm.

the face of it, were unlikely to realize outstanding accomplishments and whose efforts at first glance appeared futile or misdirected.

Pentecostals, when all is said and done, must simply bow in reverence – as one would do on being present at the birth of an infant – at the sublime beauty and perfection of God's handiwork. Despite the fact that procreation and gestation can be described dispassionately and despite the fact that these processes require at least minimal human participation, every birth is a miracle that far transcends the ephemeral, finite perceptions, passions, efforts, and abilities of the human parents.

Not surprisingly, J. Philip Hogan, at the conclusion of his lengthy term of service, simply bowed in amazement and unqualified admiration before what God had done – as often as not – despite his and his colleagues' best efforts. Initially inclined by his training and assumptions to believe that the destinies of the Christian church lay in the hands of highly motivated, visionary, and resourceful men and women, he admitted at the end of his administrative career to be perceiving more clearly the deft hand of God, the facile coordination of the Spirit, behind what on the face of the enterprise appeared to be the achievements of missionaries and their sending churches. After all, he and his colleagues in the global venture were simply 'unprofitable servants,' the meek and humble from every nation, whom God used on a historically discernible scale to accomplish his purpose among the nations.

Select Bibliography

Note: Journal or magazine articles by JPH, where cited in the footnotes without bibliographical details, refer to the Hogan clippings file kept in the DFM section of the Assemblies of God Archives, Springfield, Missouri. Bibliographical information is based on a taped interview with David Hogan which is kept in the Assemblies of God Archives, as well as author interviews with J. Phil Hogan and Virginia Hogan.

Adeney, D.H., *China: The Church's Long March* (Ventura, CA: Regal Books, 1985)

Ahlstrom, S.E., *A Religious History of the American People* (New Haven: Yale University Press, 1972)

Anderson, R.M., *Vision of the Disinherited: The Making of American Pentecostalism* (New York: Oxford University Press, 1979)

Annis, S., *God and Production in a Guatemalan Town* (Austin: University of Texas Press, 1987)

Barrett, D.B., *World Christian Encyclopedia* (New York: Oxford University Press, 1982)

Blumhofer, E.L., *The Assemblies of God: A Chapter in the Story of American Pentecostalism*, vol.2, *Since 1941* (Springfield, MO: Gospel Publishing House, 1989)

Blumhofer, E.L. and Balmer, R., eds., *Modern Revivalism* (Urbana: University of Illinois Press, 1993)

Burgess, S.M., McGee, G.B. and Alexander, P.H., eds., *Dictionary of Pentecostal and Charismatic Movements* (Grand Rapids, MI: Zondervan, 1988), abbr. *DPCM*

Cameron, W.B., *Modern Social Movements* (New York: Random House, 1966)

Campolo, T., *How to Be Pentecostal Without Speaking in Tongues* (Dallas: Word Publishing, 1991)

Clark, E.T., *The Small Sects in America* (New York and Nashville: Abindon-Cokesbury Press, 1949)

Cox, H., *Tongues of Fire: The Rise of Pentecostal Spirituality and the Reshaping of Religion in the Twenty-first Century* (Reading, MA: Addison-Wesley Publishing Company, 1995)

DPCM, see Burgess, McGee and Alexander, eds.

Elliot, E., *Through Gates of Splendor* (New York: Harpers, 1957)

Fife, E. and Glasser, A., *Missions in Crisis* (Chicago: Intervarsity Press, 1961)

Garrard-Burnett, V. and Stoll D., ed, *Rethinking Protestantism in Latin America* (Philadelphia: Temple University Press, 1993)

Harrell, D., *All Things Are Possible: The Healing and Charismatic Revivals in Modern America* (Bloomington, IN: Indiana University Press, 1975)

Hembree, R., *Mark* (Plainfield, NJ: Logos International, 1979)

Herberg, W., *Protestant, Catholic, Jew: An Essay in American Religious Sociology* (Chicago: University of Chicago Press, 1955)

Herring, H., *A History of Latin America*, 3rd ed. (New York: Alfred A. Knopf, 1968)

Hodges, M., *The Indigenous Church* (Springfield, MO: Gospel Publishing House, 1953)

Hollenweger, W., *The Pentecostals* (Minneapolis, MN: Augsburg Publishing House, 1972)

Hutchinson, W.R., *Errand to the World: American Protestant Thought and Foreign Missions* (Chicago: University of Chicago Press, 1987)

International Encyclopedia of the Social Sciences, 15 vols. (New York: Macmillan Company and Free Press, 1968)

Johns, C.B., *Pentecostal Formation: A Pedagogy Among the Oppressed* (Sheffield: Sheffield Academic Press, 1993)

Johnstone, P., *Operation World* (Grand Rapids, MI: Zondervan Publishing House, 1993)

Mariz, C.L., *Coping with Poverty* (Philadelphia: Temple University Press, 1994)

Martin, D., *Tongues of Fire: The Explosion of Protestantism in Latin America* (Oxford: Basil Blackwell, 1990)

Marty, M., *A Nation of Behavers* (Chicago: University of Chicago Press, 1977)

McGavran, D., *The Bridges of God* (New York: Friendship Press, 1955)

McGee, G., *This Gospel Shall Be Preached*, vol. 1, *A History and Theology of Assemblies of God Foreign Missions to 1959* (Springfield, MO: Gospel Publishing House, 1986); vol. 2, *A History and Theology of Assemblies of God Foreign Missions Since 1959* (Springfield, MO: Gospel Publishing House, 1989)

Miller, D., ed., *Coming of Age: Protestantism in Contemporary Latin America* (Lanham, MD: University Press of America, 1994)

Nichols, N. and Bang, J., *God's Faithfulness in Ningpo* (Springfield, MO: Gospel Publishing House, 1938)

Nida, E., *Understanding Latin Americans* (Pasadena, CA: William Carey Press, 1974)

Percy, J.O., *Facing the Unfinished Task* (Grand Rapids, MI: Zondervan Publishing House, 1961)

Petersen, D., *Not By Might Nor By Power: A Pentecostal Theology of Social Concern in Latin America* (Oxford: Regnum, 1996)

Poloma, M.M., *The Assemblies of God at the Crossroads: Charisma and Institutional Dilemmas* (Knoxville: University of Tennessee Press, 1989)

Read, W.R., Monterroso, V.M. and Johnson, H.A., *Latin American Church Growth* (Grand Rapids, MI: William B. Eerdmans Publishing Co., 1969)

Reid, D.G., ed., *Dictionary of Christianity in America* (Downers Grove, IL: Intervarsity Press, 1990)

Rubenstein, M.A., *The Protestant Community on Modern Taiwan* (Armonk, NY: M.E. Sharpe, Inc., 1991)

Sanders, R.I., *Meet the Mossi* (Springfield, MO: Gospel Publishing House, 1955)

Scherer, R.P., *American Denominational Organization* (South Pasadena, CA: William Carey Library, 1980)

Shepard, C.E., *Forgiven* (New York: Atlantic Monthly Press, 1989)

Siewert, J.A. and Kenyon, J.A., eds., *Mission Handbook 1993–1995* (Monrovia, CA: MARC, 1993)

Stoll, D., *Is Latin America Turning Protestant?* (Berkeley: University of California Press, 1990)

Tucker, R.A., *From Jerusalem to Irian Jaya* (Grand Rapids, MI: Zondervan Publishing House, 1983)

Wagner, C.P., *Look Out! The Pentecostals Are Coming* (Carol Stream, Ill: Creation House, 1973)

Wilson, E.A., *Seventy-five Years of Dreams and Destinies* (Santa Cruz, CA: Bethany College of the Assemblies of God, 1994)

Winehouse, I., *The Assemblies of God: A Popular Survey* (New York: Vantage Press, 1959)

Winter, R.D., *The Twenty-five Unbelievable Years, 1945–1969* (South Pasadena, CA: William Carey Library, 1970)

Winters, G.P., *It Is Your Affair, God: Acts of the Holy Spirit in Zaire* (Nampa, ID: Good Impressions, 1989)

Zaretsky, I.I. and Leone, M.P., eds., *Religious Movements in Contemporary America* (Princeton, NJ: Princeton University Press, 1974)

Index

Isiro (formerly Paulis) 105
Israelis, perceptions of Pentecostals 10
Italian Assemblies of God 122–4
Italian Pentecostals 12
Ito, Akiei (General Superintendent,
   Yokohama Assemblies of God)
   189

Jamaica, missionary outreach in 54
James, Will 24
Japan 67, 135–6
Javier, Eli (General Superintendent,
   Philippines Assemblies of God) 188
Jesus Movement 86
Jeyaraj, Y. 121
Jimmy Swaggart Children's Fund 169–70
Jimmy Swaggart Ministries 167–76
   financial support for DFM 174–5
Johnstone, Patrick, *Operation World* 3
Jones, Jr., Bob 11
Jorguenson, Eleanor (wife of Melvin
   Jorguenson) 99
Jorguenson, Melvin 99

Kalambule, Laiton 118
Kennedy, John F. (President of USA) 95
Kersten, Milton 124, 125
Keys, Leyland R. (pastor, Glad Tidings
   Bible Institute) 35
Kingswriter, Delmar 118–19
Kraemer, Hendrik, and guidance of the
   Holy Spirit 135–6
Kruschev, Nikita (Premier of USSR) 95
Ku Klux Klan 27
Kuzmic, Peter (Director, Evangelical
   Theological Seminary (Osijek,
   Croatia)) 184, 191, 192
L'Amour, Louis 24, 25
Latin America
   Assemblies of God expansion in
      189–90
   expansion of Pentecostalism 189–90
Latin America ChildCare (LACC) 139,
   146, 148–52, 175
Latin American Church Growth study
   (1969) 5–6
Latter Rain movement 86
Lau, Patrick (Superintendent, Singapore
   Assemblies of God) 187
Lausanne Conference (Switzerland),
   International Conference on
   World Evangelization (Lausane
   Conference) (Switzerland) (1974)
   128, 133, 134
lay leadership 85

Lazaro, Manuel (Superintendent,
   Assemblies of God in Tanzania)
   186
Lee, Daniel (magistrate and member of
   Ningpo Assemblies of God) 39
Lehmann, Harold 46
Lehmann, Henry 132–3
Lehmann, Naomi 133
Leopoldville (Congo) 98
Lernoux, Penny, accuses Pentecostals of
   social strike 138
Lewis, Gayle (VH's father) 18, 26
Lewis, Oscar, *The Children of Aánchez*,
   Mexican opposition to publication
   110
Lewis, Virginia *see* Hogan, Virginia
   (JPH's wife)
Liceo Cristiano Reverendo Juan Bueno
   148–50
Life publishers 129
Light for the Lost (LTFL) 81–2, 85, 123
Lillian Trasher Orphanage (Assuit,
   Egypt) 146–7, 175
Lindsell, Harold 11
Lombardi, Giacomo 122
Louis, Monsier (friend of Lillian Hogan
   and Gail Winters) 100
Lowenberg, Paul 18
Luce, Alice 53

McAlister, Robert 166
McDonnell, Kilian 195
McGarran, Donald 4, 58–60, 63, 91
McGee, Gary B. ix, 154
   Assemblies of God and social concern
      139, 144
   Global Conquest, impact 72
   indigenous churches to be
      self-supporting 116
   missiology of Assemblies of God 54
   on Noel Perkin's achievements 53
McIntire, Carl 11
McPherson, Aimee Semple 13, 22, 27–28
Malawi, Assemblies of God in 118–19, 186
Malayalan district (South India),
   Assemblies of God in 120
Malaysia, Assemblies of God in 187–8
male dominance, effects of
   Pentecostalism on 141–2
Malz, Carl 130
Manacas Bible Institute (Cuba) 95, 96
Mangbetu tribe 105
Manila, Assemblies of God in 188
Manzano, Bob (head of PTL missions
   department) 166

A Vision of Hope
An insight into the life of Samuel Habib, one of the foremost leaders of the Christian community in Egypt.
David W. Virtue

The story of Samuel Habib, one of the Arab World's greatest contemporary Christian leaders and his plan for peace in the strife-torn Middle East where the cross and the crescent meet and where the Bible, Koran and Torah vie for centre stage.

'Sam Habib has been able to provide leadership in the secular world . . . and for the Protestant churches of Egypt simultaneously. This combination has made it possible for him to sustain a catalytic influence . . . among Muslims and Orthodox, Catholic and Protestant Christians that has made his voice heard in governmental circles.' William P. Thompson, Central Committee member, World Council of Churches

ISBN 1-870345-16-9

In Season and Out of Season

Sermons to a Nation

David Gitari

This is a challenging selection of 25 sermons preached between 1975 and 1994 by an African bishop. Although the occasions for their delivery appear routine their subject matter is far from ordinary. These sermons show that African preachers, as Kwame Bediako says in the Foreword, are 'not ivory-tower academics [but] practical theologians seeking from the Gospel answers to burning issues'.

ISBN 1-87034-511-8

The Story of Faith Missions
From Hudson Taylor to Present Day Africa
Klaus Fiedler

Born of the nineteenth-century Evangelical Awakening, and closely linked to Hudson Taylor and the China Inland Mission he founded in 1865, the faith mission movement has lost none of its vitality and relevance as it continues to play an important evangelistic role in Africa and worldwide.

Setting faith missions in Africa in the context of the many revival and missionary movements which have shaped Protestant church history, the author describes their spiritual and practical evolution over 125 years and outlines the challenge they face today.

ISBN 1-87034-518-5